U.S.-Mexican Economic Relations

U.S.-Mexican Economic Relations

PROSPECTS AND PROBLEMS

Edited by
Khosrow Fatemi

PRAEGER

New York
Westport, Connecticut
London

Library of Congress Cataloging-in-Publication Data

U.S.-Mexican economic relations : prospects and problems / edited by
  Khosrow Fatemi.
    p. cm.
   Bibliography: p.
   Includes index.
   ISBN 0-275-92955-8 (alk. paper)
   1. United States—Foreign economic relations—Mexico. 2. Mexico—
Foreign economic relations—United States. I. Fatemi, Khosrow.
II. Title: US-Mexican economic relations.
HF1452.5.M6U15   1988
337.73072—dc 19   88-311

Library of Congress Catalog Card Number: 88-311

ISBN: 0-275-92955-8

First published in 1988

Praeger Publishers, One Madison Avenue, New York, NY 10010
A division of Greenwood Press, Inc.

Printed in the United States of America

The paper used in this book complies with the
Permanent Paper Standard issued by the National
Information Standards Organization (Z39.48-1984).

10 9 8 7 6 5 4 3 2 1

To my wife, Marcella.
Were it not for her continuous
encouragement and unwavering
support, this book would have
never become a reality.

Contents

Tables and Charts

TABLES

CHARTS

Preface

This volume is, for the most part, a product of an international symposium on "North American Economies in the 1990s" held in Laredo, Texas in the summer of 1987. The symposium was cosponsored by Laredo State University. My special thanks go to several members of the university for their support, and also for their invaluable assistance. Manuel T. Pacheco, president of Laredo State University, by providing continuous encouragement and by his willingness to invest the university's prestige and resources in this project, was instrumental in bringing to fruition the Symposium, and eventually this book. I am also grateful to Leo Sayavedra, academic vice president, and many members of the university's administrative and secretarial services. My colleague Sandra Richard, Chair of Business Division, was both inspiring and accommodating. Finally, my special thanks are to Phillip Lane, director of the Institute for International Trade, for his ever-present willingness to help.

I am also grateful to many symposium participants for their assistance in evaluating and refereeing the papers presented at the symposium for inclusion in this book. They were Zewdineh Assefa, Pan American University; Klaus P. Fischer, Hofstra University; H. Peter Gray, Professor Emeritus, Rutgers; Donald Hakala, East Texas State University; Michael Hammig, Clemson University; Belmont Haydel, Rider College; Charles Hegji, Auburn University at Montgomery; Joseph Horton, University of Scranton; Irene Lange, California State University, Fullerton; Stanley Lawson, St. John's University; Rafael Lecuona, Laredo State University; Jean-Guy Loranger, University of Montreal; Shah M. Mehrabi, Mary Washington College; Faisal A. Nasr, University of Texas at Austin; Gary Noreiko, University of Southern Colorado; Brother Leo Ryan, DePaul University; Rendl-Marcus, Professor Emeritus, City University of New York; David Timmins, Instituto Tecnico de Estudios Superiores de Monterrey; M. Reza Vaghefi, University of North Florida; Mahmood Zaidi, University of Minnesota; and M. Raquibuz Zaman, Ithaca College.

Finally, a very special note of appreciation to my secretary, Blanca Saucedo and my student assistant, Susan Weiland. Their willingness to spend a countless number of hours on this project was beyond my expectations and very helpful.

Needless to say, none of the above bears any responsibility for the contents of this book. That goes to the editor along with the individual contributors of each chapter.

PART ONE
INTRODUCTION

1

Introduction

Khosrow Fatemi

There may not be any integrative agreements formally binding the United States and Mexico together, but a great deal of interdependency—an "invisible integration"—does exist between them. The two countries are indeed interdependent, an interdependency that covers every aspect of the sociopolitical and economic spectrum. Sociologically, about 10 percent of the U.S. population is of Mexican ancestry and shares Mexico's cultural values and attributes; economically, the United States is the source or destination of almost two-thirds of Mexico's foreign trade as well as being the major source of technology and foreign investment for Mexico; and politically, the two countries share similar ideologies and objectives. There is divergence to be sure: divergence in the stage of economic development, divergence in income distribution and consumerism, divergence in culture, and divergence in many other aspects of life in the two countries; but such differences do not detract from the basic "invisible integration" that exists between the two countries.

The purpose of this book is to present an analysis of economic relations between the United States and Mexico. Following a general preview of bilateral economic relations in this introductory chapter, each succeeding part will evaluate a different aspect of economic relations between the two countries. Generally, each part will have one or two chapters dealing with specific concrete issues and one or two more on the theoretical aspects of the same issues.

AN ECONOMIC OVERVIEW

U.S.-Mexican economic relations are as comprehensive as relations between any two countries. For simplification reasons they are divided into the following six categories:

3

1. International Trade
2. Foreign Investment and Transfer of Technology, including *maquiladoras*
3. Immigration
4. Oil
5. External Debt Issue, and
6. Border Relations.

International Trade

Bilateral trade relations between the United States and Mexico have been expanding gradually in recent years. For Mexico, the American market has become the mainstay of its economic growth. During the 1980s, Mexican exports to its northern neighbor fluctuated between $10.1-$14.1 billion, accounting for as much as 67 percent of the country's total exports by 1986 and surpassing 70 percent in 1987 (Table 1.1). Mexico's reliance on the United States for its imports has been even higher. In recent years, Mexico has been importing at least two-thirds of its total imports from the United States.

Table 1.1
Mexico's International Trade (Million Dollars)

	EXPORTS			IMPORTS		
		To	U.S.		From	U.S.
Year	Total	U.S.	Share	Total	U.S.	Share
1980	$15,557	$10,072	65%	$17,687	$10,890	62%
1981	19,381	10,716	55%	21,933	13,998	64%
1982	21,209	11,129	52%	13,687	8,188	60%
1983	22,313	13,034	58%	8,200	4,958	60%
1984	24,382	14,130	58%	10,327	6,440	62%
1985	22,105	13,341	60%	13,441	8,954	67%
1986	16,579	11,163	67%	12,320	8,272	67%
1987*	21,000	15,000	71%	12,000	8,500	71%
Annual						
Average	20,316	12,323	61%	13,699	8,774	64%

Note: *Estimated by the author.
Source: *Direction of Trade Statistics: 1987 Yearbook*, 1987, pp. 283–284 and different monthly
      issues.

For the United States, trade with Mexico has also been growing and gaining in significance. Mexico is now the third highest importer of American exports (after Canada and Japan). It is also America's fourth highest source of imports (after Japan, Canada, and Germany). (See Table 1.2.)

Mexico's export earnings have shown more fluctuations in recent years than before, mostly because of the volatility of oil prices. For example, in dollar terms, Mexico's total oil exports (crude oil, petroleum products, and natural gas) amounted to $14.6 billion in 1985. It dropped to only $6.1 billion in 1986, a reduction of 57 percent. In contrast, by volume, crude oil exports for the two years were 1.45 and 1.29 million barrels per day (bpd) respectively, a drop of only 12 percent. Consequently, Mexico's non-oil exports have been growing more steadily, showing some acceleration in this growth since 1982. While the average annual increase for the decade has been 12.5 percent, the rate has been more than twice that during the last two years. In 1986, for example, non-oil exports were 33 percent higher than in 1985.

Mexico's second source of foreign exchange, after oil, has been tourism, and here again, the major supplier has been the United States. In 1986, Mexico's income from tourism was $1,167 million, an estimated 80 percent of which came from American tourists.

Trade between Mexico and the United States will continue to follow an expanding trend. The existence of two widely divergent economies next to each other will greatly contribute to an expansion of trade between the two

Table 1.2
United States International Trade Major Trading Partners, 1986

DESTINATION FOR U.S. EXPORTS		SOURCE OF U.S. IMPORTS	
Country	%	Country	%
Canada	20.9	Japan	22.1
Japan	12.4	Canada	17.7
Mexico	5.7	Germany	6.7
Britain	5.3	Mexico	4.5
Germany	4.9	Britain	4.1
Others	50.8	Others	44.9
	100%		100%

Source: Direction of Trade Statistics, 1986 Yearbook.

countries. In very simple terms, Mexico is richly endowed with what the United States needs: oil, raw materials, and cheap labor. And conversely, what the United States produces—for example, technology, heavy machinery, and high-tech products—Mexico needs. This scenario inevitably leads to more trade and, for better or worse, to greater interdependence between the two countries. Noneconomic considerations such as diversification of source of supply for either partner or political considerations may lead to short-term interruption of growth, but in the long run, helped—albeit slightly—by Mexico's entry into General Agreement on Tariffs and Trade (GATT), the trend line will continue to show appreciable increases.

Foreign Investment and Transfer of Technology

Closely related to foreign trade are the inflows of U.S. capital and technology into Mexico. It is now estimated that total foreign direct investment in Mexico amounts to $15 billion, of which 67 percent is invested by American multinational companies. This total also indicates a 200 percent increase since the early 1980s. One important factor contributing to this rapid growth has been the recent introduction of swap or debt capitalization arrangements.[1] Through discounting of existing debt and converting it into equity, swap arrangements have made certain investments less expensive in Mexico. This change should be reflected in higher investment totals in the coming years.

Another important and longer term reason for the rapid growth of foreign direct investment in Mexico has been the increase in the number of *maquiladora* plants.[2] For the Mexican economy, *maquiladoras* provide capital, technology, and employment. For their United States partners, they provide cheap labor and access to the American market on a duty-free basis. Presently, there are about 900 plants operating under this concept. Their annual foreign exchange earnings for Mexico is estimated by the Mexican government to be $1.3 billion and their value-added contributions to the Mexican economy to be $1.4 billion. The Mexican decision in 1986 to allow *maquiladoras* to market a portion of their production in Mexico—rather than having to re-export all of it—has made them much more attractive to foreign investors.

One of the more controversial aspects of the transfer of technology through *maquiladora* operations is the perceived impact of these plants on the employment picture in the United States. Specifically, do *maquiladoras* create jobs for Mexican workers at the expense of American workers? Or, do they also create employment opportunities for the American workers by creating demand for more parts and components that are produced in the United States and by American workers? The rapid growth of *maquila* plants in recent years—from 57 in 1967 to about 900 twenty years later—is an indication of their usefulness to many sectors of both U.S. and Mexican economies. Furthermore, the general consensus among the students of the field is that *maquiladoras* have not yet reached or even approached their full potentials, and will continue to grow in the foreseeable future.

The impact of *maquiladoras* on the illegal immigration of Mexican workers to the United States is also subject to some controversy. Do *maquiladoras* provide employment for Mexican workers in Mexico by acting as a buffer zone of employment and economic stability and by "providing Mexicans with jobs and reducing the incentive for them to enter the United States as wetbacks," as has been argued?[3] Or, do they attract more Mexican workers to the frontier zone than the region can accommodate and therefore increase the likelihood of further illegal immigration, as others have postulated. The 250,000 Mexican nationals who are currently working in different *maquila* plants attest to the validity of the first argument. Yet, there is little empirical evidence to suggest that without these *maquiladora* plants these workers would have emigrated to the United States.

One of the more serious apprehensions of U.S. investors, that is, the lack of confidence in the Mexican government, particularly its policies vis-à-vis foreign direct investment, has subsided substantially in recent years. This is partly due to the effectiveness of the new policies adopted by the Mexican government, and partly due to the support it has received from the International Monetary Fund (IMF). The expected continuation of such policies by the new administration of Carlos Salinas de Gortari should attract even larger sums of United States investment, and greater amounts of U.S. technology into Mexico.

Immigration

The migration of Mexican workers into the United States, be it temporary or permanent, legal or illegal, has been a source of irritation between the two countries, and for good reason. The Immigration and Naturalization Service estimates that there are 6 million Mexican nationals living in the United States illegally. Other sources put the figure much higher, in fact more than twice that. Added to these figures are millions more who live and work in the United States under different bilateral or other arrangements: permanent residents, foreign scholars, temporary migrant workers, etc. Not surprisingly, however, the controversy is focused almost exclusively on the first group and is generally centered on a seemingly simple question: Do illegal immigrants contribute to the U.S. employment, or do they take jobs away from American workers?

The general consensus among the students of the field is that the migration of Mexican workers to the United States is negatively correlated to economic conditions in Mexico. In other words, adverse economic conditions in Mexico make even the possibility of underground employment in the United States that much more attractive to the unemployed—and probably "unemployable"—Mexican youth. So long as economic conditions remain as divergent as they presently are, the dream of "high" earnings will be sufficient to attract thousands of Mexican workers to the United States. The two governments may be able to reduce the flow of new migrants, but it is highly unlikely that they can stop it. For example, preliminary estimates indicate that the most comprehensive measure taken in recent years, the Immigration Reform and Control Act of 1986, has succeeded in reducing the apprehension of illegal aliens—and presumably the influx itself—by only one-fourth. This change was attributed by the Immigration and Naturalization Service to the Act's controversial employer sanctions, whereby all employers are required to ascertain the citizenship of all new employees. All employers hiring illegal workers will be subject to a fine and/or imprisonment.

Another aspect of migration of Mexican workers to the United States, often forgotten in the confusion surrounding the illegal immigration, is the negative effect that migration has on the Mexican economy. This impact may not be substantial for the millions of unskilled migrants, but Mexican migration to the United States is not limited to this group. There are also thousands of highly skilled Mexican professionals who migrate to the United States every year. As large as the Mexican labor pool may be, it cannot help but be adversely affected by this loss.

On the other hand, in both the cases of unskilled undocumented workers and the highly skilled professional Mexicans working in the United States, the Mexican economy has benefited from the remission of foreign earnings back into Mexico. It is estimated that this remission is between 0.5-1.0 percent of the country's GNP. By comparison, oil's contribution to Mexico's GNP is 8 percent.

Irrespective of its merits or problems, barring drastic measures by both countries, and until major opportunities develop in Mexico, immigration of Mexican workers into the United States will continue to remain an issue in bilateral relations between the two countries.

Oil

As late as the early 1970s, the Mexican oil production was hardly enough to meet the country's domestic requirements, particularly in the light of its rapid industrialization efforts. During the decade following 1975, however, production increased by more than 2.1 million barrels per day (bpd), giving Mexico the capacity to export about 1.5 million bpd (Table 1.3). At $15 per barrel, this would generate $8.2 billion per year in badly needed foreign currencies. It has also made oil the country's largest source of foreign exchange earnings. Bilateral economic relations between Mexico and the United States have been altered, rather substantially, and the "invisible integration" strengthened, by Mexico's new position as a major oil exporting country. On the Mexican side, the United States has been the destination of more than one-half of the country's oil exports. From the American side,

Table 1.3
Selected Petroleum Statistics of Mexico

Year	Total Production (000 bpd)	Total Revenues ($ bil.)	Total Exports (000 bpd)	Exports to U.S. (000 bpd)	U.S. Share (%)
1979	1,461	$ 3,987	531	431	83%
1980	1,936	10,413	825	533	65
1981	2,313	14,585	1,098	522	48
1982	2,748	16,594	1,570	685	44
1983	2,689	16,165	1,535	826	54
1984	2,780	16,466	1,518	748	49
1985	2,735	14,606	1,490	816	55
1986	2,428	6,133	1,289	699	54
1987*	2,526	10,000	1,350	657	49

Note: *Estimated by the author.
Sources: *Monthly Energy Review*, August 1987; *Review of the Economic Situation in Mexico*, Mexico City: Banco Nacional de Mexico, June 1987 (for revenue figures); *Annual Statistical Bulletin*, Vienna: OPEC (different issues).

Mexico has been one of the country's top three sources of oil imports (first in 1984 and 1985, third in 1986 and 1987). Mexico is currently supplying about one-eighth of the United States' total oil imports (Table 1.4).

Mexico's increased oil production has provided an added impetus for greater interdependency between that country and the United States, both directly through more oil trade, and indirectly through expanding Mexico's ability to import U.S. products. In fact, the indirect impact of Mexico's oil exports on its economic relations with the United States has been even greater than its direct impact. Mexico's ability to import $8-$9 billion from the United States annually, and thus create even greater interdependency with the United States, is a definite result of increased oil revenues. In effect, increased oil revenues have had a multiplier effect on U.S.-Mexican economic relations. As oil prices stabilize around $20 per barrel, as they are expected to do for the remainder of the 1980s, Mexico's ability to import American products will be enhanced. (At $20 per barrel, assuming total exports of 1.5 million bpd, Mexico's annual foreign exchange income from oil will be $11.0 billion, compared to $6.1 billion in 1986.) Part of this added income may be used to retire outstanding debt, but much of it will also be used to increase imports, most likely from the United States.

Table 1.4
U.S. Oil Imports by Source (000 b/d)

Year	Total	From Mexico	% From Mexico
1980	6,909	533	8%
1981	5,996	522	9
1982	5,113	685	13
1983	5,051	826	16
1984	5,437	748	14
1985	5,067	816	16
1986	6,224	699	11
1987*	6,015	657	11

Note: *Estimated by the author.
Source: *Monthly Energy Review*, August 1987, p. 43 (Table 3.3b).

The External Debt Issue

In the latter half of the 1970s, Mexico became, what seemed then, the main beneficiary of the myopic euphoria of the international banking community. Oil price increases of the early 1970s had given international bankers more money than they could diligently manage. It was at this time that the "recycling of petrodollars" was indeed the major concern of the international banks. They were looking for potential borrowers, and no country was a better choice than Mexico. It was a rapidly industrializing country; it had easy access to the very large U.S. market; the prices of its export products were increasing; and most significantly, it had oil. On its part, Mexico was also willing to borrow, and borrow it did. By 1981, Mexico's $80 billion external debt was the second largest among the developing countries. One year later, the country was forced into accepting restrictive IMF-dictated policies, as this was the only way it could avoid default.

Mexico's foreign debt is currently estimated to be well over $100 billion (Table 1.5). Of this total, approximately 80 percent is to U.S. banks and herein may lie the most serious source of potential conflict between the two countries. The bleak picture of Mexico's international economy—specifically its ability to meet its foreign debt obligations—has improved drastically in recent months. Since 1982, Mexico has been able to accumulate more than $16 billion in foreign currencies and Special Drawing Rights (SDRs). A remarkable accomplishment, even though it is hardly enough to meet debt service obligations for one year. At prevailing interest rates, Mexico's external debt situation requires interest payments of approximately 1 billion dollars per month.

Table 1.5
Mexico's External Debt (million dollars)

	1977	1981	1986	% Increase 1986/1977
Deposit Money Banks	1,817	10,156	8,739	381%
Development Banks	10,950	21,231	27,310	149
Non-Banking Inst.	n.a.	48,880	57,050	
IMF Credit	419	n.a.	3,319	692
IMF Holding of Peso	789	642	4,485	468
Official U.S. Claims				
on Mexico (net)	2,024	15,702	16,691	724

Source: *International Financial Statistics: 1987 Yearbook*, 1987.

The biggest challenge facing the new Mexican administration is to continue making these payments without suppressing imports to the point of disrupting the country's social stability. Stoppage of these payments, if it were to happen, may also create the biggest challenge for U.S. policymakers. Will the U.S. government bail out the affected banks? Or will it let these banks—and by extension the U.S. economy—go through a major crisis? The delicacy and enormity of the issue will linger on until the Mexican debt becomes manageable. In the meanwhile, it could be an impediment to greater integration of the two economies, at least for the short run.

Border Relations

There is no doubt that the U.S.-Mexican border region is the best manifestation of the "invisible integration" between the two countries. It is perfectly clear that both sides of the border seem to be prospering from the economic activities of the other side. For example, between the last two U.S. censuses, 1970 and 1980, per capital personal income in the United States grew 47.8 percent, while for all but two of the Standard Metropolitan Statistical Areas (SMSAs) bordering Mexico this increase was much higher. At the same time, the population in the slowest growing SMSA was increasing at three times the national average. In McAllen, Texas, for example, population growth for the decade was 56 percent, compared with the national average of 11 percent. In addition, McAllen's per capita income for the same period registered a growth of 60.4 percent, contrasted with the national average of 47.8 percent.

During the same decade, the Mexican cities on the border grew even more rapidly. Tijuana's growth was 96 percent; Matamoros' was 87 percent; and

Mexicali's was 85 percent. The slowest growth was in Ciudad Juarez, 68 percent. No doubt, such a high rate of urbanization in northern Mexico was strongly induced by its proximity to the United States.

An important contribution to the development of the border region has been the rapid growth of industrialization on both sides of the border through *maquiladoras*. Employment benefits of *maquiladoras* for the Mexican border cities is more apparent, but as important is the impact for the American side. For example, it is estimated that as much as 60 percent of every dollar paid to the *maquiladora's* Mexican workers is spent in U.S. cities bordering Mexico. Whereas such estimates may be questionable, other indications of heavy expenditures by Mexican nationals in U.S. border cities are not. In many such cities, per capita retail sales are *higher* than per capita income, in some cases substantially. Laredo, Texas, for example, has the *lowest* household effective buying income among U.S. SMSAs, $15,494 in 1986. It also has the *highest* per household retail sales in the country, $31,462, almost twice the national average of $16,462. If Laredoans were to follow the national trend and spend 66.8 percent of their household income in retail sales, Laredo's average would be $10,355 per household, that is, one-third of the actual amount. The other $20,107 spent in Laredo shops is obviously by out of town, in this case out of country, shoppers.

Laredo may be an exaggerated case, but it is certainly not atypical of the border with the possible exception of the border's largest two cities, San Diego and El Paso. By whatever criteria it is measured, the "invisible integration" of the border region is a reality. It is also an indication of the potential that these relationships, synergetic, albeit asymmetrical and symbiotic, have.

CONCLUSIONS

Economic relations between the United States and Mexico have been gradually and steadily expanding during the recent past. The resultant interdependency—or "invisible integration"—has had many advantages and some disadvantages for both sides. Both sides have benefited from this gradual integration, even though the process may not have been equal, some say fair, in its benefits to the two sides; and herein may lie the core of the criticism of the concept. For Mexico, the asymmetric nature of this relationship has been a cause of concern and serious disenchantment. For Mexico, a developing nation with many economic problems and a proud heritage, the dichotomy is how to benefit from its proximity to the United States without changing the relationship from interdependency to Mexico's dependency on the United States.

Such displeasures notwithstanding, U.S.-Mexican economic relations are destined to expand in the coming years and decades. Their unquestionable growth will generate the need for more analytical studies of the issues involved such as the present book. In the remaining chapters different aspects of U.S.-Mexican economic relations will be discussed by several scholars of the field. The diversity of their respective backgrounds matches the diversity of the issues involved, thus providing the reader with a balanced articulation of the topic; and that has indeed been the sole objective of this volume.

NOTES

1. The basic concept of swap arrangements is "that foreign banks or other holders of [Mexican] dollar debts can sell these to potential investors at a substantial discount." The investor can resell the debt to the Mexican government, also discounted, though not nearly in the same proportion. The seller receives the dollar equivalent in pesos (calculated at free exchange rate) to be used for investment in Mexico through the acquisition of equity in a Mexican corporation.

"For instance, if a foreign bank were willing to sell $10 million dollars of Mexican public-sector debt at a 40 percent discount, the potential investor would pay the bank $6 million, and the bank would issue a debt cancellation note to the Mexican government. The government, in turn, would discount this note. If negotiated discount were 20 percent, the government, through its agencies, would pay the investor the equivalent of 8 million pesos. The investor would then use the pesos for the purchase of 'qualified capital stock' in a Mexican corporation" *Review of Economic Situation in Mexico*, May 1987, p. 113.

2. A special provision of U.S. customs laws allows products produced in *maquila* plants in Mexico, or similar operations elsewhere, to enter the United States without paying any tariffs or being subject to quantitative restrictions.

3. Mitchell A. Seligson, and Edward J. Williams, *Maquiladora Workers in the Mexico-United States Border Industrialization Program* (Austin: University of Texas Press, 1981), p. 3.

PART TWO
EXTERNAL DEBT ISSUES

Undoubtedly, one of the most important questions dominating the economic—and eventually political—relations between the United States and Mexico in the foreseeable future will be the foreign debt issue, specifically, Mexico's debt to U.S. banks. Of more than $100 billion that Mexico owes to foreign lenders, about 80 percent is to American banks. What Mexico does about this, or more realistically, what the two sides can agree to do about this issue, will have serious and long-lasting repercussions for the relations between the two countries. Mexico's obvious dilemma is how to solve its foreign debt problem without creating more damaging political and social ones. A list of possible solutions to any developing country's external debt includes some myopically simple and attractive ones. Unfortunately, some of these "simple and attractive" remedies—for example, a complete default on foreign liabilities—could be detrimental to the country's general economy, and sooner or later its polity. Consequently, Mexico's options are limited to those which, while solving, or at least alleviating, the debt problem, do not result in a worsening of the country's general economic performance by increasing inflation, deepening the recession, or by causing social unrest and/or political instability. In other words, there can be no revolutionary panaceas. The process will have to be slow, methodical, and at times painful.

An articulation of an evolutionary process for solving the external debt issue is given by Robert Looney in Chapter 2. His analysis of the economic consequences of the Mexican debt and his discussion of Mexico's options in dealing with this problem provide a model for other debtor developing nations to follow. Of particular importance is his discussion of the debt-equity swap arrangements which, pending an ironing out of technical details, may well be the best alternative that all countries with significant foreign debt can adopt. The optimistic evaluation of the Mexican economy given in Chapter 2 provides a ray of hope for all debt-ridden developing countries. It also gives credibility to the policies implemented by Mexico during the years following 1982.

In Chapter 3, Edgar Ortiz presents an evaluation of the economic policies followed by Mexico since 1982. He maintains that in addition to adopting short-term microeconomic policies to remedy short-term problems it faced, the government of Mexico, recognizing the old import substitution approach as the root of the crisis, has also opted for a new developmental model.

The author analyzes these policies in light of Mexico's economic performance in recent years and concludes that the plan for modernizing industries and increasing exports will not be effective unless measures are taken to reduce the burden of external debt on the Mexican economy. He also proposes new trade agreements to expand and stabilize world trade as a means of avoiding further problems by Mexico and other developing nations.

The final segment of Part Two, Chapter 4, is a discussion of a theoretical model developed by Jongmoo Jay Choi and Richard Ajayi. Their work is an attempt to bridge the theoretical gap between external debt and its major determinants, which in the case of Mexico, the authors consider to be oil prices and exchange rates. In their study, the authors synthesize the asset and monetary models of exchange rates, and estimate the reduced-form equation for Mexico for the period 1975–1986. The specific coefficients used in this model are foreign debt, oil prices, and exchange rates. The authors' findings indicate that the synthesized model performs markedly better than its components. In addition, they find that the coefficients used and other variables are more consistent with the asset model than with the monetary model or the tradition flow view.

2

Economic Consequences of the Mexican Debt: Implications for the United States

Robert E. Looney

INTRODUCTION

In one of the more surprising developments since the Latin American debt crisis began in 1982, Mexico in the summer of 1987 found itself with the unlikely dilemma of how to spend nearly $16 billion of foreign reserves.[1] A number of circumstances contributed to the turnaround:

1. Oil prices stabilized in late 1986, then rose with the increase in uncertainty concerning Persian Gulf shipping.
2. Following an earlier delay, the country received a $12 billion disbursement of a credit package agreed with the International Monetary Fund.
3. With successive peso devaluations resulting in an undervalued peso, non-oil exports rose at an annual rate of 30 percent.
4. Improved economic conditions and the undervalued peso resulted in a significant inflow of Mexican assets previously held abroad.

Several options appear to be open to the government, each having its pros and cons. Increased domestic spending to stimulate growth and create jobs would make inflation worse: price rises could easily reach an annual rate of 200 percent within months, with serious implications for wages, foreign exchange, and interest rates. Yet politically in an election year to idly sit on $16 billion, particularly when interest is being paid on a substantial part of that sum, seems unacceptable. Quite a different approach would be to use the reserves to buy Mexican sovereign paper on the secondary market, thus cancelling part of the country's $110 billion foreign debt. Given that most Mexican securities in the summer of 1987 were selling at about 55 to 60 percent of face value, Mexico could reduce its external debt burden by $13 to $18 billion by allocating between $8 billion and $10 billion to this purpose. This would save the country $800 million to $1 billion per year in interest payments. Unfortunately, despite its technical merits and pressure of its favor coming from the country's creditors, the debt purchase scheme seems politically infeasible without some sort of compensating arrangement with the country's creditors. Analysts stressing this fact note that a nation that has gone through five years of practically no economic growth, a drop of nearly 40 percent in the purchasing power of most salaries, and a virtual suspension of job creation will not readily accept that the best way to spend hard-earned foreign funds is to give them back to the banks. The government cannot publicly acknowledge that in 1986 the economy could not grow because of the lack of money and that in 1987 it cannot grow because of too much money. Nor can a country already suffering from double digit inflation be told that growth must be postponed since it would rekindle inflation.[2]

Castaneda has concluded that

Mexico's current predicament is more a symptom of the continued protraction of its economy than a sign of its recovery. The debt crisis has not been solved; it has just been postponed, together with economic growth. If anything, foreign reserves are up precisely because growth has been forsaken. Under these circumstances, the wisest course may be then one which President de la Madrid will, it is to be hoped, settle on. It would involve using the reserves partially to prime the economy, achieving some growth and modest job creation at the cost of a moderate increase in inflation, but saving the bulk for de la Madrid's successor.

Clearly whether or not the reserves are spent by the de la Madrid administration, the new president of Mexico, Salinas de Gortari[3] will be forced to tackle the fundamental problem that has confounded recent administrations: how to make the Mexican economy grow at levels compatible with demographic growth and social welfare.

The purpose of this chapter is to examine the relative merits of Castaneda's suggestion that saving the nation's earnings for the Salinas de Gortari administration could be de la Madrid's ultimate tribute to what may well prove to be his most redeeming virtue: *le sens de l'etat*, as opposed to the portfolio manager's despair in the face of idle assets. Hopefully in the process of examining this issue some conclusions can be drawn as to the role of external debt in Mexico's recent economic performance, and guidelines established as to the country's best medium-term strategy for dealing with its external obligations.

PHASES OF MEXICAN DEVELOPMENT

Any discussion of Mexico's current debt problems would be incomplete without some reference to the development strategies that lead to the current situation. Many observers[4] trace the current debt crisis back to the Echeverria Administration (1971–1976). Echeverria sought to address many of the distributional problems associated with the country's attempts at import substitution industrialization with a modification of this basic strategy dubbed "Shared Development." It had four pillars:[5]

1. the use of public expenditure to stimulate demand and broaden the domestic market;
2. the fuller use of existing productive capacity;
3. the deepening of import substitution; and
4. the expansion and diversification of exports to help confront the foreign exchange bottleneck.

These moves represented an effort to revitalize a strategy of insulation and to introduce a different domestic distribution of gains and losses.[6]

In retrospect it is clear that there were a number of basic dilemmas in Mexican economic policy under Echeverria. These included the desire to use fiscal policy to reform the social structure, but then doing so without creating an adequate tax base; the desire to raise exports, but seeking to do so while maintaining a fixed exchange rate in the face of accelerating inflation; the desire to strengthen public sector enterprises while trying to maintain their prices at unrealistically low levels; and striving for greater industrial efficiency under a policy of protectionism.[7] The net result was that the public sector deficit expanded from an average annual rate of 2.5 percent of GDP in 1965-1970 to 9.5 percent in 1976 and an increase in the external debt; by 1976 Mexico's public foreign debt was $20 billion. These alternative means of supporting "Shared Development" proved unsustainable, however, and in 1976 the development strategy collapsed in the midst of domestic political and foreign debt crisis.[8]

José Lopez Portillo (1976–1982) began his administration with an IMF stabilization program, and a promise of structural change. Once the petroleum revenues began coming in, however, attempts at stabilization were abandoned as Lopez Portillo decided to spend his way out of trouble through adopting a massively expensive development program.[9] As the oil revenues increased foreign borrowing also accelerated; control over spending became increasingly lax as the government undertook a major expansion in infrastructure investment.[10] Instead of cutting back expenditures in the wake of the 1981 decline in oil revenues (reaching only $14.5 billion instead of the $20 billion projected in the 1981 budget), the government continued its spending by even heavier foreign borrowing, mainly short term. By the end of 1981 the public sector foreign debt, scheduled to rise during the 12 months from $34 billion to $40 billion, actually jumped to $53 billion of which $14.5 was due for repayment in 1982.[11]

Progress in Dealing with the Debt

When President De La Madrid took office on December 1, 1982, the country was facing a dual economic crisis, domestic in origin, and external conditions were intensifying the problems. The first crisis, which could be considered cyclical, required frank and immediate attention, while the second, more structural in nature, would take years of constant effort to overcome.

Consequently, the economic and social strategy incorporated into the 1983–1988 National Development Plan centered on two interrelated lines of action: one of immediate, short-term economic measures and the other of structural change. Both involved reducing the public deficit, increasing domestic savings, and reducing trade barriers, while, at the same time, protecting productive capacity and employment, and bringing down inflation.

In an inflationary context, interest payments on debt contain a sizeable component corresponding to the inflationary depreciation of that same debt. If this factor is applied to Mexico, it is evident that during the 1983–1985 period there was significant progress in lowering the relative value of the public debt:[12]

1. The domestic public debt, after having increased 60 percent in real terms during 1982, fell 30 percent between 1983 and 1985.
2. Also during this period, foreign public debt, in relation to the gross domestic product, fell from 43.9 to 40.6 percent. This reflects a decline in the growth rate of net borrowing, which fell from levels surpassing 7 percent of the GDP in 1981 to 3.1 percent in 1983, 1.5 percent in 1984, and 0.4 percent in 1985.
3. In the 19 months prior to July 1986, the country received no net financial resources from the rest of the world.

The country has also made important improvements in public finances, in trimming the size of government, and in increasing efficiency in public enterprises.[13] Between 1983 and 1985 the total public sector deficit decreased from 18 percent of the GDP to 9.2 percent.

4. A better way of evaluating the adjustment is in the primary deficit (total deficit minus interest payments on the debt). In 1981, the primary deficit amounted to 8.1 percent of the GDP in 1986; despite the fall in oil prices it was anticipated that there would be a surplus of 3.9 percent.
5. The largest part of the reduction in the fiscal deficit came from cuts in government spending on goods and services before interest payments; spending has declined almost eight percentage points of GDP since 1981.
6. The system of state subsidies was also completely revised. Between 1982 and 1985, government transfers to public companies—excluding support for debt service—declined three percentage points of GDP. In real terms this means that transfers declined by 40 percent between 1982 and 1985.
7. Finally, an effort has been made to reduce the gap between the general price levels for consumer goods and the prices of public goods and services, especially in energy. This has reduced implicit subsidies and eliminated distortions in relative prices.

To stop capital flight, the government has set interest rates well above the inflation rate. In addition, the government, beginning in the summer of 1986, introduced a new type of government savings instrument whose value in Mexican pesos is tied to the value of the dollar. In other words, Mexicans are now able to invest their money within the country assured that the money will grow as if it were held in dollars in a U.S. bank account.[14] The authorities have also created incentives for export-oriented companies and companies generating new jobs. Government subsidies on gas, electricity, mass transportation, and basic foods are being phased out. They are also divesting themselves of many state run firms.

On another front the government has enjoyed some success in its debt-capitalization program.[15] Launched in June 1986, this program allows debt to be converted into capital by foreign investors. Conversion is authorized if the applicant can persuade the government that it will create new jobs, increase exports, or introduce advanced technology. Depending on the nature of the project, the debt is exchanged for pesos at 76–100 percent of face value (unlike the Chilean regime, introduced a year earlier, which exchanges at par).[16] By late 1986 some $200 million in external debt had been converted under this system and the government had more than 70 applications pending.

A parallel scheme was suggested to the Mexican government by the International Finance Corporation (IFC): a closed-end fund which would buy up foreign loans, and convert them into peso-denominated direct investments in Mexican companies. The IFC itself would be the direct investor, though it would make a secondary offering of its own shares to private investment. Clearly, this indirect procedure only slightly obscures the fact that in opting for debt-equity swaps Mexico has had to overlook many of its selective restrictions on foreign investment, another traditional banner of the country's nationalism.[17]

Most importantly the country's debt-for-equity swap plan not only rids the state of costly firms, but adds needed dollars to the treasury and is a strong stimulus in luring direct foreign investment. Debt-for-equity agreements amounted to $850 million in foreign investment in the last nine months of 1986. Primarily because of fears of inflation, the program ceiling for 1987 was set at $1.5 billion.[18] While optimists contend that this program could liquidate 8 percent of Mexico's external debt, and that the country could get rid of a major source of federal budgetary deficits[19] by offering discounts of 5 to 25 percent to foreign investors wishing to purchase shares in 55 state-run firms currently facing indebtedness and liquidity problems, it is not at all clear that the program will make more than a token dent in the country's external debt.[20] At most, foreign bankers and Finance Ministry officials estimate debt swaps will retire about $3 or $4 billion of Mexican debt. Officials characterize the debt-for-equity scheme as a temporary measure that may become more restrictive and eventually be eliminated entirely.[21]

While demand for Mexican equity remained strong through most of 1987, the Mexican government seems unlikely to raise its self-imposed ceiling on the supply of such swaps. In part the main reservations Mexican authorities have with the program (in addition to purely nationalistic concerns) involve the fact that

1. The country may be simply foregoing foreign exchange, since most swap investment would have arrived anyway in real dollars. This is most likely the case in the automotive industry but less clear in tourism, and in the *maquiladoras*, which have become the new foci of debt-swapping.
2. The cheap investment pesos may fuel a surge in inflation.[22]
3. Debt swaps give multinational subsidiaries with preexisting expansion plans a steep discount in a local currency that is already substantially undervalued. There is no evidence, moreover, officials acknowledge, that the program is attracting investors not already established in Mexico.[23]

Finally, by joining the General Agreement on Tariffs and Trade (GATT), the country hopes to increase trade with the United States, which already accounts for 60 percent of their total trade, and to expand and diversify trade with Europe. The major measures under the GATT agreement include:[24]

1. The basis of the current protection system is primarily on tariffs, compared with the previous structure that relied mainly on import licenses. About 89 percent of the items covered by tariffs, amounting to about 65 percent of the value of imports, are now license-free. In 1982, only 20 percent of the value of imports escaped quantitative restrictions.
2. Import tariffs have been cut from an interval ranging from 0 to 100 percent to one between 0 and 45 percent in 1986.
3. Beginning in April 1985, there was a gradual reduction in tariff levels; by the end of 1988, the levels will fall to a maximum of 30 percent.

In summary, since 1982 Mexico has progressively moved toward a pragmatic external approach to its massive debt problems. Debt restructuring with international creditors and foreign governments, mostly the United States and Japan, has had top priority. In terms of internal policies, reforms have been undertaken in the fiscal and industrial sectors. Mexico has slowly moved toward supply-side economics by cutting both personal and corporate income taxes to stimulate increased investment and consumption.[25]

In addition:

1. Public spending as a proportion of GDP has been reduced from 32 percent in 1981 to 19 percent in 1986; real public investment from 11 to 3 percent of GDP over the same period.
2. Public sector enterprises in the same period were reduced from 1,155 to 820 with a further 123 companies due to be sold or closed immediately.
3. Real wages were cut by about 45 percent for half of the 25 million workers with full-time jobs.

4. Subsidies have been cut back radically and even dangerously. For instance, Conasupo, the government company that produces or buys and distributes subsidized staple foods, has cut subsidies by a full 70 percent since 1982. In 1986 the maize subsidy for tortillas, the staple diet of the poor, were about one-quarter of their 1985 levels.

5. Imports have been liberalized with 62 percent in volume now free from import licenses while the country has overcome a generation of nationalist inspired trade isolationism and applied to join the General Agreement on Tariffs and Trade (GATT).

6. The more liberal trade policy is helping to diversify the economy away from oil so that by mid-1986, 30.8 percent of exports were manufactured goods, up from 17.77 percent in 1981.

7. The government in 1984 handed back to the private sector an additional 339 companies taken over by the state when the banks were nationalized in 1982. This entailed privatization of most of the country's brokerage and insurance houses, which by now have become a dynamic alternative to the state banks and channel a fifth of national savings.[26]

The 1986 Rescue Package

Mexico has been very successful in achieving its external goals. In fact Mexico was the first and so far only country to gain IMF approval of repayment linked to its principal export, oil. In the negotiations with the Paris Club, the country also achieved limited legitimacy concerning other new debt servicing principles. Two of the more far reaching and provocative principles were the priority of a minimum growth rate over strict payback requirements; and the potential of debtors deferring payment of interest.

More precisely Mexico's latest major loan package (which was finally approved in March 1987) and involved as much as $7.7 billion has as its principal provisions:

1. A longer time schedule is allowed to repay $43.7 billion in existing loans to Mexico, extending to 20 years, with no principal due for the first seven years.

2. Interest rates are reduced on the $43.7 billion in old loans, and on the $8.6 billion in loans made in 1983 and 1984, and on the $7.7 billion in new money. The interest rate will be 13/16 of one percentage point above the London interbank offer rate (LIBOR), the standard measurement for banks' cost of funds.

3. Of the contingency loan fund $500 million would be available, if the Mexican economy grows slower than its growth targets during the first quarter of 1987 and $1.2 billion would be available if export receipts—principally oil—are lower than expected.[27]

The 1986 crisis initiated widespread debate about the causes, consequences, and costs of the debt. Popular public point of view was that Mexico could not and should not have to face more years of harsh austerity just to satisfy the IMF and commercial bankers, but more conservative elements of the Mexican government felt that it was critical that Mexico meet the demands of the IMF and obtain the loans necessary to avoid a default. Others argued that the loans were necessary, but felt that concessions should be made by the IMF and the international banking community. This faction maintained that Mexico had attempted to restructure its economy and had imposed austerity. The unfortunate collapse of oil prices in 1986, they insisted, should be a responsibility shared by the commercial banks and the international financial institutions.[28] In essence, the new loan package provided for loans of over $12 billion for the period 1986–1987, and appears consistent with U.S. Treasury Secretary Baker's Third World debt program:

The Baker plan . . . emphasized that the debt crisis could only be resolved through sustained growth by the debtor countries—that austerity alone would be self-defeating in the longer run. To achieve the requisite growth, the plan prescribed orthodox programs of economic reform and structural adjustment for the debtor countries, including greater reliance on the private sector, curtailment of state subsidies and price controls, measures to stimulate both foreign and domestic investment, and export promotion and trade liberalization. The plan also called on private banks and international institutions to step up sharply their lending to indebted countries. The banks were urged to provide new commercial credits of $20 billion over a three year period, while the World Bank and the Inter-American Development Bank would contribute an additional $9 billion in loans.[29]

The rescue package called for the commercial banks to generate approximately $6 billion of new loans. The IMF and World Bank loans were contingent on the commercial bank loans being secured. This package also contained some concessions for Mexico. The World Bank agreed to provide additional credit if real economic growth was less than 3.5 percent in 1987. The IMF loan of $1.6 billion guaranteed additional credit if oil income fell below $9 billion. In exchange for this jumbo loan package, the IMF required Mexico to continue to sell off and reduce the number of state-owned enterprises, to liberalize trade, to attract more foreign investment, and to reduce its domestic deficit by three percent of GDP.

The program has come under fairly severe criticism. Critics charge that it only addresses the short-run problem of servicing immediate debt obligations, and will take the pressure off the economy only if oil prices stiffen or even increase, that the global economy continues to grow, and that interest rates do not rise, all questionable assumptions.

Furthermore, critics assert that adding another $12 billion to Mexico's debt will merely increase the nation's long-term debt service obligations. More importantly, they argue that this loan package will not reverse the negative transfer of capital from Mexico to the advanced nations; instead, it will merely perpetuate this negative flow. The critics also warn that this package will simply draw United States banks further into the debt quagmire. Moreover they argue that the Mexican people should not have to suffer through more years of austerity and a further decline in their already low standard of living.

IMPACT OF EXTERNAL DEBT AND FISCAL POLICY ON THE ECONOMY

Clearly the long-run impact of Mexico's external debt on the country's future growth will in large part depend on how the debt is used, and whether or not the debt actually results in new productive resources becoming available for capital formation. A particularly important question is: Has external debt and/or government deficits "crowded out" private sector investment? FitzGerald's work,[30] drawing largely on Mexican Treasury data, suggests that in Mexico's case government deficits tend to displace or crowd out private consumption. His empirical results indicate that private savings increased to pay for the deficit. According to FitzGerald, however, the increase in savings came at the expense of private consumption rather than private investment. Thus government deficits have had a stimulating effect on growth by mobilizing savings for increased levels of investment.

The results obtained by FitzGerald led him to conclude that development finance in Mexico was unlike the orthodox view.[31] Under this view, savings is the constraint on investment. If the government finances the deficit through the use of savings, investment is crowded out. Savings, being the residual after consumption, thus determines investment. In the Mexican case, FitzGerald concludes that consumption and savings are residuals after investment and deficit levels have been met. Thus investment and the deficit determine the levels of consumption and savings.[32]

However, using International Monetary Fund data, Looney and Frederiksen[33] found evidence for the more orthodox view of savings and investment in Mexico. Their findings indicated that both changes in savings and the level of savings were closely related to changes in GDP and the level of GDP respectively. Contrary to FitzGerald, they found that increases in savings were associated with decreases in the deficit. In addition they found that increases in government expenditures reduced private savings. With regard to the level of savings the government deficit had a minor negative impact. Government borrowing, as to be expected, was strongly related to the level of saving.

In sum then, the picture that develops from these results is one of little direct crowding out. Private savings seems to be undertaken primarily to finance investment—the orthodox view of savings. While not tested directly, there is some evidence to suggest that increased access to credit through the banking system stimulates savings and in turn private investment. The only crowding out seems to be increased savings (decreased consumption) through the inflation effect of an expansion in government expenditures.[34]

With regard to investment, Looney and Frederiksen found a pattern similar to that of consumption and savings, that is, the level of investment appears largely determined by changes in GDP. Importantly, it does not seem that government financial actions significantly crowded out investment. Government credit from the banking system was positively related to investment as were increases in the deficit (when changes in GDP were included in the estimating equation).

In general government activities (both on the expenditure and financial side) do not appear to have crowded out investment, other than through the adverse effect of inflation diverting funds away from capital formation. . . . It appears that Mexico is typical of the Keynesian case, increases in the deficit were accompanied by increases in consumption. Apparently enough slack existed in the economy so that as deficit spending increases, the available resources were more fully utilized. There were subsequent increases in national income and consumption. The results also indicate that private investment is adversely affected by inflation (the latter presumably stemming from government deficits.[35]

Looking at different time periods however, Looney and Frederiksen concluded that for the later periods (1965–1981), as opposed to earlier periods (1951–1965), the impact of government fiscal policy was shifting from positive to negative:

In general the results for the later periods suggest, contrary to FitzGerald, that the government deficit may over time be weakening in its impact on expanding the GDP. If so the impact of the deficit on investment and growth in Mexico may now be a net negative. The implication is that Mexico will not be able to overcome its current economic crisis until the government's fiscal position is under control.[36]

As noted, the empirical work of FitzGerald, and Looney and Frederiksen were largely concerned with short-run impacts of the government's deficit on savings and investment. One of the more interesting results of this analysis was the finding by Looney and Frederiksen that several of the mechanisms linking the government sector to private sector activity seem to be breaking down; that is, the positive links that government expenditure, particularly its allocations to infrastructure,[37] may be breaking down, and in fact, turning negative. To test this hypothesis a longer term estimation procedure was utilized, that is, it can be demonstrated that an equation of the Koyck[38] form:

$$\text{(a) } y = ax + byL + z$$

where (y) represents a macroeconomic aggregate such as consumption investment or gross domestic product; and (x) represents a government fiscal variable such as borrowing, or expenditures. The formula implies an exponential decay scheme whereby the effect of a once-and-for-all change in government fiscal activity (expenditures, deficits, external borrowing, etc.) would affect private consumption, investment, and growth not only during that period, but would also have (in declining terms) an impact on their level in future years. It can be shown that this result stems directly from the inclusion of national income lagged one year (byL) on the right hand side of the equation.[39]

Impact patterns along these lines are easy to imagine in Mexico's case where debt-supported government expenditures might be felt heavily during the first few time periods, decaying gradually thereafter.

To test for a general secular decline in the effectiveness of government expenditures in stimulating growth, a dummy variable was added to the regression equation. Much of the literature on Mexico treats each six-year presidential term (*sexenio*) as a fairly homogenous policy environment in which presidential economic programs[40] can be fairly easily categorized, that is, the stabilizing development of Diaz Ordaz, the shared development of Echeverria, the high growth policies of Lopez Portillo, and the austerity programs of De La Madrid.[41] A dummy variable (*DUMP*) was created to capture each presidential *sexenio*.[42] The Diaz Ordaz years, 1966–1970 = 0; the Echeverria years, 1971–1976 = 1; the Lopez Portillo years, 1977–1982 = 2; and the De La Madrid years, 1983–1988 = 3. Each government fiscal variable (x in equation [a]) was in turn multiplied by this political dummy to create a variable depicting any potential change in the slope of the fiscal-macroeconomic relationship.[43] The final equation used for estimation was therefore:

$$(b)\ y = ax + byL + dx + z$$

where dx = the dummy (*DUMP*) times the fiscal variable, (x). Statical significance of this variable would indicate a secular (by *sexenio*) change in the manner in which government fiscal activities impact on the economy. The fiscal variables examined in the regression equations were:
GEP = Government expenditures (line 82, IFS);
BDP = Net government domestic borrowing (line 84a, IFS);
BFP = Net government foreign borrowing (line 85a, IFS).
DGEP, DBDP, and *DBFP* represent these fiscal variables multiplied by the political *sexenio* dummy, *DUMP*.

EMPIRICAL RESULTS

Estimates of the distributed lag impact of fiscal developments debt on various macroeconomic aggregates over the 1966–84 period produced the following results.

Private Consumption (*PCNP*):

(1) $PCNP$ = 1.05 $PCNPL$ + 0.29 GEP − 0.17 $DGEF$ − 0.02 RHO
          (24.36)   (1.19)   (−2.74)   (−0.08)
          $r^2 = 0.975; DW = 1.85$

(2) $PCNP$ = 1.05 $PCNPL$ + 1.35 BDP − 0.79 $DBDP$ − 0.20 RHO
          (54.27)   (2.19)   (−3.20)   (−0.83)
          $r^2 = 0.979; DW = 1.94$

(3) PCNP = 1.07 $PCNPL$ + 0.99 BFP − 1.28 $DBFP$ − 0.45 RHO
          (125.28)   (1.11)   (−4.5)   (−2.131)
          $r^2 = 0.995; DW = 2.16$

Gross Capital Formation ($TINP$):

(4) $TINP$ = 1.17 $TINPL$ + 0.02 GEP − 0.09 $DGEP$ + 0.09 RHO
          (4.71)   (0.05)   (−1.14)   (0.37)
          $r^2 = 0.832; DW = 1.72$

(5) $TINP$ = 1.12 $TINPL$ + 0.60 BDP − 0.52 $DBDP$ − 0.04 RHO
          (14.91)   (0.89)   (−1.90)   (−0.18)
          $r^2 = 0.874; DW = 1.87$

(6) $TINP$ = 1.16 $TINPL$ − 0.30 BFP − 0.83 $DBFP$ − 0.43 RHO
          (31.32)   (−0.25)   (−2.03)   (−2.00)
          $r^2 = 0.963; DW = 2.19$

(7) $TINP$ = − 0.14 $TINPL$ + 0.89 $PCNP$ − 0.01 $DPCNP$ − 0.13 RHO
          (−1.04)   (6.48)   (−0.60)   (−0.171)
          $r^2 = 0.819; DW = 2.00$

Gross Domestic Product ($GDPNP$):

(8) $GDPNP$ = 1.10 $GDPNPL$ − 0.07 GEP − 0.13 $DGEP$ + 0.31 RHO
          (26.01)   (−0.22)   (−1.54)   (1.34)
          $r^2 = 0.971; DW = 1.62$

(9) $GDPNP$ = 1.07 $GDPNPL$ + 1.11 BDP − 0.80 $DBDP$ + 0.15 RHO
          (60.18)   (1.36)   (−2.14)   (0.63)
          $r^2 = 0.978; DW = 1.76$

(10) $GDPNP$ = 1.08 $GDPNPL$ − 0.38 BFP − 1.11 $DBFP$ − 0.24 RHO
          (113.51)   (−0.26)   (−2.10)   (−1.04)
          $r^2 = 0.995; DW = 2.08$

(11) $GDPNP$ = 0.12 $GDPNPL$ + 1.20 $TINP$ + 0.04 $DTINP$ + 0.21 RHO
          (2.29)   (17.23)   (1.25)   (0.98)
          $r^2 = 0.970; DW = 1.43$

(12) $GDPNP$ = 0.26 $GDPNL$ + 1.12 $PCNP$ + 0.05 $DPCNP$ + 0.43 RHO
          (1.97)   (6.25)   (2.17)   (1.98)
          $r^2 = 0.981; DW = 1.50$

In general the results indicate:[44]

1. Given the low t-values on the *bx* term, government expenditures or borrowing have had, at best, only a marginally positive impact on private consumption over the period examined. In addition there has been a decreasing effectiveness in the ability of the government to increase private sector consumption with the negative sign on the dummy term, indicating that private consumption as a proportion of government fiscal activity is decreasing considerably with each successive presidential *sexenio*. In terms of the strength of fiscal policy, private-sector consumption has been most adversely affected over time by external borrowing, followed by domestic borrowing, with government expenditures having the least negative impact.

2. Gross capital formation has not been stimulated by government expenditure or borrowing. If anything, the negative slopes on the dummy terms indicate that government fiscal actions are increasingly crowding out productive investment. On the other hand, private-sector consumption appears to be a major factor stimulating increased levels of investment. In contrast to fiscal policies, private consumption has not experienced diminishing returns over time in affecting investment.

3. Gross domestic product has also not been positively affected by government expenditures or borrowing. As with investment, whatever impact government actions have had on GDP appear to be encountering decreasing effectiveness; that is, GDP as a percentage of government expenditures or borrowing has been decreasing with each successive presidential *sexenio*.[45] On the other hand both investment and consumption have had a strong positive impact on GDP, with no signs of diminishing returns.

To sum, it appears that whatever positive impacts government expenditure and borrowing may have historically had on the economy, these effects are no longer present. In fact there is evidence that Mexico is increasingly facing diminishing returns in terms of the government's ability to inject a net positive stimulus to the economy. Apparently any near term revitalization of the economy will have to be derived from an autonomous expansion of private rather than public-sector expenditures.

CONCLUSIONS

The empirical results above suggest several principles that should serve as the basis of resolving the Mexican government's current short-term dilemma of the best use to be made of the country's large reserve position, together with the longer term problem facing both the United States and Mexico as to the resolution of the country's external debt situation.

In terms of the short-run problem, it is apparent that when Carlos Salinas de Gortari assumes office in late 1988 he must tackle the fundamental problem that has confounded the present administration as well as its predecessors: how to regain the high rates of growth that characterized the Mexican economy over the 1955–1970 period. Since the early 1970s successive governments have attempted to solve this dilemma by either exporting oil, or increasing the country's external debt. Although there has been some progress in transforming the structure of the Mexican economy, there is little reason to believe that simply increasing government expenditures will return the country to a self-sustaining high growth path. As Castaneda notes, whatever policies he chooses, Salinas de Gortari will need all the foreign reserves and breathing room he can get. Saving the nation's reserves for his successor could be President De La Madrid's wisest move.

In terms of longer run policies for dealing with the varied issues surrounding the country's external debt, the options appear to be (a) default, (b) a further variant of the current Baker-type stabilization program agreed to in March 1987, or (c) a combination of (a) and (b).[46] The default option can probably be rejected out of hand for political reasons, although it is not apparent that from a purely economic viewpoint there would be any great costs to Mexico.[47] The first offspring of the Baker Plan was the "growth oriented" adjustment plan for Mexico put into effect in March 1977. Another version of this approach to external debt is the Bradley Plan. As in the Baker Plan, Mexico would be required to liberalize its international trading arrangements and generally adopt market-oriented reforms. Clearly any approach to alleviating the debt problem that is likely to revive economic growth in Mexico (and other indebted countries) is welcomed. Yet the Baker and Bradley type proposals raise some disturbing questions both as to their feasibility and their desirability.[48]

Countries get into debt servicing problems for two kinds of reasons: bad luck and bad management or bad policies. (Among the latter we include those that get into trouble by design.) Bad luck includes such external (to borrowing countries) shocks as the rise in world wide real interest rates (largely made in the USA), adverse shifts in the terms of trade (the decline in the oil price in the case of Mexico) . . . . The proposals are unfair in that they do not make the magnitude or the terms on which the relief is provided contingent on whether the country's problems are due to bad luck or bad management. Past policy performance is not taken into account. Future policy reform and performance is of course put at the center of the stage, but it is doubtful whether this can be taken too seriously, precisely because past policies (or how a country got into the current mess) are not taken into account. By treating the existing debt as a bygone and focusing exclusively on (promises of) future policies for trade liberalization, privatization, fiscal probity etc., these proposals contribute to an environment in which countries are more likely deliberately to build up their debt once more to unsustainable levels in the expectation of a Bradley Plan Vintage II when the next crisis hits.[49]

The empirical analysis above, while acknowledging that Mexico has had its share of bad luck,[50] also identifies a long-run secular decline in the effectiveness of government expenditures as a major cause of the country's current debt problems. Until this limitation to growth is overcome, it is unlikely that the current stabilization effort or future Baker-Bradley type programs will be of any real value in solving the country's growth difficulties.

If solutions (a) and (b) to the debt problem are not viable, what is left? Pragmatic Mexicans realized some time ago that a number of political and economic reforms need to be enacted before the country will be able to return to any type of growth path resembling that achieved in the 1955-1970 period.[51] Controls on capital flight, privatization of inefficient and corrupt state-controlled industries, a lowering of trade barriers, and tax reform and price controls have been instituted or are being considered.[52] It will be politically impossible to fully implement these reforms without a significant reduction and eventual elimination of the debt burden. A long-term debt moratorium (like a Chapter 11 bankruptcy filing in the United States) would guarantee Mexico a new start and some hope of success.[53] In return, however, Mexico would be required to exchange at a rate of 50 cents on the dollar, an increasing volume each year of debt for equity, and in fact encourage the expansion of such programs.

The empirical analysis above indicated that any long-term solution to Mexico's growth-debt problems must involve a gradual contraction of the public sector in the economy and an expansion of private sector activity. Using this general principal, several guidelines for a long-term solution to the country's economic problems are apparent:

1. Reforms must be adequate in scope to end the negative capital flow from Mexico to the advanced industrial nations. Clearly this will involve tax and other measures to increase the private rate of return on investments in Mexico.

2. Any new money loaned to Mexico must be used for productive investment that increases capital formation and the competitive productive capability of the nation. To increase the attractiveness of these loans, the United States government should provide the guarantee.

3. To reduce the increasing burden posed by public sector deficits, the government will have to make a more determined effort to raise domestic revenues, both through tax reform and increased tax collection.[54]

If implemented, these policies should enable the country to achieve a long-run solution to its debt problems, while at the same time assuring a sustainable flow of external capital.

NOTES

1. Jorge Castaneda, "The Unlikely Dilemma of How to Spend It," *Financial Times*, August 26, 1987, p. 16.

2. Castaneda, "The Unlikely Dilemma," p. 16.

3. Larry Rohter, "Waiting Game Is Over In Mexico As Presidential Choice Is Named," *New York Times*, October 5, 1987, p. 1; David Gardner, "Youth and Ability Win Day for Salinas," *Financial Times*, October 6, 1987, p. 6.

4. See, for example, Redvers Opie, *Mexican Industrialization and Petroleum* (Mexico City: ECANAL, August 1979).

5. David Mares, "Mexico's Challenges," *Third World Quarterly*, July 1987, p. 795.

6. Mares, "Mexico's Challenges," p. 795.

7. Travier Marquez, "La Economica Mexicana en 1977 y su Futuro," Madrid, October 1977 (mimeo).

8. For a complete account of this period see Robert E. Looney, *Mexico's Economy: A Policy Analysis with Forecasts to 1990* (Boulder, CO: Westview Press, 1978).

9. Cf. Robert E. Looney, "Mexican Optimism and Economic Reality: An Analysis of the Industrial Development Plan," *Rivista Internazionale di Scienze Economiche & Commerciali*, May 1984.

10. Robert E. Looney, "The Mexican Oil Syndrome: Current Vulnerability and Longer Term Viability," *OPEC Review*, Winter 1985. See also Robert E. Looney, "Scope for Policy in an Oil Based Economy: Mexican Stabilization Policies in the 1970s," *Socio-economic Planning Sciences*, 1987.

11. An analysis of the events leading up to the 1982 crisis is given in Robert E. Looney, *Economic Policy Making in Mexico: Factors Underlying the 1982 Crisis* (Durham, NC: Duke University Press, 1985).

12. Pedro Aspe, "Charting Mexico's Economic Progress," *The Wall Street Journal*, August 8, 1987.

13. Aspe, "Charting Mexico's Economic Progress."

14. William Stockton, "Mexico's New Bid to Stem Capital Flight," *New York Times*, July 28, 1986.

15. In the Mexican case, debt swaps work this way: A foreign company buys Mexican government debt on the secondary international market at the usual discount (in 1987 this was about 55 cents to the dollar) and redeems it within Mexico for pesos. For the highest priority investment projects defined as the purchase of state enterprises, the government will supply pesos at the loan's full face value. In the lowest ranking of the nine investment categories defined under the plan, Mexico will hand over the peso equivalent of 75 percent of the loan's dollar value. Most transactions approved so far have fallen under the third category, which gives a 92 percent rate for projects oriented toward exports or high technology or that will be located in designated industrial development zones. Also included in this category is foreign equity participation in existing Mexican-owned enterprises. The pesos must be used for approved capital investments, not for import financing, foreign debt payment, or as a cheap source of local working capital. The pesos are paid out directly to the foreign investor's local suppliers, creditors, and contractors. Cf. "How Debt Swaps Work," *Journal of Commerce*, December 16, 1986.

16. Eduardo Crawley, "Mexico," in World of Information, *The Latin America and Caribbean Review*, 8th ed., (Saffron Walden, Essex: World of Information, 1987), pp. 95–96.

17. Crawley, "Mexico," p. 96.

18. "Heels Dragged on Local Debt Swap," *Latin America Weekly Report*, July 16, 1987, p. 4.

19. "Mexico," *Latin America Weekly Review*, October 2, 1986, p. 2.

20. William Orme, "Debt-Equity Swaps as a Passing Mexican Fancy," *Journal of Commerce*, December 16, 1986.

21. Orme, "Debt-Equity Swaps."

22. David Gardner, "Bankers Rush for Mexican Equity," *Financial Times*, June 2, 1987.

23. William Orme, "Swaps Spur Foreign Investment in Mexico," *Financial Times*, January 5, 1987.

24. Aspe, "Charting Mexico's Economic Progress."

25. "Mexico," *Latin America Weekly Review*, November 20, 1986, p. 5.

26. David Gardner, "Mexico Looks to IMF for Appreciation of Its Efforts," *Financial Times*, July 1, 1986.

27. Anne Swardson, "Banks Agree to Lend Mexico As Much As $7.7 Billion," *Washington Post*, March 21, 1987.

28. John C. Pool, and Steve Stamos, *The ABC's of International Finance* (Lexington, MA: Lexington Books, 1987), p. 113.

29. Art Pine, "Mexico-IMF Reach Tentative Agreement on Economic Restructuring Framework," *The Wall Street Journal*, July 15, 1986.

30. E. V. K. FitzGerald, "The Fiscal Deficit and Development Finance: A Note on the Accumulation Balance in Mexico," *Working Paper No. 35*, Cambridge: Cambridge University Center of Latin American Studies, 1979; E. V. K. FitzGerald, "A Note on Capital Accumulation in Mexico: The Budget Deficit and Investment in Finance," *Development and Change*, July 1980, pp. 391–417; and E. V. K. Fitz-Gerald, "Looney and Frederiksen on Mexican Fiscal Policy: A Reply," *World Development*, March 1987, pp. 405–406.

31. While the mainstream of the FitzGerald model is non-Keynesian, he did demonstrate for at least one variable and one time period (nonhousing rate of depreciation for 1960–1976) the presence of a Keynesian relationship. He also confirmed the result using Hacienda data and model. See FitzGerald, "A Note on Capital," p. 412.

32. FitzGerald, "The Fiscal Deficit," pp. 14–15.

33. Robert E. Looney, and P. C. Frederiksen, "Fiscal Policy in Mexico: The Fitz-Gerald Thesis Reexamined," *World Development*, March 1987, pp. 399–404.

34. Looney and Frederiksen, "Fiscal Policy in Mexico," p. 401.

35. Looney and Frederiksen, "Fiscal Policy in Mexico," p. 401.

36. Looney and Frederiksen, "Fiscal Policy in Mexico," p. 404.

37. Robert E. Looney, and P. C. Frederiksen, "The Regional Impact of Infrastructure Investment in Mexico," *Regional Studies*, No. 4, 1981, pp. 285–296.

38. Cf. L. M. Koyck, *Distributed Lags and Investment Analysis* (Amsterdam: North Holland, 1954).

39. Potluri Rao and Roger Miller, *Applied Econometrics* (Belmont, CA: Wadsworth Press, 1970), Chap. 7.

40. See, for example, Leopoldo Solis, *Economic Policy Reform in Mexico* (New York: Pergamon Press, 1981).

41. Cf. Wayne Cornelius, "The Political Economy of Mexico Under De La Madrid: Austerity, Routinized Crisis, and Nascent Recovery," *Mexican Studies*, Winter 1985, pp. 1–28.

42. The available data on government finances cover only the years 1966–1984, and are therefore not comprehensive for the entire span of the De La Madrid and Diaz Ordaz administrations. Estimates are from the *International Financial Statistics* (1986 Yearbook and August 1987 volumes).

43. A similar analysis is contained in Robert E. Looney, and P. C. Frederiksen, "Consequences of Military and Civilian Rule in Argentina: An Analysis of Central Government Budgetary Trade-Offs, 1961–1982," *Comparative Political Studies*, April 1987, pp. 34–46.

44. All of the equations are estimated in constant 1980 prices.

45. Robert E. Looney, "Mechanisms of Mexican Economic Growth: The Role of Deteriorating Sources of Growth in the Current Economic Crisis," *Journal of Social, Political and Economic Studies*, Spring 1987.

46. The more traditional IMF Stabilization Programs are dealt with in Robert E. Looney, and P. C. Frederiksen, "Feasibility of Alternative IMF-Type Stabilization Programs in Mexico, 1983-1987," *Journal of Policy Modeling*, October 1983.

47. Cf. Anatole Kaletsky, *The Costs of Default* (New York: The Twentieth Century Fund, 1985); and Arthur MacEwan, "Latin America: Why Not Default?" *Monthly Review*, September 1986, pp. 1-13.

48. A full analysis of these proposals is given in W. H. Buiter, and T. N. Srinivasan, "Rewarding the Profligate and Punishing the Prudent and Poor: Some Recent Proposals for Debt Relief," *World Development*, March 1987, pp. 411-418.

49. Buiter and Srinivasan, "Rewarding the Profligate," p. 413.

50. See also Robert E. Looney, "Mexican Economic Performance During the Echeverria Administration: Bad Luck or Poor Planning?" *Bulletin of Latin American Research*, May 1983.

51. Cf. Jorge Castaneda, "Mexico's Coming Challenges," *Foreign Policy*, Fall 1986, pp. 120-160; and Carl Migdail, et al., "Mexico Is Going to Make It," *Washington Quarterly*, Winter 1986, pp. 171-186.

52. Pool and Stamos, *The ABC's of International Finance*, p. 117.

53. Pool and Stamos, *The ABC's of International Finance*, p. 116.

54. William Orme, "Tax Evasion Takes Its Toll of Mexico's Revenue," *Financial Times*, August 21, 1987, p. 4.

3

Foreign Debt and Trade: The Case of Mexico

Edgar Ortiz

Determined to restore equilibrium and recover the nation's long-run growth patterns, the Mexican government, from the start of the debt crisis in 1982, has been both applying harsh adjustment policies and promoting a new development model. The latter is based on industrial modernization, freer trade, furthering foreign direct investments, and a greater participation from the private sector, diminishing, consequently, the share of the state in the economy. The goal is to leave behind the old import substitution model, seen as the root of the crisis. A radical change is sought in order to make the economy more productive and highly competitive in the international markets. Greater exports are sought to increase foreign exchange revenues both to ease the pressure of debt payments, as well as to ensure adequate levels of imports needed for development.

However, perspectives for making free trade an engine for growth seem weak and limited. Six interrelated problems can be associated with it:

1. adjustment policies have weakened the economy;
2. debt continues to increase and absorb most foreign revenues;
3. investments in the industrial sector and in science and technology have been rather curtailed;
4. industrialization and foreign trade plans have been severely undermined, by insufficient financing, and the consequent allocation of a large portion of the national budget to debt servicing;
5. trade increases depend above all on repressing domestic demand and wages, and overvaluing the dollar; and
6. unfavorable international trends.

To all these problems must be added the weak entrepreneurship in the private sector and excessive dependency on the U.S. economy and its markets.

As in the case of other Latin American countries, Mexico has been applying orthodox policies to correct its macroeconomic disequilibria. Other
alternatives have not been considered; monetarist adjustment policies have
been instrumented under the conditionality imposed by the International
Monetary Fund. Results show a complete failure. Indeed, contrary to its
own logic, stabilization policies aimed at the short run have already been
applied for six years, becoming a way of life that has violently weakened the
economy at high social costs and undermining the nation's sovereignty.

In a nutshell, on the aggregate the economy now operates at levels below
those of 1980. As shown in Table 3.1, GDP in 1986 amounted to 878,085.0
million pesos, which is only slightly above the 841,854.5 million pesos of
output reached in 1980; in dollars, GDP for 1986 was $149,102.3 million
while in 1980 it was $186,327 million. Moreover, the situation seems to have
worsened throughout the years. Inflation rates, for instance, have not
receded, but rather increased in the last three years. It reached an all-time
high of 105.0 percent in 1986, higher than the previous record of 95.8 percent, the initial year of the crisis and much higher than 59.2 percent, the
lowest inflation rate for the 1982-1986 period, obtained in 1984.[1]

All these results have been naturally accompanied by lower investments,
which remained at 1975 levels. Thus, the ill effects of repressing demand
now will be felt well into the future. The picture gets even more blurred by
the fact that social costs have been high. Salaries now equal, in real terms,
those of 1960. Similarly, unemployment and disguised unemployment are
high and continue to increase. Conservative estimates for open unemployment are 8 percent, while some estimate it as high as 17.0 percent and the
unemployment-disguised employment rate between 50-60 percent of the
labor force.[2] To these facts must be added a sensible loss of sovereignty.
Due to its continued need to negotiate new debts and renegotiate old ones,
Mexico has been forced to inhibit and postpone its own goals and aspirations; these have become subsumed to the conditionality imposed by the
IMF (and indirectly by private bank lenders) and U.S. government views,
since representatives of this government intervene in debt negotiations or
elaborate unilateral political alternatives such as the Baker Plan.

Unfavorable international conditions, such as sharp decreases in oil
prices, and earthquake damages can be partly blamed for poor and jeopard-
izing results. However, the main reason seems to rest upon the limitations
of orthodox policies: they concentrate on trade imbalances, ignoring that
the major source of current disequilibria are exceedingly high debt
payments. They ignore the long-run structural roots of the crisis and emphasize the short run, and ignore the international nature of the crisis, in
spite of the fact that it is imperative to solve it globally.[3]

Under those circumstances—conceptual and empirical—it is hard to con-
ceive new foreign trade can improve its role in the economy. The entire
system has accentuated its previous rigidities and has become even more
vulnerable to internal instabilities or external shocks. Massive investments

would be necessary in infrastructure, technological development, and capital goods. However internal resources for such purposes are limited, as the performance of the economy proves. Substantial foreign debt acquisitions are also out of the question, for international liquidity is low and Mexico is considered a high-risk country. Hence, trade levels most likely will only show moderate increases from their current levels: exports of $16 billion in 1986 (10.7 percent of GDP), similar to levels obtained in 1980 (8.2 percent).

New debt acquisitions and debt service payments are also a constraint for future trade. As a result of stabilization policies imports have been sharply cut. From an all-time high of $23.9 billion in 1981, imports decreased dramatically to $8.5 billion in 1983 and remained at $11.4 billion (7.7 percent of the GDP) in 1986. Since 1982 Mexico has been able to generate high trade surpluses. Accumulated surpluses amount to $46.4 billion. Thus, there has been an "overadjustment" process. Under normal circumstances, these revenues would have been applied for importing goods, many used for development. Moreover, imports would have also benefited trading partners, mainly the United States, which now resents these cuts, particularly in the border area.[4] Unfortunately, this has not been the case. Large amounts of foreign exchange revenues have been devoted to pay debts. As shown in Table 3.1, debt services have increased sharply since 1970. In that year debt payments remained at manageable levels: 21.2 percent in relation to exports and 1.9 percent in relation to GDP. Debt services now absorb 73.3 percent of export revenues and amount to 7.8 percent of GDP. Similarly, the ratio of total foreign debt to GDP has also increased dramatically throughout the years, from 10.5 percent in 1970 to 80.8 percent in 1983 and 67.8 percent in 1987. Mexico is indeed overcommitted with debts and is deviating needed resources for growth to debt payments. In fact, net debt flows have been negative since 1982 ($4.9 billion total) so that trade surpluses seem hardly enough to patch them up. It also can be affirmed that with these types of transfer Mexico and other developing nations are subsidizing economic recovery of the lending developed countries.

Significant debt levels have been renegotiated. After four rounds of negotiations, $23.7 and $48.7 billion of public debt, and $12.0 billion of private debt have been restructured under better terms.[5] However, debt has continued to increase. Therefore, debt payments will remain high. Further resources will have to be diverted from trade surpluses. Since imports are closely related to growth and industrial output that could be geared for exports, this means that Mexico will continue to be involved in a vicious circle of restrained trade-high debt payments. The situation has been maintained somewhat under control, but it cannot go on indefinitely. If trade is to become an engine for growth (and a means for ensuring payments), first the debt problem must be solved.

Exports will also remain low because of low industrial investments and inadequate support to science and technology. Two ill effects can be related

Table 3.1
Mexican Debt and Trade Trends

	1970	1975	1980	1985	1986
Gross Domestic Product-pesos[ab]	444,271.4	609,976.8	841,854.5	912,334.0	878,085.0
Manufacturing GDP[ab]	105,203.0	148,057.7	209,681.9	223,031.4	207,144.7
Gross Fixed Investments[ab]	100,956.0	150,859.0	235,974.0	164,212.4	162,581.2
Gross Domestic Product-dollars[cb]	35,541.7	88,003.9	186,327.2	166,173.6	149,102.3
Exports[cd]	1,373.0	2,934.7	15,307.5	21,663.8	16,031.0
Imports[cd]	2,460.7	6,851.0	18,486.2	13,212.2	11,432.4
Trade Balance[cd]	-1,087.7	-3,916.3	-3,178.7	8,451.6	4,598.6
Current Account Revenues[cd]	3,254.4	7,134.8	25,021.8	30,774.4	24,265.4
Current Account Balance[cd]	-1,187.9	-4,442.6	-6,760.8	1,236.7	-1,270.4
Total Foreign Debt[cd]	3,745.0	20,093.0	50,713.0	97,500.0	101,165.0
Debt Service [cd]	692.0	2,091.0	9,200.0	13,970.6	11,746.5
Net Debt Flows[cd]	-349.0	3,478.0	986.0	-10,470.6	-8,081.5
Terms of Trade	96.7	97.8	127.8	91.9	65.6
Terms of Trade[e]	100.0	96.1	123.5	71.5	54.6
Federal Financial Deficit/GDP	3.8	10.0	7.8	9.5	16.3
Debt Service/Exports (%)	50.4	71.2	60.1	64.5	73.3
Debt Service/Current Acct. Rev. (%)	21.2	29.3	36.8	45.4	48.4
Debt Service/GDP	1.9	2.4	4.9	8.4	7.8
Total Foreign Debt/GDP (%)	10.5	22.8	27.2	58.7	67.8

Notes: a = million pesos; b = constant 1970 values; c = million U.S. dollars; d = Nominal;
e = adjusted for international interest rates.

Source: Developed by the author based on information in: Banco de Mexico, *Indicadores Economicos* and *Informe Anual*, various issues, 1970–1987, and press releases from Banco de Mexico y Secretaria de Hacienda y Credito Publico, reported in "El Financiero," various issues, 1985–1987.

to it: limited output levels, and obsolescence and low productivity. As shown in Table 3.1, gross fixed investments have remained stagnant since 1983. Indeed, 1986 investment levels (207.1 billion pesos) are slightly below the 209.7 billion pesos of investments during 1980. Similarly, industrial investments have declined sharply. Due to continuous cuts in domestic demand, industry now operates at 60 percent of its full capacity, and replacement of equipment has declined nearly 25 percent since 1982.[6] This is also reflected in a lower industrial output that in 1986 amounted to 207.1 billion pesos (23.6 percent of GDP), which is 7.7 percent lower than the output obtained in 1981 (24.7 percent of GDP). Low output levels and limited replacements of plant and equipment hinder productivity. Indeed, this has been promoted only through severe cuts in real wages. As already pointed out, in real terms, wages are at 1960 levels, and correspond to 41.7 percent of 1976, the peak for the 1960–1986 period. The decline in real wages since 1982 has been 50.7 percent.[7]

Low output levels limit the possibility of taking advantage of both domestic and foreign market opportunities. No sound market penetration policies can be developed. Similarly, obsolescence and low productivity hinder the goal of achieving international competitiveness. To radically transform the industrial sector, large investments are needed, but capital formation is low, to a great extent due to a diversion of resources to debt payments, as previously suggested.

This problem gets compounded by the lack of a sound policy in science and technology. Goals are not only unclear and unrealistic, but also investments in this area have decreased to 5 percent of GDP (1 percent in 1982). Moreover, dependency on foreign technology is extremely high. Payments for foreign technology are usually higher than domestic investments in this area: 0.7 percent and 0.6 percent of GDP in 1985 and 1986, respectively.[8] All this prevents the development of alternative endogenous technologies.

Consequently, future nontraditional exports will be selective and will not show a spectacular growth. Most likely, these will be led by multinational corporations. Although from 1982 to 1985 their investments remained low at $400–600 million per year, in 1986 apparently there was a sharp increase. Foreign direct investment now nears $17.0 billion; in 1986 alone increases amounted to $1.2 billion; to this must be added $1.1 billion of foreign direct investments resulting from swaps from debt to shares.[9]

Due to high-debt commitments, a goal of the Mexican government has been to generate trade surpluses. Indeed, as previously pointed out, there has been an overadjustment process and surpluses have been diverted to debt servicing. However, it is important to note that because of unfavorable international conditions, surpluses have been attained by restricting imports sharply. That is, export levels have fallen short of goals set at the National Industrialization and Foreign Trade Program, 1984–1988, while imports have been considerably below the goals set in that plan. Although this is true for the entire 1984-1986 period, considered in the national plans, this situation is best depicted by the results obtained in 1986. Real trade surpluses were $4.6 billion while planned trade surpluses were of $8.8 billion. This situation was partly mitigated by a healthy growth in non-oil exports (104.0 percent since 1982), which were $9.7 billion in 1986, above the goal of $8.5 to $8.9 billion.[10]

Thus, it has been impossible to maintain trade goals. Surpluses have been generated by pressuring down imports and promoting exports through overvaluing the dollar. But the problem does not remain there. Due to lower exchange revenues, the government has had to cut important development programs, including those planned on trade and industrialization. Indeed, debt servicing/GDP has varied between 7.5 percent and 12.9 percent of GDP for the 1982-1986 period. This ratio has tended to decrease to 7.8 percent in 1986, as a result of debt restructuring. However, debt has been continuously high so that large proportions of the national budget have been devoted to foreign debt payments: 19.4 percent in 1986.[11] This figure explains by itself public deficit. As shown in Table 3.1 in relation to GDP, public deficit has constantly increased since 1984. Now it averages 16.3 percent of GDP, which is almost as high as the deficit—seen as the root of the crisis—was before adjustment processes began in 1982 (17.6 percent). This figure is also considerably higher than the goals set by adjustment policies (3.5 percent to 7.5 percent) and expectations.[12] Although foreign debt payments explain the size of public deficit, domestic debt also must be taken into account, for its acquisition is closely linked to foreign debt obligations.

Indeed, in 1986 domestic debt increased dramatically so that it amounted to 46.4 percent of GDP. As a result, total debt servicing is expected to take more than half of the national budget, assuming inflation levels of 90.0[13] percent which has been already surpassed.[14] In short, public deficit is not the result of overspending, but of high-debt payments. In fact, operating revenues and expenditures show significant surpluses.

Under these circumstances, due to the lack of funds, the government has been forced to cut some programs, many related to industrial modernization and trade. As pointed out before, investments in sciences and technology are 0.5 percent of GDP, while original goals called for investments around 1 percent of GDP in this area.[15] The government also cut its investments to 4 percent of GDP in 1986 (11.0 percent in 1980 and 5 percent in 1960). Moreover, industrial investments from the public sector are mostly limited to five enterprises: Pemex, Comision Federal de Electricidad, Sidermex, Fertimex, and Azucar.[16] Thus, plans for industrial modernization have been practically put aside. The picture does not improve in the private sector. It has been estimated that only 5 percent of the industrial equipment is modern.[17] Nevertheless, private industrial investments have been stagnant, as previously mentioned. This has been partly because of insufficient financing. Internally capital formation has remained low and most of it has been diverted to financing public deficit. Indeed, the reserve requirement averages 90 percent; thus, the banking system has been unable to channel resources to the productive system. In addition, it is worth noting that the most dynamic private enterprises have high foreign debt obligations ($19.7 billion in 1982). Thus, although official mechanisms (FICORCA)[18] were created to alleviate this problem and $12.0 billion of private debt was renegotiated in 1984, these firms have had to cut their internal resources for investing. In brief, foreign trade has also limited possibilities to contribute significantly to Mexico's economic growth, because unfavorable trade conditions and high debt payments have limited public and private resources destined to industrialization and foreign trade plans.

Exports might also remain low because current efforts have resorted to dangerous and artificial incentives. First, nontraditional exports have been promoted, cutting sharply into internal demand. That is, trade increases in non-oil exports have not been generated as a result of output surpluses. Simply, significative amounts of what used to be produced for internal demand are now directed for exports. Obliged by sharp contractions in internal markets firms have directed a significant amount of their output to external markets. Demand repression in some sectors has been quite severe. In the auto industry, for example, domestic sales have declined 55.5 percent in relation to 1982.[19]

However, an indefinite repression of domestic consumption is not feasible, neither materially, nor politically. Internal demand will increase due to the nature of population growth and greater awareness of personal needs. Further, some social unrest is already present in some sectors of the Mexican population. Thus to preserve political stability restrictive demand policies will have to be eased. Some output will have to be therefore redirected to satisfy national needs.

Similarly, non-oil exports have indeed increased in the last few years. In 1982 the share of oil exports was 75.0 percent. By 1985 this share had declined to 67.5 percent and in 1986 this share declined to 39.3 percent, as a result of sharp decreases in oil prices. However, it is worth noting that since 1982 non-oil exports have increased over 104.6 percent, from $4.7 billion in 1982 to $9.7 billion dollars in 1986 (see Table 3.2).

As promising as these figures are, it is important to point out that such growth is largely due to high overvaluation of the dollar (38.2 percent in 1986). This situation cannot be sustained for long. It has promoted lower imports, which have prevented adequate levels of investment and technological innovation. In addition, Mexico will have to change this policy since it is now a member of GATT.

Restrictions on wages is another artificial means by which non-oil exports have been promoted. Their secular trend was pointed out before. Here, it must be emphasized that such a strategy cannot be sustained indefinitely for two reasons: first, in order to avoid social unrest and second, because the

Table 3.2
Main Trends of the Mexican Trade Balance (million dollars)

	1970	1975	1980	1985	1986
Total Exports	1373.0	2934.7	15307.5	21,663.8	16,031.0
Oil exports	40.4	468.9	10560.4	14,766.6	6,307.2
Non-oil exports	1332.6	2465.8	4747.1	6,897.2	9,723.8
Public Sector Exports	225.0	615.1	11670.0	15,777.9	7,649.5
Oil	27.0	411.6	10555.7	14,683.8	6,217.7
Non oil	198.0	203.5	1114.3	1,094.1	1,431.8
Private Sector Exports	1148.0	2319.6	3637.5	5,885.9	8,381.5
Oil	13.4	57.3	5.3	82.8	89.5
Non Oil	1134.6	2262.3	3632.2	5,803.1	8,292.0
Total Imports	2460.7	6851.0	18486.2	13,212.2	11,432.4
Public Sector	596.4	2278.2	6982.2	4,386.6	3,343.8
Consumer goods	85.2	104.0	1211.3	558.6	100.6
Intermediate goods	206.7	1339.8	4260.5	2,912.8	2,011.2
Capital goods	304.5	834.4	1510.4	915.2	932.0
Private Sector	1864.3	4572.8	11504.0	8,825.6	8,088.6
Consumer goods	442.8	346.4	1214.8	523.1	445.9
Intermediate goods	591.2	2732.3	6767.2	6,052.9	5,620.6
Capital goods	830.3	1494.1	3522.0	2,249.6	2,022.1
Trade Balance	-1087.7	-3916.3	-3178.7	8,451.6	4,598.6
Public Sector	-371.4	-1663.1	4687.8	11,391.3	4,305.7
Private Sector	-716.3	-2253.2	-7866.5	-2,939.7	292.9

Source: Developed by the author from information in: Banco de Mexico, *Indicadores Economicos* and *Informe Anual*, various issues, 1970–1987; Secretaria de Programacion y Presupuesto, *Anuario Estadistico de los Estados Unidos Mexicanos*, various issues, 1970–1984; *Manual de Estadisticas Basicas del Sector Comercio*, 1982; *Boletin de Informacion Economica*, various issues, 1985–1987; "Sumario Estadistico," Comercio Exterior, various issues, 1978–1987.

substitutionality between labor and technological innovation is limited in the international markets.

To this situation must be added the fact that labor groups from other countries also seek to defend their interests. Artificial means for promoting exports to their countries aid in their cause. In the case of Mexico this could lead to lower exports because large proportions of exports is the result of intrafirm trade of multinationals based in Mexico and the United States. Thus, to penetrate markets and maintain a high participation in them, productivity and high quality products should be developed. On the other hand, all gains artificially attained will be rapidly lost.

Finally, unfavorable international trends might also prevent an adequate growth of Mexican exports. First, economic growth of potential importers has been sluggish. In fact, economic growth of the developed nations continued to decline in 1986. GDP growth averaged 4.7 percent in 1984, 3.0 percent in 1985, and 2.4 percent in 1986. Similarly, potential markets in developing countries are also limited, for their growth has been unstable and low, averaging 3.5 percent in 1986.[20] Second, many developed countries have adopted protectionist rules that affect industrial exports from developing nations. Third, international prices for primary goods have shown a declining trend. Finally, world trade has been unstable and characterized by trade wars.

Mexico does not escape this environment. Indeed, its terms of trade (TOT) have declined severely in the last few years. As shown in Table 3.1, TOT declined from a peak of 127.6 in 1981 to 65.5 in 1986. This situation is even more dramatic when increases in real international interest rates are taken into account. Then, the decline is from 127.3 in 1981 to 54.6 in 1986, that is, a decrease of 72.7 points. Sharp drops in prices of exports of primary goods lie behind this fact. However, the major cause is the dramatic fall in oil exports on an average, for Mexico, from $25.35 per barrel in 1985 to $11.87 in 1986.[21]

Mexico's international trade problems get compounded by two more facts, unrelated to the debt problem, but not dissociated from it: lack of entrepreneurship by its private sector, and high dependency on the United States. In relation to the first problem it must be mentioned that the lack of an endogenous technology is partly due to the limited interest of the private sector. The private sector finds it easier to associate itself with foreign capital and to buy technology from it, as explained before. It does not promote productivity either. Rather it seeks protectionism so that local goods are not competitive internationally; hence, artificial schemes must now be used to promote exports, as previously explained. In brief, Mexican entrepreneurs have been short-sighted and *malinchistas* (xenophilous)[22], for often local scientists have developed sound technology, but foreign technology has been preferred.[23]

Similarly, U.S.-Mexican economic relations are complex and asymmetrical. Traditionally, around 70 percent of Mexico's foreign sector is related to business with the United States. Thus, the Mexican business cycle has been greatly influenced by U.S. economic activity.[24] Moreover, since the relationship has been asymmetrical, the United States has often given unfair treatment to Mexican goods. The situation has not changed. As a major actor in a world trade and due to its huge trade deficit, the United States has adopted many protectionist measures. Many affect Mexican exports directly. Although Mexico has liberalized its import codes and joined the GATT, it appears that the United States has decided to hinder trade with Mexico; recently, unfair compensatory tariffs or nontariff barriers were placed on Mexican goods. This has been extended even to oil exports, for a special $.30 tax was levied on Latin American oil imports. The tax is still in effect despite the fact that GATT has already demanded suspension and payments of retributions. To all these problems, a partial solution is to diversify markets. However, this needs a long-run approach and currently the opportunities are limited, either because of trade instability as previously suggested, or because most developed countries compete among each other with similar trade and foreign direct investment policies.

The preceding comments do not mean that Mexico should increase trade barriers and become autarkic. They mean that trade should be placed in its right dimension to make it an effective aid for growth. For this, in addition to reviewing shortcomings of policies taken, it is necessary to analyze trade patterns and potential markets. Indeed, closely examining trade patterns, one can find deep structural changes in the last few years.

However, not all indications are good or bad. The decrease in the share of oil exports, previously pointed out, is healthy, but close attention must be paid to the fact that the relative change per se is superficial, since oil prices have fallen sharply, decreasing total exports and the share of these goods in that total.

Similarly, it is worth noting that trade surpluses have been generated largely by the public sector, while the private sector has consistently shown a deficit. Trends for the private sector changed slightly in 1983 and 1986, but this was not only the result of increased exports, but also of severe import curtailments. Finally, in both the private and the public sectors, it is obvious that the main imports are now intermediate and capital goods. In these two categories, in 1986 the public sector imported $2.9 billion; the corresponding figure for the private sector was $7.6 billion; together these two constituted 92.6 percent of total imports. (See Table 3.2.)

Such trends suggest that public enterprises might be the best option for promoting growth and trade equilibrium, particularly considering that trade imbalances have consistently been caused by high imports of capital goods. Since 1980 accumulated trade deficit for capital goods imports add up to $25.0 billion. Since 1983 this is the only sector that has not been balanced; its share of total exports has averaged around 25.0 percent. Since capital goods industries require high investments, often beyond the capacity of the private sector, public corporations could be created for developing a strong endogenous capital goods industry, less dependent on imports. This policy should be complemented with science and technology development. High possibilities exist for establishment of linkages with the public higher education institutions. Further, promotion of industrialization under integration schemes with other Latin American countries should also be considered. As a result, capital goods exports (now 4 percent of the total) could also increase; imports of capital goods would also decrease, diminishing overall import needs, too.

The fact that both consumer imports and exports have decreased from 55.6 percent of total exports and 21.4 percent of imports in 1970 to 14.7 percent and 7.4 percent, respectively, in 1986 is also revealing and encouraging. During the oil boom period these imports tended to increase sharply. However, previous and current results prove the fact that surpluses can be generated and that ample markets exist for these goods. The same cannot be said about intermediate goods. Overall, the ratio of these exports to total exports has varied from 36.7 percent in 1970 to 81.3 percent in 1986. The share of intermediate imports has been stable in the last few years, remaining at about 68.0 percent, but in 1970 this share was only 32.4 percent. There has been a tendency for surpluses, but this is distorted by the fact that oil exports are considered under this category. Moreover, it can be seen that most intermediate goods imports are made by the private sector, $5.6 billion that was 49.2 percent of total imports and 73.6 percent of intermediate goods imports. Both the public and the private sector must make radical efforts to further integrate the national industry, developing higher levels of its inputs. This could also lead to higher exports as the result of developing products that are inputs for industries of other countries.

One important clarification must be made in this respect. A great deal of intermediate goods trade is made between subsidiaries of multinational corporations. Mexico should closely study these circuits to take advantage of them. It should aim to have positive net flows, producing at the right level of the production circuit and aiming at products with high returns.

Analyzing the sectoral participation of imports and exports (Table 3.3) is also revealing. A clear trend toward a greater participation of manufacturing exports on total exports is indicated. In 1970 manufacturing exports amounted to 34.6 percent of the total. During the oil boom period and the first year of the crisis this share decreased sharply (17.7 percent and 15.9 percent in 1981 and 1982, respectively). However, an increasing trend is evident since 1983 so that by 1986 manufacturing exports accounted for almost half of all Mexican exports. Nonetheless, such changes might be superficial, as previously suggested, for they have been favored by repression of domestic markets and overvaluation of the dollar.

The picture is further disheartening considering that manufacturing imports are nearly 90 percent of total imports. Some variations are perceptible, but overall since 1970 this trend seems to be true. As a result, trade balances for this sector have always been negative. In 1980 and 1981 alone, deficit in this sector increased sharply to $12.6 and $17.6 billion, respectively. This can be explained partly by the fact that during that period international markets were easy, which allowed Mexico to increase its imports.

However, the fact remains that trade deficits of the manufacturing sector were huge. Adjustment policies have tended to decrease such deficits, but they remain high. Accumulated trade deficit for this sector added up to $20.2 billion for the 1982–1986 period and $50.4 billion for the 1980–1986 period. These were mostly balanced by income earned from mining exports,

Table 3.3
Mexican Sectoral Exports and Imports (million dollars)

EXPORTS

Year	Total	Agriculture	Mining	Manufacturing	Other
1970	1,373.0	665.6	231.7	475.6	.1
1975	2,934.7	835.9	756.8	1,217.6	124.4
1980	15,307.5	1,545.5	10,313.7	3,382.9	65.4
1985	21,663.8	1,299.9	13,691.6	6,650.8	21.5
1986	16,031.0	2,148.1	6,139.9	7,726.9	16.1

IMPORTS

Year	Total	Agriculture	Mining	Manufacturing	Other
1970	2,460.7	147.6	120.6	2,190.1	2.4
1975	6,851.0	828.9	505.6	5,513.2	3.3
1980	18,486.2	2,011.8	255.9	16,002.8	215.7
1985	13,212.2	1,585.5	184.9	11,322.9	118.9
1986	11,432.4	983.2	182.9	10,186.3	80.0

BALANCES

Year	Total	Agriculture	Mining	Manufacturing	Other
1970	-1,087.7	518.0	111.1	-1,714.5	-2.3
1975	-3,916.3	7.0	251.2	-4,295.6	121.1
1980	-3,178.7	-466.3	10,057.8	-12,619.9	-150.3
1985	8,451.6	-285.6	13,506.7	-4,672.1	-97.4
1986	4,598.6	1,164.9	5,957.0	-2,459.4	-63.9

Source: See Table 3.2.

oil and gas in particular. As income from this traditional sector decays, it is likely that industrial imports and industrialization could not be fully supported, which would be similar to the situation prevailing before the oil boom.[25]

In other words, chances for developing a strong industrial sector (and outward-oriented as promoted by policymakers) are low. The needs for industrial imports are too high and unbalancing. Thus, the first step to modernize the industrial sector should be to eliminate deficit there. The government and the private sector should join forces in developing a strong industrial sector in both consumer and intermediate goods. Technology development is an option. Results will take place in the long run. For this reason, in the short run a careful evaluation of industrial exports and imports should be made to increase exports in all potential areas, and decrease imports in redundant areas, or in areas where domestic firms can quickly respond to domestic production needs both for imports and exports.

Confirming previous analysis, Table 3.4 shows that industrial exports indeed increased throughout the years. Moreover, Mexico's main industrial exports used to be food, beverages, and tobacco (30 percent), and chemical and pharmaceutical goods (16.0 percent). The share of these industrial goods has fallen in 1986, to 12.6 percent and 10.9 percent respectively.

On the other hand, the share of metal goods, machinery, and vehicles has increased sharply from 7.7 percent in 1970 to 31.3 percent in 1983 and 40.6 percent in 1986. These figures, however, hide the fact that most exports in this category correspond to vehicles and their replacement parts: $2.1 billion that is 66.4 percent of these lines of goods ($3.1 billion in total) and 27 percent of total industrial exports. In addition, it is worth noting again that most of this trade is between Mexican subsidiaries and their parent corporations in the United States. For instance, Mexico's explosive growth in automotive exports is due not only to favorable circumstances, but also due to a greater integration of the Mexican subsidiaries of Chrysler, General Motors, and Ford with their parent companies in the United States. Indeed, domestic demand for autos has decreased sharply to levels below 1983 (272,815 units in 1983 and 258,835 units in 1986). However, exports increased from 22,456 units in 1983 to 72,429 units in 1986.[26] Another indication of this is the fact that Chrysler Corporation sometimes exports 97 percent of its output.[27] This confirms the fact that exports increased as a result of survival strategies and artificial incentives. Since this cannot be

Table 3.4
Mexican Industrial Exports (million dollars)

	1970	1975	1980	1985	1986
Total	475.6	1,217.6	3,382.9	6,650.8	7,726.9
Food, beverages, tobacco	144.0	106.9	770.2	738.2	973.6
Textiles, garments and shoes	38.8	172.4	201.0	206.2	347.7
Wood and Furniture goods	9.7	28.3	57.9	93.1	108.2
Paper and printed goods	19.9	40.6	86.2	99.7	139.1
Oil goods	31.1	22.5	427.0	1,336.8	649.1
Petrochemical	1.2	4.8	116.7	106.4	85.0
Chemical and Pharmctl.	76.0	200.3	394.6	671.7	842.2
Plastics and rubber	4.2	9.0	21.3	46.5	85.0
Non metalic mfg.	23.9	61.3	128.9	312.6	378.6
Steel	37.1	68.9	71.5	239.4	455.9
Minerals processed	30.8	133.3	121.2	399.0	479.0
Metal goods, machinery, vehicles	36.6	328.7	938.3	2,354.7	3,137.1
Others	22.3	40.6	48.1	46.5	46.4

Source: See Table 3.2.

maintained forever, future automotive exports might be endangered. Nonetheless, the positive lesson is that Mexico can export cars and parts, and that significant market gains have been made in the United States.

To avoid instabilities and to take advantage of other opportunities, detailed analysis should be made. The shift and share and the origin and destination of industrial goods should be determined. Detailed analysis is necessary to determine exactly the nature and size of industrial investment's substitutes for exporting; detailed analysis is also necessary to determine which markets to serve and how to serve. Research is also needed to determine the degree of integration between U.S. and Mexican firms, so that sound industrialization and trade plans can be developed. Finally, as previously suggested, market research should be made to develop products and conquer potential foreign markets.

In short, recent trade patterns show encouraging tendencies. Surpluses are being generated and significant increases have been made in industrial exports. However, warning symptoms also persist. Above all, capital and intermediate goods imports are still high and produce deficit, as a net result of exchanges with the same types of goods from other countries. An overadjustment process has taken place. However, because of its artificiality and negative effects, it cannot be maintained for long. To make trade a significant contributor to growth, foreign debt problems should be solved, that is, payments should be eased. Only in that way can trade acquire its real dimension, become stable, if properly managed, and yield some surpluses that could be used for furthering development and cancelling debts. Lack of attention to the foreign debt problem would only create and deepen existing vicious circles of disequilibria in the external sector.

In conclusion, debt and trade are highly interrelated. Mexico's government plans call for modernizing the industrial sector and increasing exports as a means to promote development. Moreover, debt obligations and development goals are contradictory under the current policies being applied. As long as debt keeps increasing and debt services increase, too many resources will have to be diverted to debt payment. Moreover, as this policy is privileged through harsh adjustment policies, the economy will only be weakened. It will not be able to restore equilibrium and growth. In the external sector, trade surpluses might be generated and nontraditional exports might grow. However, gains would be superficial and could not be maintained for long. Sooner or later the debt-forced trade vicious circle of plundering resources from Third World countries, including Mexico, would break. For these reasons, a global approach is necessary. All parties responsible for the debt problem—lenders and borrowers—should negotiate realistic terms of payments. Similarly, new trade agreements are necessary to expand and stabilize world trade, to price fairly primary goods, and to eliminate artificial trade barriers. The most appropriate way for this would be to create a special international organization in which lending and borrowing countries negotiate on an equal basis, taking into consideration political and technical aspects of both debt and trade. The United Nations Assembly would be the most appropriate institution to create this organization. A global approach of this sort would yield mutual benefits for both lending and borrowing countries, as world trade would increase and peace and political stability would be promoted.

NOTES

1. Banco de Mexico, *Indicadores Economicos*, 1982–1987, various issues. In the analysis that follows some aggregate economic indicators are in pesos, due to data availability (Table 3.1). All debt and trade figures are in U.S. dollars.

2. *Uno mas Uno*, "La desocupacion es ya de 17%: la SPP," Martes 15 de Julio de 1986; p. 1. Unemployment rates estimates based on research from the labor movement.

3. Edgar Ortiz, "Mexico's Financial Crisis: Origins and Perspectives," in *Mexico's Economic Policy: Past, Present and Future*, ed. William E. Cole (Knoxville: University of Tennessee, 1987).

4. W. Charles Sawyer and Richard L. Sprinkle, "The Effects of the Mexican Economic Crisis on Trade and Employment in the United States," *Journal of Borderland Studies*, Vol. 1, No. 2, Fall 1986, pp. 66–74.

5. Secretaria de Hacienda y Credito Publico, "Estrategia del Financiamiento del Desarollo," *El Mercado de Valores*, Ano XLVI, No. 52, Diciembre 29, 1986, pp. 1214–1232.

6. Derived from information released by Secretaria de Energia Minas e Industrial Paraestatal. See *El Financiero*, "Capacidad Productiva y Competetividad en Disminucion; el Margen, Estrecho: SEMIP," Miercoles 1 de Julio de 1987, p. 35.

7. Edgar Ortiz, "Estabilizacion y Cambio Estructural," *Economics and Finance: Current Issues in the North American and Caribbean Countries* (Mexico City: CIDE, 1987).

8. *El Financiero*, "Pagaron Empresas Publicas y Privadas 317 mil 200 mdp por Transferencia de Tecnologia," Jueves 3 de Septiembre de 1987, p. 39.

9. *Uno mas Uno*, "48% de la inversion extranjera en 1986, solo pago con acciones," Martes 21 de Abril de 1987, p. 1.

10. Goals mentioned in this section are taken from *Programa Nacional de Fomento Industrial y Comercio Exterior*, 1984–1988 (Mexico City: Poder Ejecutive Federal, 1984).

11. The ratio of foreign debt services to public budget has been derived from information in Secretaria de Hacienda y Credito Publico, "Estrategia del Financiamiento," pp. 1214–1232.

12. For a summary and analysis of adjustment goals see Edgar Ortiz, "Crisis y Deuda Externa. Limitaciones de las Politicas de Estabilizacion y Alternativas para el Desarrollo y la Renegociacion del Endeudamiento," Simposio Internacional, Crisis y Deuda Externa: Los Puntos de Vista de Mexico y Estados Unidos, Mexico, FCPS/UNAM, May 1986.

13. *El Financiero*, "Cambios Financieros en las Empresas por la Reforma Fiscal," Lunes 24 de Noviembre de 1986, p. 58.

14. *El Financiero*, "Inflacion de 8.2% en Agosto; Alcanzo 133.9%, Anualizada," Jueves 10 de Septiembre de 1986, p. 30.

15. *El Financiero*, "Paragon Empresas Publicas," p. 39.

16. *El Financiero*, "Capacidad Productiva," p. 35.

17. *El Financiero*, "70% de la Planta Industrial es Obsoleta; Solo el 5% es Moderna, Asevera la CTM," Martes 25 de Agosto de 1986, p. 23.

18. Fideicomiso para la Cobertura de Riesgos Cambiarios. A trust fund established by the government in 1983 to cover exchange risks related to debt obligations from private enterprises.

19. Marc Scheinman, "Mexico's Explosive Growth in the Automotive Exports," in *North American Economies in the 1990s* (Symposium Proceedings), Vol. II, ed. Khosrow Fatemi (Laredo, TX: Laredo State University, 1987), pp. 767–785.

20. International Monetary Fund, *World Economic Outlook, 1986*; and OECD, *Economic Outlook, 1986*. (Compiled in Banco de Mexico: Informe Anual, 1986, p. 57.)

21. Banco de Mexico, *Informe Anual, 1986*, pp. 108–113. The oil price is an average for Istmo and Maya oil exports.

22. Pejorative for xenophile. Malintzin (Malinche) was Hernan Cortes' Indian lover.

23. *El Financiero*, "Malinchismo Industrial" de los Empresarios Mexicanos," Miercoles 26 de Agosto de 1986, p. 43.

24. Cesareo Morales, "El Comienzo de una Nueva Etapa de las Relaciones Economicas entre Mexico y Estados Unidos," in *Mexico Ante la Crisis*, Vol. I. ed. Pablo Gonzalez-Casanova and Hector Aquilar-Camin (Mexico City: Siglo XXI, 1985), pp. 64–88.

25. Raul Morales Castaneda, "El Sector Externo y la Crisis Economica Actual en Mexico: Una Perspectiva Historica," *Analisis Economico* 6 (UAM-Atzcapotzalco), pp. 227–321.

26. Scheinman, "Mexico's Explosive Growth," pp. 767–785.

27. *El Financiero*, "Chrysler de Mexico, el Mayor Exportador de IP Durante 86–87," Miercoles 1 de Abril de 1987, p. 28.

4

Debt, Oil, and Exchange Rates in the Monetary and Asset Models: The Case of Mexico

J. Jay Choi and Richard Ajayi

INTRODUCTION

External debt, undoubtedly, is among the most pressing and potentially explosive issues facing many developing countries today. With the emergence of the debt problem as a major policy issue, there has also been a concomitant growth in the literature on this subject. But much of the attention in the literature centers around the ability of borrowing nations to service their debts and the implications of default for the stability of the international financial system. Little has been done on the issue of the relationship between debt and exchange rates.

A similar gap is also found in the literature on exchange rates. Various models of exchange rates focus on money, inflation, and variables affecting the flow of the balance of payments, but these models do not focus on debt. This chapter examines the effect of external debt and its major determinant, oil prices, on exchange rates within a synthesized model of asset and monetary theories of exchange rates. The resulting model is then estimated for Mexico over the period 1975–86.

A theoretical underpinning of debt and exchange rates is found in the asset theory of exchange rates. In this view, the exchange rate, at a point in time, is determined by international asset market equilibrium, but, over time, the cumulative current account balance or the country's net foreign asset position also matters. An alternative theoretical framework is the monetary model. This model is important in its own right, but it is also a special form of an asset model under certain assumptions. Therefore, it would seem necessary to consider both models as a benchmark for an analytic framework. In this chapter, we rely on this backdrop to develop a synthesis of asset and monetary models of exchange rates. The reduced-form equation is then estimated for Mexico, an oil-exporting country with a large external debt and a history of currency devaluations, especially in the past decade. Estimation results indicate that the synthesized model performs markedly better than either the asset or the monetary model. The reason for the better performance is the introduction of debt and oil prices. There is also some evidence that the coefficients of debt and interest rates are more consistent with the asset model than the monetary model or the traditional flow approach.

THE THEORETICAL MODEL

We wish to analyze the effect of external debt and other variables on exchange rates within a fundamental model of exchange rate determination. We choose to synthesize the asset and monetary models of exchange rates, both because of their importance as standard exchange rate models and their consistency in incorporating variables of our current interest.

Our model basically follows the integrated analysis of Frankel[1] with some modifications especially with respect to debt and oil prices. The role of each sector in the synthesized model is established as follows: An equilibrium in money markets defines a long-run equilibrium exchange rate. Asset market conditions specify a short-run exchange rate as dependent on expectation as well as long-run factors. An equation for exchange rate expectation is then introduced to complete the model.

We start with the standard monetary model[2] and assume the two money-market equilibrium conditions are as follows:

$$(1)\ m = P + \phi y - \lambda r$$

$$(2)\ m^* = P^* + \phi y^* - \lambda r^*$$

where (m) is the log of money supply, (P) represents the log of general level of prices, (y) the log of real national income, (r) is the real interest rate, and the asterisks denote foreign variables. The two coefficients, (ϕ) elasticity of money demand with respect to real income and (λ) semi-elasticity of money demand with respect to real interest rates, are assumed to be identical for both domestic and foreign countries. If we also assume that the purchasing power parity holds, then,

$$(3)\ e = P - P^*$$

where (e) is the log of exchange rate defined as the domestic currency value of a unit of foreign currency. We can then obtain the standard monetary model of exchange rates as follows:

$$(4)\ \bar{e} = (m - m^*) - \phi(y - y^*) + \lambda(r - r^*).$$

This equation may be called a long-run equilibrium exchange rate equation, because it is based on an assumption that commodity prices are completely flexible. This assumption is justifiable only in the long run. In the short run, prices may be sticky for various institutional reasons. The implication of sticky prices is that a short-run adjustment in the money market is greater than would be warranted from a long-run standpoint. This extra adjustment burden leads to currency overshooting in the short run.[3] An unexpected easy domestic monetary policy, for instance, causes a long-run depreciation of domestic currency via inflation; however, with sticky prices, the resulting decrease in domestic interest rates causes a net capital outflow, thus contributing to a further depreciation of domestic currency in the short run. The dynamic path of adjustment toward a long-run equilibrium requires an assumption on expectation.[4]

An implicit assumption of the monetary model is the perfect substitutability of assets. This assumption shifts the full adjustment burden to money markets. The asset model of exchange rates, in contrast, recognizes that domestic and foreign assets are imperfect substitutes. The imperfect asset substitutability is an important characteristic of a developing economy under financing constraints. With perfect substitutability the external debt problem would not be an issue.

The asset model of exchange rate[5] can be stated as:

$$(5)\ B/EF = h(r - r^* - \hat{e}, - z)$$

where (B) is the supply of domestic assets, (F) is equal to the supply of foreign assets, (E) is the level of exchange rates, $(\hat{e})$ is the expected rate of changes in (E), and (z) is the risk factor. From this we obtain:

$$(6)\ e = - kz + h(r - r^* - \hat{e}) + (b - f)$$

where (k) is an arbitrary constant, (b) is the log of (B), and (f) equals the log of (F). At the long-run steady state equilibrium, $\hat{e} = O$ such that (e) is fully determined within this asset model. In the short run, however, the level of exchange rate depends on $(\hat{e})$.

We assume that $(\hat{e})$ follows the partial adjustment process subject to an extraneous random shock (X), according to the following:

$$(7)\ \hat{e} = - \theta(e - \bar{e}) - gX$$

where (θ) is the speed of adjustment parameter and (g) is an arbitrary constant. For Mexico, the random shock is mostly in the form of exogenous changes in world prices of oil. This specification of oil price shock may not be completely satisfactory from a theoretical standpoint. However, this method offers ease of handling and a different specification would probably not matter much for an empirical work.

To obtain the reduced-form equation, rewrite equation (7) as:

$$(8)\ e = \bar{e} - (1/\theta)\ (\hat{e} + gX).$$

Equation (4) can then be substituted for $(\bar{e})$. Similarly, we can solve for $(\hat{e})$ in equation (6) and substitute the result into equation (8). We then obtain our synthesized model:

$$(9)\ e = qkz + q\phi h(m - m^*) - q\phi\theta h(y - y^*)$$

$$+ qh(\lambda\phi - 1)(r - r^*) - qD - qhgX$$

where $q \equiv 1/(\phi h + 1)$ and $D \equiv f - b$. According to the monetary model, $(m - m^*)$ and $(r - r^*)$ should have positive coefficients while $(y - y^*)$ should have a negative coefficient. According to the asset model, both $(r - r^*)$ and (D) should have negative coefficients while the (z) term should be positive. In the synthesized model, the signs of these coefficients are the same as in the component models with the exception of $(r - r^*)$, which has an ambiguous sign because of the conflict of signs in the separate models. The oil price term should have a negative coefficient because of its positive influence on the Mexican economy and its currency.

EMPIRICAL ANALYSIS

Equation (9) is ready for estimation. Estimation was done on quarterly data from the third quarter of 1975 to the second quarter of 1986, an 11-year period when the Mexican peso was under 'managed floating'. Data definitions are as follows: (e) is the log of the units of Mexican pesos per one U.S. dollar, (M) is the log of money supply $(M1)$, (y) is the log of industrial production index, (r) is the real interest rates measured by the Treasury Bill rates minus the four-quarter rates of changes in consumer price indices, (D) is the log of the absolute value of the cumulative Mexican current account deficits, and (X) is the price of crude petroleum in U.S. dollars in the world market. Asterisks denote similar U.S. variables. Data sources are the *International Financial Statistics* published by the International Monetary Fund, and the *Statistical Abstract of Latin America* published by the UCLA Latin American Publication.

Before actually estimating the synthesized model, establishing some sort of benchmark would be helpful. We first ran the purchasing power parity equation using the Cochrane-Orcutt iterative technique to reduce autocorrelation. The estimation result, reported below, is not too bad on the surface, but it leaves us wondering whether more basic structural

$$e = 2.6128 + 1.1814\,(P - P^*)\quad R^2 = .90$$

$$(22.7)\quad (18.6)\qquad\qquad SE = .10$$

factors are not in operation. Contrary to the prediction of purchasing power parity, the constant term is not only statistically significant but also is very large. The coefficient of the price term is also greater than one and hence overpredicts exchange rates relative to the basic theory.

To explore this further, we ran the basic monetary and asset models separately using both the ordinary least square (OLS) and the Cochrane-Orcutt (CORC) techniques. The results, reported as the first two equations in Table 4.1, are not too encouraging and in fact are worse than that of purchasing power parity. The OLS results show autocorrelation so that the coefficients of the independent variables are not so reliable. On the other hand, those results from CORC exhibit low R-squares. In equations estimated by CORC, the asset model, however, shows somewhat better overall performance than the monetary model. Moreover, in both the OLS and CORC equations, the coefficient of real interest rates is consistent with the asset rather than the monetary model. In the asset model, a rise in domestic interest rates causes a net capital inflow and hence an appreciation of domestic currency. In the monetary model, a rise in domestic interest rates creates an excess supply condition in the money market and hence a depreciation of domestic currency. In the present estimation, a rise in Mexican real interest rates relative to their foreign counterpart is associated with an appreciation of the Mexican peso, thus supporting the prediction of the asset model.[6]

The next three equations in Table 4.1 show the results of equation (9), the synthesized model.[7] We can immediately see that these results are markedly better than those of the separate estimations. This is particularly true when external debt is included as an additional independent variable. An increase in t-value is also evident in individual variables. Money, in particular, has a dramatically higher t-value in the synthesized model, especially in CORC equations with the debt factor. The negative effect of real interest rate differential on dollar exchange rates (or a positive effect on the peso) is again confirmed with higher t-values. There is a change of sign, though, in the case of income. The insignificant negative effect (of income on dollars) is now positive and statistically significant in equations (3) and (5). This new result is at odds with the monetary model and consistent with the traditional flow balance-of-payments view. In the traditional flow view, an increase in domestic real income raises imports and hence the domestic-currency value of foreign currency. In the monetary model, an increase in income raises domestic money demand and hence the foreign-currency value of domestic currency.

External debt is shown to raise the value of the Mexican peso. This may sound a little bit odd, but it is actually consistent with the asset model. In the context of an asset model, external debt implies an excess of foreign demand for Mexican assets, and this pressure for capital inflow boosts the external value of the Mexican peso. This, however, is in conflict with the traditional flow view that net external borrowing is used to finance the current account deficits. Such an action is accompanied by a depreciation of the country's currency.

Table 4.1
Estimation Results of the Synthesized Model

$$e = a_0 + a_1 (m-m^*) + a_2 (y-y^*) + a_3 (r-r^*) + a_4 D + a_5 X$$

	Technique	a_0	a_1	a_2	a_3	a_4	a_5	R^2	SE	DW
1	OLS	3.969	1.3227	-2.2048	-0.0095			.957	.23	.64
		(89.8)	(27.0)	(-6.03)	(-4.39)					
	CORC	15.874	0.3668	-0.0448	-0.0051			.162	.12	1.35
		(3.15)	(1.38)	(-0.76)	(-2.07)					
2	OLS	-3.748			-0.0145	0.5353	(0.4437)	.335	.92	0.04
		(-1.76)			(-1.71)	(0.57)	(0.28)			
	CORC	3.595			-0.0056	-0.0498	-0.1316	.191	.11	2.03
		2.36			(-2.72)	(-0.23)	(-0.41)			
3	OLS	14.354	1.8623	2.3431	-0.0126	-1.0786		.984	.14	1.32
		(10.7)	(24.5)	(3.73)	(-9.07)	(-7.75)				
	CORC	13.239	1.8077	1.8896	-0.0114	-0.9617		.964	.14	1.77
		(7.32)	(18.0)	(2.40)	(-5.83)	(-5.13)				
4	OLS	9.598	1.6271	0.4255	-0.0107		-1.0709	.969	.20	0.67
		(6.42)	(17.9)	(0.56)	(-5.73)		(-3.77)			
	CORC	12.275	0.4536	0.2411	-0.0050		-0.5670	.237	.12	1.43
		(3.97)	(1.72)	(0.39)	(-2.00)		(-1.68)			
5	OLS	14.522	1.8726	2.4388	-0.0126	-1.0186	-0.1420	.984	.15	1.33
		(10.5)	(23.7)	(3.69)	(-8.97)	(-5.68)	(-0.54)			
	CORC	13.261	1.8131	1.9335	-0.0113	-0.8590	-0.1926	.964	.14	1.77
		(7.22)	(17.6)	(2.41)	(-5.69)	(-3.21)	(-0.53)			

Notes: Numbers in the parentheses are t-values
OLS = ordinary least square, and CORC = Cochrane-Orcutt iterative estimation technique.

A random increase in world price of oil is shown to have a weak positive impact on the Mexican peso. This is as it should be because Mexico is an oil exporter and the demand for oil is price-inelastic at least in the short run. Thus far, oil price change has been treated as a random shock, but it could also be a risk proxy for Mexico. The latter possibility may account for somewhat low t-values for oil prices. However, when oil price is included without the debt term, its significance level increases somewhat. Finally, we wish to note that we also tried the relative price between oil and domestic goods. This experiment, however, proved unsuccessful because oil prices denominated in Mexican pesos represent more of Mexican inflation than any random shock in the world market.

SUMMARY AND CONCLUSION

The connection between external debt and exchange rates has not received much attention in international finance literature. The literature on debt is primarily concerned with the debt-servicing capacity of the borrowing country and its implication for the viability of the international financial system. The debt-servicing capacity of the borrowing country, especially an oil-exporting country such as Mexico, depends on oil prices in the world market. The models of exchange rates focus on money, inflation, and variables affecting the flow of balance of payments, but not on debt or oil prices. To introduce external debt and oil prices, we develop a synthesis of the asset and monetary models of exchange rate determination. The model is then estimated for Mexico over the period 1975-1986. Estimation results indicate that the synthesized model performs markedly better than its component models, monetary or asset. In conflict with the traditional flow view but consistent with the asset model, external debt is shown to have a significant positive impact on the value of the Mexican peso. Other results include real interest rate differential having a positive impact on the peso. This result supports the prediction of an asset model but rejects that of the monetary model. Finally, an increase in oil prices in the world market has a favorable but weak effect on the peso.

NOTES

1. Jeffrey Frankel, "Monetary and Portfolio-Balance Models of Exchange Rate Determination," in *Economic Interdependence and Flexible Exchange Rates*, ed. J. Bhandari and B. Putnam (Cambridge, MA: The MIT Press, 1983).

2. Harry G. Johnson, "The Monetary Approach to the Balance of Payments," in *Further Essays in Monetary Economics*, ed. H. Johnson (Cambridge, MA: Harvard University Press, 1973); see also, Jacob A. Frenkel, "A Monetary Approach to the Exchange Rate: Doctrinal Aspects and Empirical Evidence," *Scandinavian Journal of Economics*, Vol. 78, No. 2, May 1976, pp. 200-224.

3. Rudiger Dornbusch, "Expectations and Exchange Rate Dynamics," *Journal of Political Economy*, Vol. 84, No. 6, December 1976, pp. 1161-1176.

4. Dornbusch, "Expectations and Exchange Rate Dynamics," pp. 1161-1176. Dornbusch shows that the dynamic approach to a long-run equilibrium is obtained under the assumption of rational expectation.

5. Pentti J. K. Kouri, "The Exchange Rate and the Balance of Payments in the Short Run and in the Long Run: A Monetary Approach," *Scandinavian Journal of Economics*, Vol. 78, No. 2, May 1976, pp. 280-304; see also, William Branson, "Asset Markets and Relative Price in Exchange Rate Determination," *Sozialwissenschafter Annalen*, 1977, pp. 69-89; and Rudiger Dornbusch, "Exchange Rate Economics: Where Do We Stand?" *Brookings Papers on Economic Activity*, No. 1, 1980, pp. 143-194.

6. The use of nominal interest rates is not appropriate in view of the high rate of inflation in Mexico relative to the United States. That is, the nominal interest rate is just a proxy for inflation in Mexico.

7. We also tried the purchasing power parity model modified for debt and oil prices. The result is not much different from what is reported here.

PART THREE
CROSS-BORDER RELATIONS: FROM IMMIGRATION TO DRUGS

Nowhere do the relations between the United States and Mexico play a more significant role than they do in the border region between the two countries. This region stretches for almost 2,000 miles from San Diego/Tijuana on the Pacific Ocean to Brownsville/Matamoros on the Gulf of Mexico and includes millions of inhabitants on either side of the border. On the U.S. side, the economy of the border region—with the possible exception of the two largest cities on the border, San Diego and El Paso—is so intensely interwoven with the economy of Mexico that any change in the Mexican economy will affect the border region as much as, if not more than, similar changes in the U.S. economy. For example, after the fall of the Mexican peso in 1982, the entire border region underwent several major economic crises of its own. Most border cities went through a recession far deeper than what the rest of the country experienced. For many months during 1983-1986, unemployment rate in most parts of the region was highest in the United States, sometimes two or three times the national average.

The dependence of the U.S. border region on Mexico is not a one-way process. Mexico's border region with the United States is also heavily dependent on its northern neighbor. Furthermore, this interdependence is not limited to economic issues. There is a great deal of interaction in cultural, social, and even political issues. For example, the United States side of the border region is comprised of mostly Mexican Americans with strong cultural and social ties with their relatives and friends south of the border. Such ties greatly influence the political, sociological, and economic behavior of both groups and have important repercussions for both countries.

Two of the more problematic issues facing the United States and Mexico, particularly the border region, are labor issues or immigration, and the more recent problem of drug trafficking. In Chapter 5, Walter Greene and Jerry Prock discuss the immigration issue by analyzing one of the most comprehensive and more controversial solutions applied to it in recent decades, that is, the Immigration Reform and Control Act of 1986. The background information contained in this chapter, along with the authors' critical evaluation of the law, provide an excellent introduction to this critical issue facing both nations.

In Chapter 6, Ronald Ayers approaches the labor issue from an educational perspective. He hypothesizes that the border region presents labor force participants with unique risks that inhibit the greater pursuit of education. He uses the concept of a human capital earnings function to expound his hypothesis. His conclusion is that to achieve the desired level of education—and therefore, economic improvements—in the region, financial inducements alone will not suffice. Proper public policy must include other incentives for higher levels of education.

In Chapter 7, Dale Bremmer and Randall Kesselring develop a theoretical model to address the issue of labor flow restriction along the U.S.-Mexico border. Their approach is to apply the general economic theory of factor mobility to international labor migration. Proponents of factor mobility theory have long argued that factor mobility leads to increased productivity. However, this principle is usually applied to capital and internal labor migration and has not received sufficient application to international migration of labor. They attempt to bridge this gap by developing a theoretical model of legal and illegal immigration from home to host country. Their model demonstrates that the imposition of effective immigration limits results in lost output for both home and host countries.

In the final chapter of Part Three, Ana Maria Perez Gabriel discusses the increasingly important issue of drug trafficking across the border. Specifically, she analyzes the recent agreements between the United States and Mexico to combat the problem and evaluates the implications of such limiting agreements on trade for the border region. The author argues that some of the agreements signed between the two countries are actually in violation of the Mexican Federal Constitution and, therefore, have no legal basis. She further argues that some of the same laws also violate both U.S. and Mexican international trade commitments, such as their respective obligations to GATT.

5

The Immigration Reform and Control Act of 1986: Its Implications and Prospects

Walter E. Greene and Jerry Prock

U.S. IMMIGRATION REFORM

The legal boundary between the United States of America and Mexico has shifted several times during the past 200 years. Wherever the border was, there were few legal restrictions on crossing the border from Mexico to the United States until 1917. In 1917 the U.S. imposed an $8 per head tax and a constricted literacy test on Mexican immigrants.

The immigrants from Mexico had no real impediments until the 500-man Border Patrol division of the Immigration and Naturalization Service was created in 1924. U.S. labor needs, particularly in agriculture, were the primary force behind border immigration policy throughout the 1930s, 1940s, and 1950s. Then, in 1965 the U.S. passed a new immigration bill that limited visas to 20,000 persons from any one nation. This move pushed two-thirds of the normal annual Mexico-U.S. migration into an "illegal" status.[1]

Merely changing the status from legal to illegal did not stem the flow of migration. The people had a reason to cross the boundary between the two nations no matter what the governments said. Most illegals are day workers such as maids, gardeners, and laborers in general. They come across at dawn and go home to Mexico at nightfall. "We know where police are watching," explains Sandra Lopez, who mops floors in an El Paso office building, "but if you get caught, you try again. A week ago I was caught three times. It means only that you will be late for work. But I have a nice boss. His mother lives in Juarez. He understands such matters."[2]

It is worthwhile to point out that they even help each other. In cities along the border like Brownsville, Juarez, Nogales, and Nuevo Laredo, where the principal cross points are located, a favorite pastime for the young is to burn a tire, for warmth and to signal a gathering point for slipping into the United States.[3]

For those who come, the lure is the same. Fifty dollars earned in the United States can support a family of six for two weeks in rural cities in Mexico, where the minimum wage is $4 a day. The rate of inflation in Mexico was more than 100 percent in 1986-1987. America has enormous symbolism for poor people all over the world, especially to those closest to its border. Moreover, Mexican people listen to songs and stories, and they think the streets are paved with gold in the United States.

In an effort to keep millions of illegal aliens out of the country, in August 1982, the Congress decided to carry out the first overhaul of U.S. immigration laws in three decades. The Senate voted in favor of the bill, but the House did not pass it. However, in May 1985, Senator Alan K. Simpson presented a new bill to the U.S. Congress. Finally on November 6, 1986, the Immigration Reform Act became law. The new immigration act required all employees to "prove U.S. citizenship" after May 6, 1987. "The lands along both sides of the border have become almost a third country—neither truly Mexican nor truly American—and the cultural 'third country' was creeping northward (and southward) at a steady pace last year."[4]

PROBLEMS CAUSED BY ILLEGAL IMMIGRANTS IN THE UNITED STATES

To obtain a clear understanding of why the immigration bill was passed, we need to refer to the political, economic, and social problems that the illegal immigrants have been causing throughout the years in the United States.

Estimates of how many illegal aliens are currently in the United States range from 12 million by the Immigration and Naturalization Service to 3.5 million by the Mexican-American Legal Defense & Educational Fund.[5] The rate of entry is growing; in fiscal year 1986 the U.S. Border Patrol apprehended 1.77 million illegal aliens.

In the last decade, the Hispanic population in the United States has increased an estimated 60 percent to 18 million, with 4 million voters nationwide, 2.5 million yet to be registered. Forty percent of this population is 18 years of age or younger.

Hispanics are fast becoming a heavy electoral muscle that is felt at every political level. They are a new key factor in presidential politics. They are concentrated in nine states that control 193, or 71 percent of the 270 electoral votes needed to elect a president. Hispanic groups led the 1984 drive that derailed the immigration legislation, the Simpson-Mazzoli Bill.

The consequence of the Hispanic surge is just as profound in U.S. education, health, and welfare. For the past two decades, San Diego, California, has treated parts of Tijuana's sewage at an annual cost to California's tax payers of 1 million dollars. Other border towns have complained of similar drains. For Texas, the cost of educating more than 29,000 offsprings of undocumented Mexican aliens is estimated to be 76 million dollars per year. A large part of the money goes to provide bilingual education for those who do not yet speak English. In Roma, Texas, 98 percent of the enrollment is Hispanic, and the district's annual $12 million budget is stretched thin with the addition of about 200 more students each year. Brownsville, Texas, is building two new schools, yet the city population has actually decreased. Guards on the International Bridge catch 6 to 10 students crossing every day to go to school in the United States. Hospitals also strain to meet the influx of needy newcomers. During the first five months of 1985, Memorial General Hospital in Las Cruces, NM, delivered some 45 infants free of charge to illegal alien parents. Each infant costs local taxpayers $1,400 and becomes a U.S citizen. In Los Angeles County, where illegal immigrants are thought to account for 13 percent of the 7.9 million residents, officials estimate that health-care costs for aliens top $100 million a year. However, unemployment blamed on illegal immigrants is, for some people, the most serious problem.

In April 1986, a Texas television station in the Lower Rio Grande Valley visited a food stamp distribution center. That night they reported that of 38 applicants receiving food stamps that day at the one center, only one was a U.S. citizen. One other person did possess a Green Card (Work Permit); however, it was out-of-date. The remaining 36 were illegals either living illegally in the United States or commuting from Mexico. The poverty level in the Rio Grande Valley of Texas based on a 1984 census and poverty rate published by the Department of Human Services indicates that more than 25 percent of all people living in the Lower Rio Grande Valley are under the Poverty Guidelines and 27 percent or more (39 percent in Starr County) receive food stamps. Despite the above, the evidence of immigrants' receipt of public assistance income is inconclusive.[6]

Along the border, what is Anglo is partly Hispanic, and what is Hispanic is partly Anglo. In El Paso, 63 percent of the population is of Hispanic descent. Crowds cheer the U.S flag when it is paraded across a stage, then cheer just as lustily for the Mexican banner.[7] In Laredo, a singular American event, Washington's birthday, brings into focus the meshing of two cultures. It features a "Noche Mexicana" with Latin entertainment.[8] In Nogales, most residents have Mexican ancestry and may have relatives in Mexico. Now, there are many people with blond hair and blue eyes speaking Spanish. "It becomes very hard," says Veronica Guerra, an educational consultant in El Paso. "Our people tell us, you speak too much English, you are losing your origins. Yet Anglos are presssuring us to be what we call in Second Barrio, a 'Tio Taco', an Uncle Taco, like Uncle Tom." The use of Spanish is fast becoming a necessity. Some experts believe that about 20 percent of the Anglo population in South Texas is now bilingual.

NECESSITY OF MEXICAN LABOR

Although there are complaints that illegal aliens are taking jobs away from Americans, thereby increasing unemployment in the United States, many U.S. businesses, both industrial and agricultural, say they desperately need these workers. Along the border, the measure is highly controversial. Tens of thousands of Mexicans are used on construction projects and to harvest crops. In a recent study, the Urban Institute has found that illegal aliens fuel the economy and do not deprive others of jobs. The Institute said that, despite the influx of Mexicans, Southern California can meet less than half of its expected labor needed in this decade. It has also determined that the presence of Mexican workers has led to higher profits for business and lower prices to consumers.[9] "If I had to pay Anglo wages to harvest my crops," says a grower near Vinton, Texas (a town near El Paso), "I'd go belly up. You would pay beef-filet prices for your salad."[10]

Illegal aliens, because they are fleeing poverty, are willing to accept much less pay. Also, most of the jobs that illegals are getting are jobs that otherwise would go undone. In other words, this kind of employee is difficult to find in the United States, and employers would have to pay U.S. laborers the minimum wage required by the law.

There is also some evidence that immigrants do not just take jobs; they also create them. Illegal aliens are good at lubricating an economy because they supposedly stay off welfare and slip into all sort of economic nooks and crannies. sometimes taking two or three part-time jobs. However, there is still a big controversy about how good or bad Mexican labor is for the United States. Nevertheless, the cry of "worker shortage" in the seasonal agricultural worker area grew so strong that in June 1987 the INS changed its policy on documentation and started letting agricultural workers cross the border based on their word that they had worked in U.S. agriculture before.

AN OVERVIEW OF PREVIOUS IMMIGRATION BILLS

After two aborted bills and several compromises, finally the Immigration Reform Act (P.L. 99–603) was signed by President Reagan on November 6, 1986. It consists of three parts. Part one discusses the legalization of aliens who resided in the United States prior to January 1, 1982, as illegals and how they can qualify for citizenship. Basically, they must report to a legalization center for processing with proof of U.S. residency prior to January 1, 1982. They must have no felony convictions and must not have left the United States for more than 30 days total since January 1, 1982. (If foreign citizens were here legally, then they may not apply for U.S. citizenship under this act.)

Part two is S.A.W.S., the Seasonal Agriculture Workers Sections (Section 302). This section provides that workers must apply within two years of November 6, 1986, and must have already worked for 90 days or more within this two-year period. If workers apply and do not qualify, they may reapply after 1990 but only as temporary S.A.W.S. workers.

Part three is of major concern to U.S businesses as this section applies sanctions against businesses that knowingly employ illegals. If businesses employed persons prior to November 6, 1986, there should be no problems, provided the following conditions are met. Basically, the first six months, until May 6, 1987, were designated as "the official education period." The Immigration and Naturalization Service (INS) stresses that hiring an illegal even during the education period is still an offense. The education period was set aside to prepare guidelines for documentation, for procedures to be followed, and to set up a special counsel for appeals.

During the education period, voluntary compliance is expected and the INS recommends that all employees inform all new hirees that documentation of legal work status will be required when INS guidelines are issued.[11] Any INS form can attest to status, for example, Certificate of Naturalization, Passports (either U.S. or foreign). Green cards, form I-191, form I-994, or form I-551, are best. Social Security cards are not valid by themselves, neither are drivers licenses. However, both may be used as supporting documentation since illegals are not allowed to possess a Social Security card. When the State Employment Agency refers an employee to an employer, it should have also checked the status of citizenship; therefore, the employer should make a copy of those forms, plus all other forms the prospective employee presents as proof of U.S. citizenship. It is also "suggested" that employees hired prior to November 6, 1986, be requested to supply copies of any documents they possess to support their U.S. citizenship status.

After the six-month education period, there will be a one year "Citation Period." During this period, May 6, 1987 to May 6, 1988, all employers will receive a citation upon the first offense. Basically, this will be a warning with no criminal penalties or fines, but it is a one-time only warning. Even during the one-year citation period, employers can expect to receive civil penalties on second and subsequent violations.

The law will be fully in effect as of March 6, 1988, and all civil and criminal penalties can be imposed on first offenses. Those penalties are as follows:

1. On first offense: $250–$2,000 per illegal employee

2. second offense: $2,000–$5,000 per illegal employee

3. third offense: $5,000–$10,000 per illegal employee

4. fourth offense: $10,000–or more plus 6 months per illegal employee

As with all federal laws, an employee may challenge or appeal to an administrative law judge within 30 days; and if still unsatisfied, he may appeal within 45 days to the appropriate federal district.

Discrimination occurs when employers refuse to hire individuals because they "might be" illegal aliens. Therefore, it behooves all employers to have a sound policy/procedure to verify proof of citizenship of all employees in hiring records to avoid challenges of discrimination.

REACTIONS OF DIFFERENT GROUPS TOWARD
THE NEW BILL

Everyone agrees that much is at stake, but no one really can predict future events. The division of opinion on immigration does not follow normal ideological fault lines that explain the unpredictability of the legislation. Some conservatives think immigrants take jobs from the rest of us. Others think that immigrants create jobs and become patriotic Americans. Some liberals think that immigrants take things without permission and ignore the National Labor Relations Board. But other liberals do not want to police our borders because that would be racist, antiminority, and noncompassionate. Many liberals would like to legalize all aliens because that would strengthen their bargaining position as employees and put them within reach of social workers and the welfare state.

Former employers of illegal aliens are the most affected by the new act. By far, the most powerful interest group involved is the Western Produce Growers, which relies on hundreds of thousands of illegal aliens to pick perishable crops. Insiders say the growers spent more than a million dollars last year lobbying for an amendment, which is gaining new support, to provide an open-ended supply of foreign "guest workers" to replace illegal workers.[12] Other powerful agricultural interests—the American Farm Bureau, the National Association of Agricultural Employers, the California Agricultural Producers Association, and the Florida Fruit and Vegetables Association—have declared their opposition to any comprehensive immigration legislation unless it provides for easy access to foreign labor. Hispanic groups and the American Civil Liberties Union fear that sanctions could lead employers to avoid hiring Spanish-speaking or Hispanic-looking people altogether. The U.S. Chamber of Commerce also opposes this provision and it says that it simply dislikes any regulation of business.

The League of United Latin American Citizens and The Mexican American Legal Defense and Educational Fund also oppose the bill. Their opposition is to the employer sanction provision which they say probably would be ineffective and, as a result, Hispanic people would not get the benefit of the legalization program. Businessmen also oppose sanctions because of the additional paperwork and because they believe that certain industries need cheap immigrant labor to survive. Many individual farmers and businessmen resist sanctions against illegal immigrants who, they say, take low-paying jobs no American wants. "You couldn't get your car clean in Southern California without them," asserts former Peace Corps Director Joseph Blatchford. The American Society for Personnel Administrators (ASPA) has also opposed the bill. ASPA has long been involved in dialogues with federal officials and the Hispanic caucus on illegal alien reform efforts, taking the position that it opposes the bureaucratic production of such things as national identity cards. "We already have social security cards. We don't believe the answer to hiring problems involving illegal aliens lies in passing legislations that may not be effective and which might place a heavy burden on employers," said ASPA National Vice President for Public Affairs John Millikin.[13]

One of the reasons why the immigration act passed is that some people or groups think immigrants take jobs away from Americans. Therefore, several individuals and groups backed the immigration bill. The Reagan administration supported the new bill because, as INS Commissioner Nelson said, "the deferred legislation program proposed by Senator Simpson represented a better balance with enforcements and avoided some of the serious cost issues in a time of needed deficit reduction."[14] The United States Chamber of Commerce, which opposed the earlier versions of the bill as burdensome to employers, made the strategic decision to support the Simpson measure this time in return for voluntary, rather than mandatory, recordkeeping. The AFL-CIO favors the employer sanctions as crucial to cutting off the illegal flow. The INS's view is that it is the job magnet that attracts illegals. Says Commissioner Nelson: "Once word spreads along the border that there are no jobs for illegals in the U.S. the magnet no longer exists."[15] But, the supply of labor for menial occupations is not adequate to meet the needs of U.S. farmers and businessmen. Thus the American economy will soon see:

1. a rise in the price of products or services supported by these "menial" jobs;
2. a reduction in the goods and services supplied to U.S. consumers;
3. an exportation of "menial" jobs (of course this will not be a possibility for U.S. farmers); or
4. a continuation of the support of the illegal immigration into the United States by legal and illegal institutions and networks.

Economic events in Mexico and the United States have more impact on Mexican-U.S. migration than any law. And the economic conditions have not been changed by the Immigration Reform Act. A great many people in Mexico need economic help. One way or another, the United States offers them the best chance to improve their economic condition. It may be quite some time before the full impact of this immigration legislation is known. The indications of early results are contradictory. In South Texas, the number of requests for forms to apply for legal status has been very heavy, but through July 1987 the number of applications *filed* for legal status has been much fewer than anticipated.

Unofficial reports from southern California have indicated that on the day the first phase of the act was implemented (May 5, 1987) there was a drop in the number of illegals trying to cross the border but otherwise illegal border crossings have been "business as usual." At the same time the border patrol in the McAllen, Texas district, which extends approximately 150 miles along the lower Rio Grande, reports that the number of illegals caught in the United States or trying to cross the border is down by about 50 percent relative to the same period a year earlier.

CONCLUSION

Legal immigration increased from 450,000 to 543,903 or 20.8 percent from 1980 through 1984; while the number of illegal aliens *caught* increased in the same five-year period from just over 800,000 to 4,241,489 or 430 percent.

It should be clearly understood that illegal immigrants (primarily from Mexico) are causing, without doubt, some political, economic, and cultural problems in the United States. However, illegal labor is needed in the United States because of several reasons: First of all, illegal labor is cheaper. Second, illegal labor is used in harvest and construction jobs, as well as maids, cleaning, gardeners, and car-washer's jobs, because this kind of employee is scarce in the United States. Therefore, illegals are performing tasks that would otherwise remain undone. Third, it has been found that illegals do not hurt the U.S. economy; on the contrary, they contribute to the U.S. economy because they create jobs. On the other hand, the U.S. Congress is fighting strongly to find proper regulations and legislations for illegal immigrants.

Of course, employers of illegal immigrants in different sectors of the United States are the most affected by the immigration bill. As a result, they have vigorously opposed the different provisions of the bill concerning their specific necessities. In short, it is going to be a hard problem to solve because of Mexico's current economic conditions. The new social and economic problems that may be created by the Immigration Reform Act may far outweigh any employment benefits that are gained.

NOTES

1. Ellwyn R. Studdard, "Identifying Legal Mexican Workers in the U.S. Borderlands: Perceptions & Deceptions in the Legal Analysis of Border Migration," *Southwest Journal of Business and Economics*, Summer 1986, p. 14.

2. D. Garcia, "Across the River—Into the Jail." *Newsweek*, July 7, 1982, p. 35.

3. David Jackson, "Making the Great Escape," *Time*, September 13, 1982, p. 73.

4. Kent Gilbreath, "A Businessman's Guide to the Mexican Economy," *Columbia Journal of World Business*, Summer 1986, pp. 3–14.

5. Judy Keen, "4M Would Get Amnesty," *USA Today*, October 17, 1986, p. 5A.

6. G. J. Borjas, and M. Tienda, "The Economic Consequences of Immigration," *Science*, February 6, 1987, pp. 645–651.

7. Gilbreath, "A Businessman's Guide," pp. 3–14.

8. "Debating Immigration Reform," *America*, June 16, 1984, p. 449.

9. "Immigration: How It's Affecting Us," *Atlantic*, November 1983, p. 47.

10. Ricardo Chavira, "Symbiosis Along 1936 Miles," *Forbes*, June 17, 1985, p. 29.

11. "ASPA Opposes Immigration Bill," *Resource*, October 1985, p. 1.

12. Ellen Hume, "Immigration-Control Measures Spawn Alliances that Encompass Diverse Political and Social Camps," *The Wall Street Journal*, August 28, 1985, p. 21.

13. "ASPA Opposes Immigration Bill," p. 1.

14. Robert Pear, "Senate Gets New Version of Immigration Bill," *New York Times*, May 24, 1985, p. 91.

15. George Russell, "Trying to Stem the Illegal Tide," *Time*, July 8, 1985, p. 50.

6

Problems of Human Capital Investment along the U.S.-Mexican Border: A Theoretical Perspective

Ronald M. Ayers

INTRODUCTION

It is widely believed that more education is associated with rising standards of living. It has been shown numerous times in the literature on economic development that there is a strong positive relationship between the educational attainment of a population and its per capita income. Moreover, improvements in the quality and availability of education are frequently offered in the policy literature as partial solutions to the desire for a higher level of economic development within a particular nation or region.

One example of a region within the United States that lags in numerous measures of economic development is the southwestern borderlands area. Low wages, very high levels of unemployment, and the concomitant adverse effects on the quality of life in this region have prompted policymakers at all levels of government, as well as private sector development organizations, to seek solutions to these problems.

The literature on policy-making that is pertinent to the relationship between education and economic development generally focuses on the supply side of the economic equation, while paying little or no attention to the demand side. That is, there seems to be a naive assumption, underlying much of the thought and writing addressed to these issues, that providing greater access to education will necessarily result in significant increases in the desire to take advantage of the improved access. It is the purpose of this chapter to reconsider this assumption. The theoretical structure employed to do so will be the human capital model of investment in self. The human capital model views the worker as an investor in self-education, who follows the rule of rational investment, which says that one will invest in an increment of human capital only if the expected return from that increment exceeds the expected cost of producing it. The focus of this chapter will be to elaborate upon the familiar human capital model by casting the analysis in terms of an individual optimizer who resides in the southwestern borderlands, and who faces a number of unique difficulties and constraints associated with the decision to invest in self. The hypothesis of this chapter is that the special problems confronting border optimizers grow out of the additional risks to the return on human capital investment imposed by the intimate linkages between U.S. border-area economies and the historically unstable economy of Mexico. In addition, Chapter 6 compares the human capital investor to the multinational firm which is contemplating physical investment in another country, since both the firm and the worker face risks that are essentially political in origin. Therefore, a number of concepts in the literature on political risk analysis are relevant to individuals who live and work along the border.

THE GENERAL THEORY OF INVESTMENT IN HUMAN CAPITAL

The concept of human capital and the development of the theory's analytical framework is universally acknowledged to be one of the major advances in economic analysis. This analysis embraces all aspects of improvements in the quality of human labor, and hence has been utilized in studies of education and training, human migration, and medical care. Expenditures on man that lead to future increases in productivity are viewed as investment in capital and are consequently treated as capital formation. Central to the theory is the concept of a human capital earnings function. This may be written:

$$(1)\ E_t = X_t + K_t - C_t$$

where

E = earnings at period (t)

X_t = base level of earnings assuming no human capital investment

K = total return on investments made prior to period (t) and

C = cost of investments.

The total return is the sum of the product of the rates of return and the amounts invested in each form of education and training. Modifying equation (1) accordingly we have:

$$(2)\ E_t = X_t + \sum_{j=1}^{n} r_{t-j} f_t c_{t-j} - C_t$$

The factor f_{t-j} in the second term of equation (2) is an adjustment factor for finiteness of the individual's period of participation in the labor force.

Two comments are in order before continuing further with this sketch of the basic theory. First, that part of earnings which is independent of human capital acquisition is represented by the term X_I. Typically, this term is assumed to be small in relation to total earnings. Secondly, the theory assumes that units of human capital acquired across individuals are homogeneous. Each unit of human capital acquired will add an identical increment of earnings to the various individual investors. While the end product of human capital investment is conceptualized in standardized units, the cost of producing each unit will vary significantly from one person to another.

In Chart 6.1 the horizontal axis measures the amount invested in human capital in dollars, while the vertical axis measures the marginal rate of return, or cost. The marginal benefit to investing in human capital (curve D, the demand curve for human capital) is taken, for simplicity, to be the rate of return. This rate of return is a function of marginal returns to dollars invested, and the marginal production cost of investment. Any demand curve for human capital would have negative slope for at least two reasons. The first is that human capital is embodied in the person investing. The law of diminishing marginal returns will operate because of limited memory and cognitive skills. The outcome is increasing marginal costs of producing a dollar of returns.

The second is that human capital investment is highly intensive in investor's own time. The opportunity costs associated with investment are often considerable. As the value of time normally increases with the age of the investor, the marginal cost of investing in human capital will rise.

Human capital investment is undertaken for pecuniary returns and for the monetary equivalents of psychic returns (may be positive or negative). The usual assumption of diminishing monetary equivalents implies diminishing returns to psychic benefits.

The final consideration relating to the negatively sloped demand curve concerns the considerable risk associated with the receipt of future benefits and with the expenditure of costs. Under the assumption that increments to human capital accumulation increase the marginal aversion to risk, the demand curve will be even more steeply sloped.

INDIVIDUAL INVESTMENT DECISIONS AND POLITICAL RISK IN THE BORDERLAND AREA

The economy of the southwest borderland area of the United States exhibits a close symbiotic relationship with that of Mexico. The border economy's performance is partially linked to national economic developments, originating in the United States, but it also reflects significant linkages to the cyclical and trend behavior of the economy of Mexico. The range of risks that a typical worker contemplating incremental human capital investment faces are expanded when that worker resides in the area

Chart 6.1
Supply and Demand for Human Capital Investment

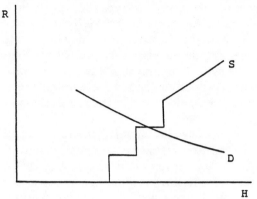

impacted strongly by developments in the Mexican economy, when compared to the risks that same worker would face should he reside in the interior, where his prospects would not be so closely tied to those of Mexico's economy. Because of geographic proximity, border-area workers are analogous to multinational firms in that they face a variety of risks that distinguish their information needs and planning horizons from those of interior workers.

Political risk analysis has been developed to explain the unique problems experienced by multinational *firms* that are contemplating overseas *capital* investment. Velez and Ayers have shown that *border-area firms* are akin to multinational firms.[1] It follows that *border-area workers* are also subject to the adverse impacts associated with the existence of political risks. Some examples of economic events with political origins in Mexico that would affect the return on human capital accumulated by the border-area labor pool include devaluations, exchange controls, import and export restrictions, changes in taxation, and changes in labor policy. Such events, originating in Mexico, affect the profitability of U.S. firms in the border area (even those that do *not* have direct linkages to Mexico), and hence affect wages and employment along the U.S. side of the border. While one might expect successful border business persons to have practiced, in some measure, policies to minimize the effects of such happenings, it is not clear that workers have open to them a sufficient range of options to incorporate into their choice calculus to leave the level, type, and quality of human capital investment unaffected. The root of the problem is that human capital cannot be separated from its owner.

The types of planning activities that workers must take to measure and deal with political risk flows out of the following proposed generalized definition of worker-specific political risk: the probability of maintaining a competitive market return on an increment of human capital investment over a specified period of time, in a U.S. labor market that will be impacted by changing economic and political conditions in Mexico. This definition is a modification of one that applies to multinational firms.

In the political risk literature the basic strategies to cope with political risk faced by firms are complementary to each other. However, when the focus changes from physical investment by firms to human capital investment by individuals, the strategies of risk aversion/risk adaptation are much more in the nature of substitutes for each other rather than complements. Multinational firms that practice a strategy of risk aversion simply do not invest to begin with in countries where risk is too great; or, they initiate a process of disinvestment in places where it is feared that risks have grown beyond acceptable limits. The equivalent response of a risk averse border resident would be to not invest in human capital at all, to limit the amount of the human capital investment, or to move away from the border and its attendant risks and seek work elsewhere. Lower expected earnings would be the result of workers taking either of the first two responses. The model of human capital investment presented in the next section of this chapter shows that this can be an optimal response. Indeed, this is the major thesis of this chapter. The latter response, however, may at first glance seem to be a solution to the problems imposed by political risk. Move away and lower the risk while receiving a market return on human capital investment. The problem with this is that the model of rational economic man portrays the worker as a utility maximizer rather than as a pure income maximizer. The decision that firms face is purely in terms of dollars and cents, but individuals who choose to leave a geographic area are confronted with psychic costs associated with separation from culture, family, and friends as well as the costs of adapting to a new culture, a different climate, and new employment relationships. When these psychic costs are added to the monetary costs of migration, the total cost may be considerable. In any case, for a worker, unlike a firm, this possibility involves an all-or-nothing decision. Since human capital is embedded in the worker it is impossible to relocate a portion of one's human capital to another physical location in the same way that it is possible to relocate physical capital through the disinvestment process.

Risk transfer involves insurance against risk. Border firms directly doing business in Mexico can "insure" against currency fluctuations by participating in the futures market for pesos. The essence of risk transfer is to put the risk on someone else. It is not clear that this option is open to workers. At first thought, one might believe that workers have transferred some risk from themselves to their employer whenever the human capital is in the form of training provided by and paid for by the firm. In the case of specific human capital this is true. Specific human capital raises the productivity of the worker but only for the one firm providing the training. Specific human capital is distinguished from general human capital, which raises the productivity of workers across many firms. Whenever the worker receives *specific* training in a competitive labor market, the employer will bear the cost of that training and will also enjoy the whole of the increase in profit brought about by the increased productivity of the worker caused by the receipt of the training. The firm that incurs the cost of providing specific training is at risk that the worker will no longer be employed by the firm in the future. In other words, there is always the possibility that the firm will have paid the cost of the training, but the benefits to the firm, which would normally accrue to it over time, may be lost. If a border firm lays off a specifically-trained new worker because of events in Mexico, we have a perfect example. In the case of general training provided by the firm, the firm always faces the possibility that the worker will quit. Therefore, the human capital model concludes that general training will be paid for by the worker in the form of lower earnings during the training period, or in the form of direct monetary expenditures by the worker. College tuition is a good example of spending to acquire general human capital. Since the worker pays one way or another, the riskiness of the expected return must be a consideration when deciding how much to invest, and the risk cannot be transferred to another party.

The third possible strategy for dealing with political risk created by proximity to the border is risk adaptation. The worker must learn to deal with risk by following investment strategies that involve an acceptable personal level of risk, by tailoring the level of investment to the risky environment, and by learning how to monitor the unfolding of events in Mexico that would be expected to impact his personal situation the strongest. Since the information costs of engaging in a strategy of risk adaptation may be quite high for an individual worker we cannot expect border workers to be as adept at this as their employers, who can spread the costs of the strategy over the entire employee pool.

A HUMAN CAPITAL INVESTMENT MODEL
WITH POLITICAL RISK

Following the human capital investment literature it is proposed that the individual maximizes net capital value. The standard net capital value equation is modified by including an adjustment for the existence of political risk:

$$Max\, NCV = \sum_{t=0}^{n} \frac{\left[\sum_{j=0}^{m} (P_j E_j)\right]_t}{(1 + i + u)^t} - \sum_{t=0}^{n} \frac{\left[\sum_{k=1}^{s} (P_k C_k)\right]_t}{(1 + i + u')^t}$$

where

NCV = net capital value

P_j = probability of earnings stream E

E_j = earnings stream

i = personal discount rate

U = earnings political risk premium

P_k = probability of cost stream C

C_k = cost stream

u' = cost political risk premium

m = total A of earnings outcomes

s = total A of cost outcomes

The standard NCV equation does not include the u and u' terms, but is similar to the equation above otherwise. In the first term the numerator contains the expected value of future earnings. Typically, since dollars earned in the future are worth less than dollars earned today, the expected value is discounted by the term in the denominator, excluding (u). However, this discounting procedure must be modified for the border because of the existence there of political risk. Hence, the discounting procedure in this analysis includes the (u) term. If we make the simplifying assumption that two typical workers, one living along the border and the other away from it, have the same expected value of earnings, then the variable (u) can take on only positive values. The variable (u) represents the possibility that actual earnings along the border will deviate from expected earnings. Since (u) is in the denominator, its presence causes the first term to be smaller than it would be otherwise. The outcome is that expected discounted earnings for the border worker are lower than expected discounted earnings for the interior worker.

The second term of the equation represents, in the numerator, the expected flow of costs associated with human capital investment. Again, let us assume that these cost flows are identical regardless of the worker's location. In the standard literature these costs are discounted by a personal discount rate. The present argument is that the discounting procedure for the border worker must include the adjustment variable for political risk, (u'). Since the less favorable outcome for the worker in this case is that the worker will have to pay higher than expected costs for an increment of human capital, the risk adjustment in the second term will result in that term becoming inflated in value relative to the value in the absence of political risk. This requires the variable (u') to have a negative value.

To what point has the discussion of the model led us? The logic of the argument is that the demand curve for human capital for the border worker will be to the left of the demand curve for an identical worker away from the border. Other things equal (such as access to education), it is rational to invest less in oneself if one resides along the border.

CONCLUSIONS

If the public policy of the states that share a border with Mexico is to bring the border areas into economic parity with the remainder of the state, spending more money on education may not be sufficient to induce the desired level of economic improvement. Proper public policy must include a search for ways of raising the return on education by reducing political risk. Only then will workers partake of enough education to bring up the level of economic development.

NOTE

1. Alex Velez and Ronald M. Ayers, "Toward More Effective Planning for Risk by Businesses: Applications to the U.S.-Mexican Border," *The Southwest Journal of Business and Economics*, Vol. 3, No. 1, Fall 1985, pp. 1-10.

7

A Theoretical Model of International Labor Flow Restrictions: The Case of Mexico and the United States

Dale S. Bremmer and Randall G. Kesselring

INTRODUCTION

The problem with illegal labor migration from Mexico to the United States is a persistent and distressing one to government administrators on both sides of the border. This problem results from the immediate proximity of two countries experiencing radically different levels of economic welfare. Indeed, the difference between the prevailing wage in Mexico and the United States is no less than astounding. With free exchange of labor and capital, this difference would diminish with time and eventually disappear. However, the two countries, acting in perverse economic fashion, intervene in this process in order to prevent just such a convergence. The United States—a country of relative labor scarcity—uses quotas to restrict inflows of labor. Conversely, Mexico—a country of relative capital scarcity—erects numerous barriers to the inflow of capital.[1]

Economic literature is filled with articles decrying the imposition of trade barriers in the product market, but applications of international trade theory to the labor market are quite scarce. Consequently, this chapter attempts the development of a simple model that emphasizes the economic costs of labor market restrictions. The model is specifically applied to the situation which exists between Mexico and the United States.

The remainder of the chapter consists of four parts. First, the assumptions of the model are stated and justified. Then, a two-country model of unrestricted labor migration is developed. Next, the model is extended to include restrictions of labor flows. Finally, conclusions are drawn and implications for the 1990s are discussed.

ASSUMPTIONS OF THE MODEL

To understand the determinants of international migration and the impact of impeding such flows, a simple mathematical model is developed.

Assume there are two countries, country (i) and country (j). Each country is endowed with the two factors, labor and capital, used in the manufacture of a single good, output. Let the endowment of labor in country (i) be L_i, while L_j denotes the labor endowment in country (j). Analogously, country (i) is endowed with capital stock K_i, while the capital stock endowment in country (j) is K_j. Labor in both countries is assumed to be homogeneous. The initial capital-labor ratio in country (i) is assumed to be greater than its counterpart in country (j).

In each country the demand for labor is equal to the marginal product of its employees. In addition, the demand for labor is assumed to be perfectly elastic, implying a constant marginal product of labor. Therefore, the real wage in each country is uniquely determined. Let w_i represent the wage in country (i) while w_j is the wage in country (j). Given that country (i) is more capital intensive, the marginal product of workers in country (i) is greater than the marginal product of workers in country (j). Consequently, w_i is greater than w_j.

Capital is assumed to be immobile; however, given the difference in wage rates, labor flows unilaterally from country (j) to country (i). Since the marginal product of employees in each country is assumed to be constant, any potential change in labor productivity due to migration is ignored. Diminishing marginal returns to labor are not encountered given the assumptions of the model.

The level of output in each country is uniquely determined by its own production function. Therefore, the output of country (i), Q_i may be written as $Q_i = f_i(N_i, K_i)$ where N_i is the number of workers in country (i). In a similar fashion, output for country (j), Q_j, is found by $Q_j = f_j(N_j, K_j)$ where N_j is the number of workers in country (j). Since labor may migrate from country (j) to country (i), N_i may be greater than L_i and N_j may be less than L_j.

The simplifying assumptions of this model avoid some interesting questions beyond the chapter's scope and best left for future research. First, the assumption of a perfectly elastic demand for labor ignores the effect migration has on w_i and w_j. Intuitively, immigration increases the number of workers in country (i) and leads to reductions in w_i. Conversely, emigration reduces labor in country (j) and increases w_j.[2] If wages are made a function of migration, then decisions to migrate are based on an endogenous expected wage which unnecessarily complicates the model. The constant wage assumption ignores the endogeneity of wages and does not require the specification of an adjustment mechanism that explains how the expected wage converges to the actual wage.

Assuming the homogeneity of labor avoids the problem of having workers of different skills and two different wage rates for skilled and unskilled workers. The question of whether unskilled immigrant labor replaces either skilled or unskilled workers in country (i) is therefore ignored. Assuming that all workers are employed avoids the question of whether the immigrants take jobs from workers in country (i), forcing them to be unemployed.

The model's structure essentially allows a static analysis of partial equilibrium and focuses attention on two key issues. First, the model explains the determinants of immigration. Second, the model's structure allows one to determine the cost of a rigorously enforced immigration quota. Here the cost of an immigration quota is measured in terms of foregone total output.

UNRESTRICTED MIGRATION MODEL

Given the wage differential, workers in country (j) have the incentive to move to country (i). The decision to migrate is based solely on the relative benefits of moving. The relative benefit from migration (r) is defined as:

$$(1)\ r = \frac{w_i - C}{w_j}$$

where (C) is the cost of moving. Here $w_i - C$ may be viewed as the net wage received by the migrant moving to country (i). (C) is assumed to be constant; however, in reality (C) is probably a function of distance and the number of immigrants already residing in country (i). The further one migrates, the higher the transportation cost. Also, with a larger migrant stock, the host country provides a better information flow to potential migrants that reduces the cost of moving.

Obviously, (r) is positively related to w_i and inversely related to w_j and (C). Migration occurs only if the net wage received in country (i) exceeds w_j, which is equivalent to (r) being greater than one. Conversely, if (r) is less than one, no migration occurs. Finally, the potential migrant is indifferent to moving if (r) is equal to one.

There are psychic costs involved in the decision to migrate; consequently, every potential migrant has a reservation value of (r). (This is equivalent to the notion of a reservation wage in labor force participation theory.) An individual will move only if (r) is above some minimum level or reservation value. However, the reservation value for (r) will vary across individuals in country (j).

Let $f(r)$ describe the percentage of the population in country (j) that is willing to migrate given a value of (r). In addition, $f(r)$ is assumed to be monotonically increasing in (r). As indicated in Chart 7.1, an increase in (r) results in a larger percentage of L_j moving to country (i). Since no migration will occur if (r) is less than one, $f(1)$ is equal to zero. As (r) increases, the reservation value of (r) for more and more individuals is surpassed and the number of immigrants increases. Since (f) is a function of (r), then $f(r)$ is directly related to w_i and inversely related to w_j and (C).

The number of persons in country (j) who are willing to move for a given value of (r) is defined as:

Chart 7.1
Comparison of Wage Rates and Willingness to Migrate in a Free Market

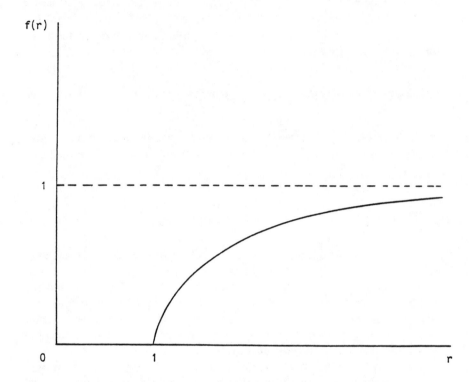

$$(2)\ M = f(r)L_j$$

where (M) is the actual number of immigrants. Larger values of w_i lead to larger values of (M) while larger values of w_j or (C) result in smaller values of (M).

Immigration from country (j) to country (i) increases the effective labor force in country (i) while reducing the number of workers in country (j). The amount of available employees in each country after immigration is defined as:

$$(3)\ N_i = L_i + M \text{ and } N_j = L_j - M.$$

Any change in the effective labor force for each country has a potential impact on the level of combined output. Let (Q) represent combined output and be defined as:

$$(4)\ Q = Q_i + Q_j = f_i(N_i, K_i) + f_j(N_j, K_j).$$

RESTRICTED MIGRATION MODEL

The previous section emphasized that a given level of benefit (r), determines the number of laborers who wish to migrate. With no quota, this is the number that actually moves. With a quota, a two-step decision process is invoked. Chart 7.2 illustrates the problem. (S) represents the supply of migrants to country (i). *Ceteris parabus*, a higher wage in country (i) would increase the level of migration to country (i) and produce a positively sloped function. At L_j the curve becomes vertical because in this simplistic model a sufficiently high wage will induce the entire population of (j) to migrate. For wage w_i, (M) people will wish to migrate. If the government imposes a quota at (M^*), $M - M^*$ people who would migrate if it were legal must now decide whether or not to illegally migrate. Hence, the maximum number of illegal migrants can be defined as:

$$(5)\ R = M - M^*.$$

Chart 7.2
Comparison of Wage Rates and Willingness to Migrate under a Quota System

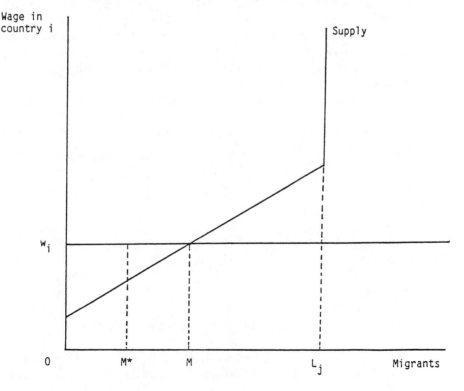

Illegal migration involves a cost which legal migration clearly does not: There is a definite risk that the illegal migrant will be apprehended and returned to his home country. Consequently, a new return equation is specified:

$$(6)\ r^* = \frac{[1 - g(E)]w_i + g(E)w_j - C}{w_j}$$

where (r^*) is the relative benefit of migrating illegally from country (j) to country (i), and g is the probability of an illegal immigrant being apprehended and returned to country (j). This probability is assumed to be a function of country (i)'s enforcement efforts (E) and must lie in the interval from 0 to 1. The first term in the numerator is the product of the wage rate and the probability of successful migration, the expected value of an attempted migration. The second term in the numerator is the product of the home wage rate and the probability of being returned, the expected value of a failed migration attempt. Summing these terms, subtracting (C), and dividing by the home wage rate provides a measure of the expected benefit to making an illegal migration attempt.

The difference between (r^*) and (r) should also be noted. If $g(E) = 0$ (a 0 probability of being apprehended and returned), (r^*) will be identical to (r). Significantly, for all positive values of $g(E)$, (r) will exceed (r^*). As a consequence, it is not possible to observe the number of people who would immigrate if it were legal. The researcher can only observe the quota plus those people who immigrated illegally and were detected (though perhaps not returned).

As a result, a new probability function similar to that illustrated in Chart 7.1 must be used to determine the level of illegal migration. If $h(r^*)$ represents the probability of an illegal migration given (r^*), then the level of illegal migration (I) is:

$$(7)\ I = h(r^*)\ (M - M^*)$$

The upper and lower limits for $h(r^*)$ can be established by substituting the known boundaries (0 and 1) for $g(E)$ into equation (6). When $g = 0$, $h(r^*)$ must accept the value 1, and when $g = 1$, $h(r^*)$ must accept the value 0. Consequently, $h(r^*)$ is restricted to values lying between 0 and 1.

The importance of this result can be seen in the following partial derivative:

$$(8)\ \delta I/\delta M^* = -h(r^*).$$

Clearly, illegal migration will respond in a predictable way to an immigration quota. Illegal migration will vary inversely with a numerical migration quota.

Once the levels of legal and illegal migration have been determined, the effective labor force in each country can be calculated. For example:

(9) $N_i = L_i + (1 - g)I + M^*$ and

$N_j = L_j - (1 - g)I - M^*.$

Inserting these calculations into each country's production function and summing provides the following result:

(10) $Q = f_i(L_i + (1\text{-}g)I + M^*, K_i) + f_j(L_j - (1\text{-}g)I - M^*, K_j)$

which is the total output for the two countries.

The primary focus of this chapter is the effect of immigration quotas on economic welfare. Treating (Q) as a measure of welfare and partially differentiating (10) with respect to (M^*) produces the primary result of interest because it indicates the effect of a labor quota on total output.

(11) $\delta Q/\delta M^* = \delta f_i/\delta N_i[\, (1 - g)\delta I/\delta M^* + 1]$

$- \delta f_j/\delta N_j[\, (1 - g)\, \delta I/\delta M^* + 1]$

The crucial issue is the algebraic sign of this derivative. Some simple manipulation produces the following result:

(12) $\delta Q/\delta M^* = (\delta f_i/\delta N_i - \delta f_j/\delta N_j)\,[(1 - g)\, \delta I/\delta M^* + 1].$

The first term on the right hand side of equation (12) is the difference in the countries' marginal products. This term must be positive or there is no motive for migration. The second term is more complex. Equation (8) establishes that $\delta I/\delta MI$ is $- h(r^*)$, which must lie between the values of 0 and $- 1$. Also, $(1 - g)$ is a probability that restricts its value to numbers between 0 and 1. The product of these two numbers must be negative and less than 1. Summing this result with one produces a positive number. Consequently, equation (12) must be unambiguously positive:

(13) $\delta Q/\delta M^* > 0.$

Summarizing, whenever a country imposes an effective immigration quota, aggregate output is reduced.

CONCLUSIONS

This simple model of migration once more reveals the inefficiencies associated with government-imposed restrictions on a free market. The use of a binding immigration quota results in foregone output, an economic cost that can never be recovered. The amount of output lost will be greater if enforcement of the quota diverts the use of capital and labor from productive activity.

These results provide insight into the current problems existing along the U.S.-Mexico border. The adoption of policies that restrict labor and capital flows result in economic inefficiencies and foregone production. These costs are imposed on both the United States and Mexico.

Prospects for the future are mixed. The recent changes in U.S. immigration laws establish penalties for employers who hire illegal migrants. If this provision effectively discourages their employment, which was its stated purpose, labor flows will be reduced, economic costs will rise, and border tensions will increase. On the other hand, recent events indicate that Mexico is loosening its restrictions on capital inflows. This could ameliorate the problem to some degree.

NOTES

1. See, for example, Wilfred J. Ethier, "Illegal Immigration: The Host-Country Problem, *American Economic Review*, Vol. 76, No. 1, March 1986, pp. 56–71; and Hearings on United States-Mexico Economic Relations (98–1297), Subcommittee of the Committee on Appropriations, United States Senate, Washington, D.C.: U.S. Government Printing Office, 1985.

2. M. Greenwood and J. McDowell, "The Factor Market Consequences of U.S. Immigration," *Journal of Economic Literature*, Vol. 24, No. 4, December 1986, pp. 1738–1772.

8

U.S.-Mexican Agreements on Illicit Narcotics Trafficking: Legal Implications on Trade for the Border Region

Ana Maria Perez Gabriel

On August 5, 1930, and October 2, 1930, an exchange of notes between the United States and Mexico marked the beginning of close cooperation for strict international control of illicit traffic in narcotic drugs. The U.S. Ambassador, Dwight W. Morrow, suggested to the Mexican Minister of Foreign Affairs, Genaro Estrada, an exchange of information and evidence, photographs, criminal records, fingerprints, *Bertillon* measurements, and mutual cooperation in detective and investigating work in relation to persons engaged in the illicit traffic of narcotic drugs. The U.S. Ambassador labeled his proposal an *informal* agreement. Mexico denied the U.S. request for photos of transgressors, fingerprints, and *Bertillon* measurements on cases arising in states where said violations were only punished by administrative sanctions such as fines or arrests not exceeding 15 days, but agreed to furnish such information on illicit narcotics smuggling cases under federal jurisdiction.

These executive agreements have come a long way! In June 1973 an exchange of letters between U.S. Ambassador Robert A. McBride, and Guido Belssaso, Director of the Mexican National Center for Drug Dependency Research, provided the Mexican National Center with a collection of reference works in the field of narcotics abuse. The collection was financed by a special grant of up to $5,000 as an American contribution to Mexican research in narcotics abuse, and to support joint Mexican efforts to curb international traffic of illegal narcotics. The U.S. ambassador proposed that his letter and the reply by the Mexican Director shall constitute an agreement between their two governments; the proposition was accepted by the Mexican official. By 1973, these agreements were effected only by an exchange of letters between the United States ambassador in Mexico City and the Mexican Secretary of Foreign Relations; in recent years, the agreements on this subject have been effected by the exchange of notes between the United States ambassador in Mexico City and the Mexican attorney general. Also

91

since 1973, the United States started providing funds—in increasing amounts—to cover costs of helicopters, training for Mexican helicopter pilots and mechanics, fuel, and other equipment. It is interesting to observe that in some agreements, the objectives exceed the specific illegal drug traffic control, as in the case of the agreement effected by an exchange of notes on August 31, 1973, involving communications equipment.[1] Also, the Agreement of October 26, 1973, provided for U.S. technical assistance financed by a grant not to exceed $75,650 and contracted to the Resource Planning Corporation of Miami, Florida, for consultants to carry out an epidemiological study of narcotics abuse in Mexico. The consultants would also be teachers in training on social science research methods for such study. It must be noted that the latter agreement called for access at any time to personnel of the Florida Corporation for monitoring work.[2] Exceeding objectives likewise were the following agreements: December 3, 1973, stated that at a total cost to the U.S. government not to exceed $3,644,000, material assistance, including helicopters, would be provided, and that Mexico would take title of helicopters once they were first used in training Mexican pilots.[3] We should observe that again access to the equipment is permitted to U.S. government personnel for verification of use and condition of service. Eventually the total was increased to $3,800,000. Further assistance included the replacing of helicopters, one destroyed and another badly damaged, on June 24, 1974, and providing also that the United States would consider requests from the Mexican government for financing spare parts and cost of fuel in Mexico's 1974 effort to eradicate the opium poppy. Through amendments, the amount was further increased and Mexico became obliged to give the U.S. embassy and U.S. government consulate raw and analyzed data obtained from the operation of a multispectral aerial photographic system to detect opium poppy cultivation. This agreement also included training of nine Mexican nationals at a National Aeronautics and Space Administration Test Facility for 60 days and additional funds of $15,500 for travelling and per diem of trainees, all amounting to $598,702.[4]

What seems even more compromising for Mexico is the acceptance of a complete video setup for classroom instructions, night viewing devices, alert transmitter, vehicle tracking equipment, portable repeaters, radios, and a portable shooting range for use at the Federal Judicial Police Training Academy and the Mexican corresponding obligation to permit access to U.S government personnel to verify usage and condition of service of equipment.[5] Likewise, Mexico accepted—among other items of technical assistance—arms and ammunition for the personnel participating in drug control activities. Mexico was also obligated to indemnify and safeguard the contractor and its personnel (Bell Helicopter Company) against responsibility for loss or damage caused to the Mexican Attorney General Office's aircraft, equipment or other property provided through said Office, with the exception of gross negligence or willful misconduct of contractor, under Mexican law. This clause of the Agreement, accepted by Mexico, is in violation of Article 1928 of Mexico's Federal Civil Code that sets forth that the State is responsible for all damages caused by its officials while on duty, that said officials are to pay for those damages which they have incurred and only in case they are unable to do so, the state shall pay for them. Under this Agreement, the Mexican government is taking up direct liability from which it does not exempt even its own official personnel.[6]

A very debatable issue, and one that implies violation of Article 13 of the Mexican Federal Constitution, is the United States government proposition, and acceptance by the Mexican government, of salary supplements to augment scale restrictions of the Office of the Attorney General for Mexican support personnel exclusively dedicated to opium poppy eradication and narcotics interdiction.[7] Another cause of violation of the Mexican Constitution is the Mexican government's acceptance that armed forces elements should engage in the narcotics eradication and interdiction activities.[8] Under Mexican laws, compensation for public services must be decreed by law and in the case at hand, the Mexican Congress has had no intervention whatsoever in authorizing said salary supplements; and civilians must be prosecuted and tried by civilian authorities.

The preceding analysis of the Agreements as to signatories and subject matter permits us to state that we are in the presence of treaties, regardless of the designation they have received, such as "agreements," "exchange of notes," and "exchange of letters." According to Article 2 of the Vienna Convention on the Law of Treaties, treaty means an international agreement concluded between states in written form and governed by international law, whether embodied in a single instrument or in two or more related instruments and whatever its particular designation.[9] Mexico, as well as the United States, is a party to this Convention and, therefore, obligated under international law to honor the agreements on narcotics trafficking control. Nevertheless, Article 133 of the Mexican Federal Constitution requires submission of treaties for Senate approval. A treaty must conform with the Constitution and be approved by the Senate to become law. The judges of the several Mexican states shall be bound thereby, anything to the contrary in the Constitution or laws of the states notwithstanding. In addition, Mexican law does not recognize the legal existence of what U.S. law has designated as "Executive Agreements." Mexican international commitments are only constitutionally possible—in domestic law—through treaties and treaties require conformance to the Mexican Constitution, including Senate approval. Executive Agreements as an enlargement of the Constitution are unconstitutional, to put it mildly.

As to the legal status of these Agreements, everything seemed to be running smoothly until the murder of the United States Drug Enforcement Administration Special Agent Enrique Camarena Salazar and his colleague, Mexican pilot Alfredo Zavala Avelar, in February 1985, and the alleged torture of DEA agent Victor Cortez Junior. The subsequent pressure by the

United States on the Mexican government for effective prosecution triggered awareness in the Mexican Congress as to the existence of the said agreements; the Senate required the executive branch to submit a complete and detailed account on them.

Article 15 of the Mexican Constitution prohibits the execution of treaties that violate fundamental freedoms of man and citizens. As already stated, Article 13 protects civilians from being prosecuted and tried by military jurisdiction. Furthermore, Articles 21 and 102 bestow competence to investigate crimes and prosecute criminals onto the attorney general (both federal and state) and on the Judicial Police, under his direct command. In addition, said federal officers are required to be Mexican by birth, pursuant to Article 16 of the Organic Law of the Attorney General of the Republic Office. Henceforth, any intervention of foreign enforcement officers in criminal prosecution in Mexico is in direct violation of the Mexican Constitution. A closer view of the access permitted to United States government personnel as convened in the aforementioned Agreements brings to our attention its very specific objective: at the request of the United States embassy, the Mexican government through the attorney general of the Republic shall provide the personnel of the United States Government access to the equipment—given as material support—for the purpose of verifying its usage and condition of service (December 3, 1973, Agreement). Furthermore, according to the October 26, 1973, Agreement, access is to be given at any time to personnel of the United States Special Action Office for Drug Abuse Prevention for monitoring work of the Resource Planning Corporation of Miami. Actually no clause of these Agreements authorizes United States Government personnel to intervene in criminal investigation or criminal prosecution in Mexico, by the Mexican attorney general and the Judicial Police under his direct command.

During the house debate on the pending Anti-Drug Abuse legislations, Maine Representative Olympia Snowe stated that the bill under discussion should deplore "Mexico's poor record of cooperation" and that $1 million in U.S. aid should be withheld until Mexico prosecuted effectively the murderers and torturers of DEA agents Camarena and Cortez, respectively.[10] Florida Representative Smith argued that Americans should impress on Mexico the necessity of serving justice in the murder of DEA agent Enrique Camarena Salazar and that aid to Mexico should be conditioned furthermore to Mexico's taking action on the kidnapping of DEA agent Victor Cortez.[11] These two statements bring up two important issues. First, no clause of the Agreements we have been discussing conditions the delivery of funds agreed upon by the way Mexico legally administers criminal justice. Mexican Penal Law does not apply higher imprisonment terms to persons guilty of homicides committed against officers, regardless of the status of the victim. Penalties are decided and determined taking into consideration the particular circumstances under which the crime has been committed. Second, every circumstance will be studied in depth, by Mexican courts in these cases. Stiffer penalties are applied for aggravated crimes, which in the case of aggravated homicide, range from 20-to 40-year imprisonment.

A further explanation is now at hand. During the Hearing of the House Committee on July 17, 1986, it was inquired why none of Special Agent Camarena's killers have yet been brought to justice. Appearing as a witness before the hearing, David Westrate, Assistant Administrator for Operations, United States Department of Justice, brought up the point that long-term investigations probably will go on for several years. Congressman Smith spoke of Mexican judges issuing *amparos* to a number of suspects and asked how long we must wait for progress in the Camarena investigation, and whether the U.S.–Mexico Extradition Treaty covered drug offenses. To have a clear perspective on the criminal proceedings against those accused of Agent Camarena's murder and in order to be able to assess if said proceedings have been stonewalled, we must first consider more deeply how the Mexican Federal Criminal Justice system functions. The system is made up of federal district judges, circuit courts of appeals, and collegiate courts of *amparo* or the Supreme Court of Justice of the Nation, depending on the jurisdiction for the specific case.

The proceeding, as regulated by the Federal Code on criminal proceedings, consists of the following stages:

1. Pre-trial investigation: Police under the direct control of the federal district attorney investigate the facts of the crime committed. The accused has a right to defense counsel. Results of the investigation are entered in a record. Once the investigation has been completed, the district attorney renders a resolution deciding if the person who has been arrested goes to trial before a judge, or he may set him free with a warning.

2. Trial (*Instruccion*) consists of a series of hearings during which the district attorney and the defense present their evidence.

3. Final Hearing on the case and rendering of a decision. The district attorney, the defense, and the judge may interrogate the accused at this final hearing. Some evidence procedure might take place again if feasible and authorized by the federal judge. The defense and district attorney present their last arguments and allegations on the case.

Once the accused stands formal trial as decreed by the judge, the accused is presented to the judge by the district attorney within the next 72 hours. After that, the trial period should last no more than 10 months, if maximum penalty for the crime charged is over two-year imprisonment; and not over 3 months if maximum penalty is less than two-year imprisonment. The complete criminal procedure should last no longer than four months if the crime is punishable by less than a two-year prison term; and less than a year if the crime is punishable by a higher prison term.

Writs of *amparo* and appeals may arise during the proceeding, *but there is no stallment of proceeding*, which continues its course to the rendering of a decision by the federal judge. Final decision may be appealed by either the district attorney or by defense attorney or by both; appeal should be presented within the next five days after decision is served to accused. If appeal is admitted, the complete original record is forwarded to the competent circuit court of appeals.

Procedure progress is as follows:

1. three days for objecting the admission of appeal; if admission is objected, the remaining parties are given the opportunity of intervention;

2. within the next three days a decree is rendered by the court on the admission;

3. eight days for presenting evidence;

4. within the next 30 days a final hearing on appeal must be held; and

5. within the next eight days, a decision on the appeal must be rendered.

Within the following 15 days, defendant may challenge the final decision that was rendered on appeal proceeding, before the Supreme Court of Justice or the Collegiate Circuit Court, through the writ of *amparo* on a legality issue or criminal due process issues. If admitted, allegations by other concerned parties may be submitted within the next ten days. Within the next ten days a complete record of the case is assigned to one of the justices of the chamber on criminal cases, and during the following ten days he must produce a draft decision on the *amparo* case. This term may be extended as required by the importance of the case or the lengthy record involved. Once the draft decision is ready, it will be discussed by the chamber at a hearing to be held within the next ten days. At this hearing the decision is voted and finally rendered, granting or denying the federal protection to the *amparo* plaintiff.

Taking into consideration the various terms as set by law, the criminal investigations and prosecutions to which the congressional hearing on the Camarena investigation refers to should be focused and analyzed.

As to the question posed during the Hearing regarding extradition of drug traffickers from Mexico, and whether the Treaty covers drug offenses, we hold that pursuant to Article 2, Section (1) of the Extradition Treaty now in force between the United States of America and Mexico, said Treaty does cover drug offenses. This Treaty was signed in Mexico on May 4, 1978, and it entered into force on January 25, 1980. Among extraditable offenses are the willful acts which fall within any of the clauses of the Appendix and are punishable in accordance with the laws of both Contracting Parties by deprivation of liberty, the maximum of which shall not be less than one year. Clause number 14 of the Appendix specifically refers to offenses against the laws relating to traffic in, possession, production, manufacture, importation or export of dangerous drugs and chemicals, including narcotics drugs, cannabis, psychotropic drugs, opium, cocaine, or their derivatives. Hence, it is clear that the Treaty does cover drug offenses, likewise extradition of drug traffickers from Mexico.

In addition to the international treaty just mentioned, Mexico has as domestic legislation the law on International Extradition, 1975, which regulates such type of extradition when no treaty is available. Extradition is legally granted for all crimes punishable pursuant to Mexican criminal law with an average prison term of no less than a year. Extradition will be denied if accused has been acquitted or pardoned or enjoys amnesty privileges. Also when there is no formal accusation, the statute of limitations has run out on the case, or the crime that has been committed falls under jurisdiction of Mexican courts. Furthermore,

1. No political prisoners may be extradited.

2. Military courts may not try extraditable offenses.

3. Requesting state must grant reciprocity on similar petitions.

4. The defendant will not be prosecuted for crimes committed previously to the extradition petition and which were not included in the said petition.

5. No Mexican national shall be extradited to a foreign country but in exceptional cases as determined by the executive.

Hard legislative work has been invested to produce the Anti-Drug Abuse Act of 1986, signed into law by President Reagan on October 27, 1986.[12] An act designed to strengthen federal efforts to encourage foreign cooperation in eradicating illicit drug crops, and in halting international drug traffic; to improve enforcement of federal drug laws and enhance interdiction of illicit drug shipments; to provide strong federal leadership in establishing effective drug abuse prevention and education programs; to expand federal support for drug abuse treatment and rehabilitation efforts; and other purposes. Of particular importance in United States-Mexico foreign relations on this matter are Title II, "International Narcotics Control," and Title IX, "Denial of Trade Benefits to Uncooperative Major Drug Producing or Drug-Transit Countries."

Title II, which may be cited as the "International Narcotics Control Act of 1986," provides for aircraft bases in Latin America for narcotics control eradication and interdiction efforts and is *solely used for said purposes*. On September 10, 1986, U.S. Representative Smith (Florida) stated before a congressional debate on this bill that the task force had learned that the 88-plane air fleet given to Mexico spent most of its time on ground, and that by retaining title to aircraft intended use of same would be ensured. His proposition became a part of this Title, which now provides that the aircraft will be given on a lease or loan basis and that the secretary of state will be responsible for a detailed account to the Foreign Relations Committees of the Congress even on aircraft that were made available prior to the enactment of this new regulation.

Fifty percent of United States assistance under the Foreign Assistance Act of 1961 as amended will be withheld from major illicit drug producing or major drug-transit countries unless the president certifies to the Congress that during the previous year (beginning with March 1, 1987, and each succeeding year) those countries have cooperated fully with the United States in preventing illicit drug sales to U.S. government personnel, or their dependents in such countries, and in avoiding illicit drugs exported to the United States. To counterattack the said certification, the Congress may issue a joint resolution of disapproval. In 1987, President Reagan's certification in relation to Mexico was the subject of a Senate debate, hence, a delay in that certification.

Issuance of diplomatic passports by the secretary of state to Drug Enforcement Administration officials and employees assigned abroad has pleased the Congress (Section 2010 of this Title). An issue is now at hand. The presence and activities of DEA personnel in Mexico are already legally debatable. Will they be considered diplomatic staff of the U.S. embassy? If so, will they be subjected to Mexico's *agrement* and will their status be regulated by the Vienna Convention on Diplomatic Relations of April 18, 1961?[13] Will they be granted inviolability as to their persons, private residences, papers and correspondence, exemption from liability to any form of arrest or detention, and immunity from the criminal jurisdiction of Mexico? They may also be declared *personae non gratae* and the United States will either recall them or terminate their functions with the embassy. Will the DEA personnel as holders of a diplomatic passport acquire diplomatic status as regulated by the Vienna Convention? Will their activities as diplomatic agents be official business which should be conducted through the Mexican secretary of foreign affairs? At this point it should be remembered that the agreements on illicit narcotics traffic control have been unconstitutionally effected through exchange of letters between the United States embassy and the Mexican attorney general. A very positive result from this new perspective will be Mexican Senate control and required approval on these agreements. These are tentative issues for consideration by the Mexico-United States Intergovernmental Commission and as set forth in Section 2024 of the International Narcotics Control Act of 1986.

Under Section 2030 of the aforementioned Act, the United States Congress has found that mutual cooperation has not been attained completely because Mexico has not responded adequately in:

1. fully investigating the 1985 murders of U.S. Drug Enforcement Administration agent Enrique Camarena Salazar and his pilot, Alfredo Zavala Avelar;

2. fully investigating the 1986 detention and torture of U.S. Drug Enforcement Administration agent Victor Cortez, Junior;

3. bringing to trial and effectively prosecuting those responsible for the Camarena and Zavala murders and those responsible for the detention and torture of Cortez;

4. using effectively and efficiently the fleet of aircraft provided by the United States government for drug eradication and interdiction; and

5. preventing drug trafficking and drug-related violence at the United States-Mexican border.

Hence, a $1 million grant was withheld from funds allocated for assistance for Mexico for the fiscal year 1987, under Chapter 8 of Part I of the Foreign Assistance Act of 1961. Apart from being an unfair judgment on Mexican criminal procedure legislation and justice, the withholding of funds whose provision was agreed upon by the two countries violates United States commitments under international law, *pacta sunt servanda.*

From reading Subtitle of Title III, Defense Drug Interdiction Assistance Act, we can observe that the Department of Defense will receive funds in the amount of $138 million to refurbish and upgrade four E-2C Hawkeye surveillance aircraft for the navy and make two of them available for the Customs Service and two for the Coast Guard; $99.5 million will be appropriated for seven radar aerostats and $40 million for 8 Blackhawk helicopters; likewise the aerostats and the helicopters will be made available to other agencies to be determined by the National Drug Enforcement Policy Board. Henceforth, it appears that involvement of the Department of Defense consists of procurement and renovation of aircraft which will eventually be under the responsibility and use of the Customs Service, Coast Guard, and Drug Enforcement authorities. This provision in the Act is congruent to the position adopted by the military at the September 10, 1986, debate on H.R. Bill 5484 (the armed forces portion of the bill) to keep its personnel from direct involvement in civilian law enforcement and keep civilians as the basic and main personnel for drug enforcement. We can conclude from reading Section 3056 that the Act (Assistance to Civilian Law Enforcement and Emergency assistance by Department of Defense Personnel) leaves the definition of an emergency circumstance to the joint determination of the secretaries of state and defense, and the attorney general. The act covers, in emergency cases, criminal activity posing a serious threat to the United States interest. In this case the assistance given by the military would enhance law enforcement. But what about *posse comitatus* law? The legal competence of the military for illicit drug trafficking control is a highly debatable issue. It is particularly so in Mexico where at present the Mexican armed forces are directly involved in such activities. On March 27, 1987, the secretary of the navy declared that expenditure for those activities was as high as 1 million pesos per hour, and 100 lives have been lost on the Pacific and Gulf Navy illicit drug trafficking eradication operations, resulting in 30 criminal arrests.[14]

In his State of the Union Address, Mexican President Miguel De La Madrid reported to Congress on September 1, 1987, that illicit narcotics trafficking control called for coordinated efforts from all countries involved; because Mexican efforts—as intensive as they have been to the extent of directly using Mexican armed forces to eradicate such illicit trafficking—are insufficient if at the same time the great demand for illicit narcotics is not undermined.

Under Mexican government auspices, a conference to discuss this important issue was held and attorneys general from 13 different countries expressed their concerns and proposals of solutions on this topic.

Furthermore, the Mexican Federal Executive has concluded coordination agreements with Mexican state governors to effectively prevent not only drug addiction but also alcohol abuse and smoking related disease. As a result of these efforts, 1,352 committees are working very actively on preventive and rehabilitation measures. Colima, Nayarit, and Zacatecas subscribed to the said agreements during the month of April 1987.

Title VIII, known as the Narcotics Control Trade Act, poses inconsistency between its tariff treatment of products of uncooperative major drug producing or drug-transit countries as determined by the United States president and Article I of the General Agreement on Tariffs and Trade,[15] to which both the United States and Mexico are contracting parties. Article I.1 of GATT specifically sets forth:

With respect to customs duties and charges of any kind imposed on, in connection with importation or exportation, or imposed on international transfer of payments for imports or exports, and with respect to the method of levying such duties and charges, and with respect to all rules and formalities in connection with importation and exportation, and with respect to all matters referred to in paragraphs 2 and 4 of Article III, any advantage, favour, privilege or immunity granted by any contracting party to any product originating in or destined for any other country shall be accorded immediately and unconditionally to the like product originating in or destined for the territories of all other contracting parties.

Under the Narcotics Control Trade Act, the president is authorized by the Congress—among other measures—to apply to dutiable products a duty not to exceed 50 percent ad valorem or the equivalent specific rate, or even apply to duty-free products a duty not to exceed 50 percent ad valorem. The president can go as far as applying any combination of said actions against uncooperative countries.

In addition to the most favored nation clause, GATT obligations include prohibition of quotas, banning the use of export subsidies to sell for less abroad than in domestic market. Exceptions to GATT obligations include waiver of obligations, temporary restraints to imports severely injuring domestic industry, balance of payments crisis, customs unions and free trade areas. No exception justifies penalizing a contracting party with additional duties on its products depending on the system used by that party to administer criminal justice within its own territory.

Which law prevails? If we assume equal rank of a treaty and a federal law, then the Narcotics Control Trade Act, as subsequent in time, prevails under the *domestic law* of the United States. However, under international law the GATT commitments are still binding for the United States. Applying increased duty rates as a penalty to Mexican products would violate GATT commitments as well as infringe Article 26 and Article 27 of the Vienna Convention on the Law of Treaties, which set forth:

pacta sunt servanda internal law and observance of treaties. A party may not invoke the provisions of its internal law as justification for its failure to perform a treaty. This rule is without prejudice to Article 46.

Consequently, the conflicting titles of the Anti-Drug Abuse Act of 1986 will have to be construed in such a manner that it will not violate United States obligations under international law.

May the sense of fairness and justice for all, which has guided the United States-Mexico international relations, prevail on this delicate issue.

NOTES

1. *Treaties in Force: A List of Treaties and Other International Agreements of the United States in Force on January 1, 1986*, U.S. Department of State, Publication 9433. (Compiled by the Treaty Affairs Staff. Office of the Legal Advisor. 24 UST 1978.)

2. *Treaties in Force*, 24 UST 2245; TIAS 7742.

3. *Treaties in Force*, 25 UST 1694.

4. *Treaties in Force*, 25 UST 1286.

5. *Treaties in Force*, 25 UST 3176.

6. *Treaties in Force*, 26 UST 1274 and 27 UST 1985.

7. *Treaties in Force*, 29 UST 5334.

8. *Treaties in Force*, 29 UST 268.

9. Noyes E. Leech, et. al., *Documentary Supplement to Cases and Materials on the International Legal System* (Mineola, NY: The Foundation Press, Inc., 1973), p. 102.

10. *Congressional Record*, September 10, 1986. The House bill is intended to strengthen federal efforts to encourage foreign cooperation in eradicating illicit drug crops and in halting international drug traffic; to improve enforcement of Federal drug laws and enhance interdiction of illicit drug shipments; to provide strong federal leadership in establishing effective drug abuse prevention and education programs; to expand federal support for drug abuse treatment and rehabilitation efforts; and for other purposes.

11. *Congressional Record*, September 10, 1986. H.R. 6538, H.R. 6539.

12. Laws of the 99th Congress, 2d sess. Public Law 99-570 (H.R. 5484), October 27, 1986.

13. Leech, *Documentary Supplement to Cases*, p. 131.

14. Arteaga Gomez, Mexican Secretary of the Navy, in an interview by the Mexican Television System on March 27, 1987.

15. John H. Jackson, *Documents Supplement to Legal Problems of International Economic Relations* (St. Paul, MN: West Publishing Co., 1977), p. 4.

PART FOUR
PRODUCTION SHARING/ MAQUILADORAS: MUTUALLY BENEFICIAL OR EXPLOITATION

By whatever name it is referred to—production sharing, *maquiladoras*, in-bond industries, border industrialization, etc.—, the concept has been shrouded in controversy since its inception in the mid-1960s. It is simple in principle: it allows the establishment of plants for the assembly and process-ing of different products in one country—in this case Mexico—which use foreign (in this case U.S.) parts and components. Both the entry of parts into Mexico and the reentry of the final product into the United States would, then, be free of any duties or quantitative limitations. The primary objective of production sharing is to create efficiency and reduce costs by utilizing factor mobility of capital. That is, building production facilities—and the shipment of parts and components to be assembled—where the less expensive labor is. In theory, and many argue in practice, production sharing helps everybody. It benefits the American con-sumer by providing him/her with cheaper products. It helps U.S. business by lowering its production costs and improving its competitiveness vis-à-vis other producers. It benefits the Mexican economy by providing employ-ment and foreign currencies. Finally, and arguably, it helps the American economy by creating employment in the United States by creating demand for U.S.-made parts and components to be assembled (finished) by the Mexican worker. It is this last controversial point that is the topic of Chapter 9 by Barbara Chrispin who presents the findings of a survey of training and development practices of several *maquiladora* industries. The survey is based on interviews of 40 government and business officials. She concludes that manpower development is occuring in at least three areas: the creation of employment opportunities; the training and development of employees; and a transfer of knowledge to technicians and administrators.

Edward George presents his views on the future of *maquiladoras* located on the U.S.-Mexican border in Chapter 10. He separates border *ma-quiladoras* from those situated inland, and argues that the tremendous growth of border plants during the last two decades notwithstanding, the future of the former group is less certain. He points out that regardless of their location, *maquila* plants must convince both U.S. and Mexican of-ficials, and the general public as to their benefits for *both* countries. The *ma-quilas* will not continue to get special tax treatment from either country unless officials are convinced of their benefits to both countries. The author pro-vides a synopsis of the areas in which *maquilas* have to prove their worthiness to survive. He concludes that provided that the Mexican government con-tinues to maintain the prevailing political and labor stability, then in the foreseeable future, the *maquila* program will continue to grow. However, most of the growth will occur away from the border and not in the border region.

9

Manpower Development in the Maquiladora Industry: Fact or Fiction?

Barbara R. Chrispin

INTRODUCTION

The *maquiladora* industry, commonly referred to as the in-bond industry, was established in 1965 as an experiment in production sharing. The Border Industrialization Program, as it then was called, permitted the establishment of plants for the assembly, processing, and/or finishing of foreign materials and components. The primary objective of this program was to provide jobs for displaced agricultural workers, following the cancellation of the Bracero Program in the United States, to mitigate social unrest along the northern border zone. Under this program, the Mexican government authorized the establishment of industrial plants that would be permitted to import into Mexico all equipment and machinery, materials, and component parts necessary for production. No duty would be collected on these imports provided all finished products were exported and none were kept or sold in Mexico. This program was originally construed as a border operation only. In 1972, however, the authorized zone for such operation was expanded to permit the establishment of plants in economically depressed areas in the interior of Mexico.

In the United States, the industry took advantage of two special tariff provisions, items 806.30 and 807.00. Under these laws, duty on U.S. products processed or assembled abroad is levied only on the value-added by the foreign processing. Generally, this includes the cost of Mexican labor and overhead. The program has made Mexico highly competitive with the Far East in production costs, due primarily to its proximity to the United States and its low labor costs.

The most recent law regulating the promotion and operation of the *maquiladora* industry was enacted in 1983. The primary objectives of the program, as stated in this law, are to generate foreign exchange, to develop employment opportunities for a rapidly expanding labor force, and to foster increased regional development. The name "Maquiladora Industry" aptly reflects these objectives. The term originates from the Spanish word *maquila*. In colonial times, this referred to the toll millers collected for processing someone else's grain. Following the Mexico City earthquake in 1985, Mexico's economic woes were exacerbated by the drop in oil prices and by the loss of tourism revenues. These events moved the Maquiladora Industry into second place in the Mexican economy as a source of foreign exchange and have made it the nation's most rapidly expanding industrial sector.

In addition to providing jobs, supporters believe the industry is training people in the industrial process and contributing to a knowledge transfer that will spill over into other parts of the Mexican economy. The purpose of this chapter is to assess the evidence supporting this argument.

METHODOLOGY

A survey of training and development practice in the Maquiladora Industry was conducted during fall 1985. Interviews were held with 40 key government and business officials, expatriate and host country, associated in some way with the development of the industry in Mexico. Three cities were selected as sites for the survey: Juarez, Chihuahua, and Guadalajara. Juarez, a border city across from El Paso, has the largest number of in-bond plants of any Mexican city. Chihuahua, approximately 300 miles south of Juarez, is one of the sites in the interior which is being promoted by the government to foster regional development. Guadalajara is recognized as the "Silicon Valley" of Mexico and supports a well-educated work force. Data from secondary sources obtained from the interviewees is used as supporting documentation.

FINDINGS AND DISCUSSION

Profile of the *Maquiladora* Work Force

Employment in the *maquiladora* industry grew to almost 200,000 employees in 672 plants throughout Mexico in 1984; the largest growth occurred between 1978 and 1984. While employees in the *maquiladora* industry represent only about 1 percent of the labor force in manufacturing, employment in this sector grew at a rate of 12.7 percent between 1975 and 1985, compared to a rate of 1.6 percent for the manufacturing sector as a whole. For the three locations under study, the average employment per plant is given in Table 9.1.

Approximately 36 percent of the total *maquiladora* work force is located in Juarez; together the three cities under study account for 44 percent of the total employment in the industry.

Table 9.1
Average Number of Employees per Maquila Plant

Location	Plants	Employees	Emp/Plant
Cd. Juarez, Chih.	155	72,495	468
Chihuahua, Chih.	26	9,874	379
Guadalajara, Jal	13	5,914	455
TOTAL COUNTRY	672	199,684	297

Source: Secretaria de Patrimonio y Fomento Industrial, Mexico, January–December 1984.

Sex

The *maquiladora* industry has been characterized as a labor force comprised primarily of women. As the following data indicate, however, the proportion of men to women has been changing. This is due in large part to the rapid growth of employment opportunities in the industry (see Table 9.2).

Similar data for the three cities under consideration are given in Table 9.3. The employee profile in Juarez shows the most dramatic changes. Due in part to industry growth, but primarily to a change in industry profile, the percentage of men and technicians has been increasing relative to the national average. Nevertheless, the employment of men remains a priority goal of the Maquiladora Association in Juarez.

Several officials acknowledged, however, that social and economic factors have contributed to a national increase in the labor force participation rate of women. This trend shows up in industry statistics, but not in national employment statistics, which are not disaggregated by sex.

Age

The age profile for employees in Juarez and Chihuahua is given in Table 9.4. In Juarez, the average age of a *maquiladora* employee remained constant

Table 9.2
National In-Bond Industry Employees by Sex and Occupation
(percentage)

	Jan.-Jul. 1982	Jan.- Dec. 1984
women	64.5	58.7
men	18.8	24.2
technicians	10.3	11.2
administrative	6.3	5.9

Source: Secretaria de Patrimonio y Fomento Industrial, Mexico, 1984.

Table 9.3
Percentage of Employees by Sex/Occupation
(January-December 1984)

	Cd. Juarez	Chihuahua	Guadalajara
women	56.60	74.89	60.74
men	25.05	9.90	17.06
technicians	11.72	8.35	11.26
administrative	6.62	6.86	4.94

Source: Secretaria de Patrimonio y Fomento Industrial, Mexico, 1984.

between 1983 and 1985; however, in Chihuahua it decreased somewhat during the same time period. Data on age was not obtained for Guadalajara. The mean age in Mexico is 18. Thus, the labor force tends to be exceptionally young. The higher age in Juarez suggests, among other things, that the length of employment in the industry is increasing and that women are staying in the labor force for a longer period of time.

Education

Recent statistics for Mexico indicate that 53.7 percent of the population over 15 have had no schooling, 29.5 percent have had first level education, 8.9 percent intermediate level education, 5.2 percent secondary level education, and 2.6 percent postsecondary education. As the following statistics show, the level of education for *maquiladora* workers is considerably higher (see Table 9.5).

While the *maquiladora* employees are better educated than the population as a whole, 50 percent of the direct-labor employees have only a primary school education, and only slightly more than 50 percent of the technicians have completed at least a secondary school education. According

Table 9.4
Average Age per Maquila Employee

	Cd. Juarez		Chihuahua	
	1983	1985	1983	1985
direct-labor	24.5	24.6	21.8	21.7
technicians	26.7	26.0	26.7	21.4
administrative	25.0	25.5	27.3	24.6
Total	25.0	25.0	23.0	21.9

Source: Desarollo Economico del Estado de Chihuahua, A.C. 1983 and 1985.

Table 9.5
Level of Education of Maquila Workers in Cd. Juarez
(percentage)

	prim.	sec.	prep.	prof.	post-prof.	Total
direct-labor	56	34	8	2	0	100
technicians	18	25	34	21	2	100
administrative	45	36	13	5	1	100

	Level	of Education	in Chihuahua			
direct-labor	52	40	8	0	0	100
technician	23	24	23	30	0	100
administrative	0	56	11	11	22	100

Source: Desarrollo Economico del Estado de Chihuahua, A.C., 1983.

to company officials, the problem is compounded by the fact that the work force lacks knowledge of how the industrial system works and possesses few salable skills.

The Industrial Environment

The *maquiladora* industry is comprised of 10 major product groups. The product groups employing the largest number of employees are electrical, transportation equipment and accessories, shoes and clothing, and other manufacturing. These four industries also employ the largest number of males, production technicians, and administrative employees. The number of employees working in each product group for 1982 and 1984 is given in Table 9.6. Between 1982 and 1984, the number of people employed by the industry increased by 54 percent but the rank order of the product groups employing the largest number of employees remained the same. However, with the exception of transportation equipment, the largest employers showed smaller rates of employment growth compared to the industry as a whole. The industries having the largest rates of increase are transportation (150 percent), furniture (108 percent), machinery (66 percent), toys and sporting goods (137 percent), and chemical (318 percent). Thus, some changes are occurring in the industry profile. There is movement from light manufacturing to heavy manufacturing. High technology products, while still a small segment of the industry, are showing rapid growth.

Training and Development

Under the provision of the Federal Labor Law, companies operating under *maquiladora* status must train at least 25 percent of their work force,

Table 9.6
In-Bond Industry Employees by Product

Processed Products	Total Employees		% Inc.
	Jan-July 1982	Jan-Dec 1984	
Food	1,547	1,753	13%
Shoes & Clothing	16,981	23,818	40%
Furniture	2,974	6,201	108%
Chemical	65	272	318%
Transp. Eq. & Acc.	11,761	29,378	150%
Machinery	1,301	2,154	66%
Electrical	76,179	108,520	42%
Toys & Sport Goods	2,607	6,172	137%
Other Mfg.	7,817	10,854	39%
Services	7,208	10,562	42%
TOTAL	129,051	199,684	54%

Source: Secretaria de Patrimonio y Fomento Industrial de Mexico, 1982 and 1983.

either for their current position or for promotion. The percentage of new employees receiving training is given in Table 9.7.

The percentage of employees who received training after they started work decreased to 47 percent in Juarez and 5 percent in Chihuahua, according to a study conducted by Desarrollo Economico. Employees evaluated their training, however, as very positive. In Chihuahua, 93 percent reported it as good and 6 percent said it was excellent; in Juarez, 62 percent responded that it was good and 20 percent said it was excellent. The proportion of employees who wanted to continue training was 98 percent in Chihuahua and 96 percent in Juarez.

Table 9.7
Percentage of New Maquila Employees Receiving Training

	Cd. Juarez	Cd. Chihuahua
Total	74%	51%
direct-labor	77%	52%
technician	72%	50%
administrative	48%	40%

Source: Desarrollo Economico del Estado de Chihuahua, A.C., 1985.

The training and development practices of companies were found to vary according to the type of employee, the nature of the task, and the product group. Companies generally classify their employees into two major categories: direct and indirect labor. Many of the direct labor workers, in addition to having little education, come from rural backgrounds and lack knowledge of how the industrial system works. While many assembly jobs in the electronic assembly plants are of limited scope and depth, those in plants using more automated techniques tend to be more sophisticated.

During the early program years, many companies relied solely on on-the-job training (OJT) to prepare their workers. The typical approach followed by many of the larger, well-known companies is to combine formal classroom training with OJT, providing the new employee with a formal orientation program as well. Workers are then put directly on the line where they receive OJT from a supervisor or trained employees. The entry-level employee is trained in a discrete operation; subsequently, the person is cross-trained on other line operations.

In the more technically advanced companies, the training period is considerably longer. Production workers at Packard, for example, receive two weeks of theoretical instruction in the classroom before proceeding to another four weeks of practical training on the line. The addition of more sophisticated machinery or increased automation tends to lengthen the training period, albeit at the expense of the number of employees required.

If performance is judged to be satisfactory following the employee's performance review, the worker is promoted to the next job level. When completely cross-trained, policies of promotion from within enable an employee to advance to trainer, to supervisor, and ultimately to inspector or quality control. At General Motors, different color smocks identify the employee's job level. Each time the employee is promoted, the color of the smock changes, providing recognition of the employee's advancement.

Quality Circles are another technique that GM has used to increase group participation and to provide feedback to group members. Circles have been introduced into several other electronic and automotive plants as well. It appears that high technology brings several advances with it, including more sophisticated methods of job design and greater employee participation.

Most managers reported that they found Mexican workers to be easily trainable and a reliable source of labor. Productivity was judged to be as high as in the United States, and quality control was often better.

Transfer of Technology

The efficient operation of plants that must compete in some of the most competitive international markets requires employees with a high level of technical and administrative knowledge. This knowledge is transmitted constantly from the parent company to the *maquiladora* plant and assimilated by the employees of these plants.

The administrative knowledge that is judged to have the most utility and application for increasing industrial development includes knowledge of procedures, policies, and systems. Some of the most important areas identified by plant managers are: production planning, control systems, inventory control, quality control and assurance, personnel administration, training and development, salary administration, international purchasing, computer systems, and import-export procedures. In general, these managers are learning modern techniques for planning, organizing, managing, and controlling industrial systems. They are also gaining specific technical knowledge designed to enhance productivity and quality. Specific examples included knowledge of: production control, materials control, quality control, statistical quality control of processes, industrial design, product engineering, planning production flow, time management, inventory planning, manufacturing processes, industrial engineering, mechanical engineering, electrical engineering, structural engineering, electronic engineering, hydraulic engineering, machine set-up, calibrating precision equipment, automatic assembly of electronic components, and plastic injection molding.

Another form of technology transfer occurs when a *maquila* employee, especially an engineer, technician or administrator, starts a new business. While no quantitative data currently exists that sufficiently addresses this issue, a study conducted by Desarollo Economico found that 42 percent of the companies surveyed included people who had established their own businesses since working in the *maquiladora* industry. Of the 33 people who had left and started their own businesses, 73 percent had started manufacturing establishments and 27 percent had established businesses in sales. The knowledge they had acquired in the *maquiladora* industry was acknowledged to have facilitated this move.

SUMMARY AND CONCLUSIONS

The development of employment opportunities is one of the most positive benefits of the *maquiladora* industry. Although the industry represents a relatively small segment of the Mexican economy, strong growth is projected to continue, thereby creating additional jobs for a young, relatively unskilled work force. Due in part to a change in industry profile, the percentage of men and technicians has been increasing. While the growing labor force participation rate of women tends to offset these gains, government incentives designed to encourage industry growth in specific product areas provide a catalyst for creating more attractive employment opportunities for male workers.

Training and the development of employees is another contribution of the *maquiladora* industry. While many of the jobs generated by the industry are acknowledged to have limited scope and depth, three forces are fostering manpower development. An industry policy of promotion from within creates more challenging opportunities for employees with potential and motivation. For these individuals, work experience compensates in part for lack of educational attainment. Additionally, the increased organizational stability of plants in the industry contributes to changes in the production process. As these plants increase their stage of organizational development, they tend to increase their technological level. Finally, the industry itself is moving into more advanced product areas. The more technologically advanced companies use more sophisticated methods of job design and provide more advanced training. In combination, these forces create greater opportunity for employee participation and decision making.

The transfer of knowledge to people at the technical and administrative levels is the most positive example of manpower development in the *maquiladora* industry. This transfer of knowledge occurs constantly between the parent companies and the *maquiladora* plants. In the process, employees are gaining technical knowledge needed to increase productivity and quality, and the administrative know-how to manage industrial systems. Some evidence exists to suggest that this technical and administrative knowledge is beginning to transfer out from the *maquiladora* industry as well. As people leave the industry and either work for other companies or establish their own businesses, a ripple effect will be felt throughout the Mexican economy.

10

The Future of the Maquilas

Edward Y. George

INTRODUCTION

Lately, the *maquilas* have been a constant item in the news invoking strong feelings for and against. Powerful lobbies on the part of business are trying to push the federal government for more facilities and more concessions to promote the growth of the *maquilas*. They are supported by officials in the states bordering Mexico and, of course, encouraged by the enthusiastic attitude of Mexican officials and businessmen both on the border and in Mexico City.

On the other hand, organized labor in the United States is vociferously attacking the *maquilas* and attempting to, at least, arrest its phenomenal growth. Besides, some Mexican intellectuals perceive the *maquilas* in terms of the dependence theory and exploitation notions, and call for the "liberation" of Mexican labor from the yoke of foreign domination.

In view of the above contradictory points of view, how can one rationally conceptualize the potential future of the *maquilas*?

It is true that the *maquilas* have enjoyed a tremendous growth rate since their inception.[1] In less than two decades they grew from a mere hope to overcome the detrimental effects of the cancellation of the Bracero Program to become the third largest foreign exchange generator in the Mexican economy, and the highest single employment sector in the Mexican border cities. With almost 1,000 plants and more than a quarter of a million employees, the *maquilas* are quickly becoming an indispensable pillar of the border economy. However, the future of the *maquilas* is not, by any means, a foregone conclusion. It depends on several factors, some of them pertain to economic factors in the United States, and how that economy is affected by international economic forces; and some pertain to socioeconomic factors inherent to the Mexican stage.

FACTORS AFFECTING THE AMERICAN SIDE

The Rate of Growth of the U.S. Economy[2]

Statistics of the number of *maquilas*, and the volume of their employment over the past two decades indicate clearly that the growth of the *maquilas* has consistently mirrored the state of the U.S. economy. The recessions of 1969/1970, 1974/1975, and 1980/1982, insofar as they affected final demand in the United States, were reflected in declines in the growth of the number of plants and volume of employment on the border. However, since the long-term trend depicting United States economy is monotonically rising, there is no reason to believe that temporary declines in plant numbers or employment volume in the *maquilas* will affect the long-term growth of the program.

Shrinkage of the American Manufacturing Base

Recent statistics of the sectoral industrial structure in the United States indicate that the manufacturing share of employment is declining while that in services is rising.[3] In order to survive and retain its competitive edge, the manufacturing sector has either to concede to the hollowing-out process, or succeed in introducing high-tech innovations based on accelerated research and development. The rising costs of manufacturing in the United States are accelerating the hollowing-out process. It is interesting to notice that the hollowing-out process is quickly becoming a common feature of manufacturing in almost all industrially developed countries. During the last few years, other industrialized countries such as Japan, Germany, and Belgium have started their own *maquilas* in Mexico. Multinational firms, wherever they originate, seek locations that offer cheaper costs of production than anywhere in the world. The continuation of this trend, which seems to be inevitable, tends to favor a continuous growth of the *maquilas*.

Shrinkage of U.S. Manufacturing Share in Both Domestic and International Markets

The shrinkage of U.S. manufacturing is resulting from:

1. the rising cost of American labor relative to that of other industrial countries;
2. the dumping of manufactured goods by other countries in the lucrative American market;
3. the slowdown in American R&D expenditures and the aging of a high percentage of U.S. plants; and
4. the aggressive growth of export markets in cheap-labor countries like Korea and Taiwan.

The erosion of U.S. market shares and the inundation of the American market with cheaper imports is the cause of the huge and rising trade balance deficit, the demand by manufacturers for the imposition of trade barriers, and the clamor by organized labor for the preservation of the number of remaining manufacturing jobs within the U.S. borders. There is no reason to believe that the American manufacturing share in the international markets will reverse its recent declining trend in the near future despite the declining dollar value. In the long run this extraneously imposed slowdown in the growth of American manufacture may be detrimental to the growth of the *maquilas*.

Speed and Proliferation of Automation and Robotics in U.S. Industry

While Japan has been using robotics extensively for some time now, U.S. manufacturers have been relatively slow in adopting robotic technology. Declining demand for manufactured products, as well as slimming profit margins have conspired against committing the huge investments needed for wide-range introduction of robotics. However, some giant Fortune 500 firms have started their move into the robotic age. As this movement gains momentum, productivity will go up while production costs will go down, eliminating the need in automated firms to export manufacturing jobs overseas. It will take some time for such a movement to mature and become widespread enough to seriously threaten the growth of the maquilas. But for U.S. manufacturing to survive in the twenty-first century, it has to introduce extensive automation and robotics. Then only industrial operations that cannot be profitably automated will be candidates for overseas relocation. This trend may eliminate many of the routine assembly operations that, so far, have been the mainstay of the *maquila* operations. Thus the growth trend of the *maquilas* may be somewhat stunted.[4]

Forceful Objections by Organized Labor

Labor unions have been feeling the detrimental impact on their ranks of the flight of manufacturing jobs south of the border. It is interesting to recall that in the sixties, organized labor was afraid of automation and the spread of computers in industry. Labor leaders, and their sympathizers then, voiced their concern about the potential dire effects of automation on the job market. However, the doom prophecies did not materialize and employment continued to grow at a normal rate. The relative decline in the manufacturing share of industrial employment is due to causes other than automation. Today, manufacturing executives who make the decision to relocate some of their operations, or even plants, south of the border, emphasize that the choice is not between staying in the United States or moving to Mexico, but between losing their market and moving overseas to survive.

They maintain that by moving some of their operations overseas they can regain their cost competitiveness in the international markets. The jobs lost to Mexican labor can be compensated for by sustained expansion at home. In the final analysis, however, organized labor does not have the muscle it used to have 20 or 30 years ago. The declining union membership has weakened organized labor. It is inconceivable in the near future that labor will be able to stem the tide of *maquila* growth.[5]

FACTORS AFFECTING THE MEXICAN SIDE

The Mexican Labor Market

The extremely high unemployment rate in Mexico coupled with the continuous flow of labor migration from the hinterland to the border made the supply of labor to the *maquilas* almost perfectly elastic at the prevailing minimum wage. In the sixties, when the *maquila* program started, the major role for women in the labor force was in the service sector as maids. The emerging *maquila* plants were mostly engaged in assembly work. The adaptability of female workers to tedious repetitive assembly routines, the abundant supply of female workers, their docility, and lack of unionization made them perfect employees for the *maquilas*. Up until the late seventies, young female workers constituted the bulk of employment in the *maquila* plants. As the industrial structure of the *maquilas* changed, the composition of its labor force started to change gradually to include a rising proportion of male workers. The gradual move from a strictly assembly routine operation to more technical work necessitated the use of more male workers who, on the average, have a higher educational background than female workers. Besides, Mexican labor unions have learned, through the bitter experience they had in such places as Nuevo Laredo, to cooperate with the *maquila* management. Today, the *maquila* labor force is moving rapidly toward a balanced sex composition. However, the scale is tipped in favor of men in the technical fields.[6]

During the last few years, the supply of labor at the border has become increasingly tighter. While most firms in the past used to hire from the area, now they have to advertise the openings in the news media. Some firms go so far as to send their recruiters to the hinterland to import their workers. A new trend is emerging, namely, the move of assembly operations away from the border to inside Mexico to insure an adequate supply of labor.

The supply of technical workers in Mexico has always been scarce. The availability of high-tech workers is even more scarce. *Maquila* management, in the high-tech areas, has found that Mexican workers are fast learners, and it is much cheaper to train a Mexican worker, even to send him to short technical seminars, to learn new techniques than to bring an American engineer from the mother firm to work in the *maquilas*. This, of course, does not mean that all the technical work is now done exclusively by Mexican technicians. However, American engineers and specialists are brought to the *maquilas* for short periods of time to set up the technical operations, train a cadre of Mexican workers, and leave.

The tightening of labor supply is forcing some industrial park operators to establish technical classes and seminars for local workers. Some firms decided to move their plants away from well established industrial parks to avoid the risk of having their trained Mexican technicians pirated by other plants.

As the number of *maquila* plants grow, and as the trend toward more technical operations gathers momentum, the supply of *maquila*-grade workers, and especially technically-oriented ones will become more scarce. Such scarcity will invariably raise the cost of labor, and thereby reduce the attractiveness of Mexico as a shelter for U.S. manufacture overseas.

Rising Cost of High Labor Turnover Rates

It has been noted that the *maquilas* had consistently higher labor turnover rates than similar industrial plants in the United States. Turnover rates now are much higher than they ever were due to:

1. The tightening of the labor market at the border which forces management to hire more and more transient workers who have no roots at the border. Such workers live in slum colonies and shantytowns at the edge of the border cities that lack the necessary amenities for decent living. The pay from the *maquilas* is not enough to compensate for the hardships of such a life, especially when the commuting trek to work becomes too expensive and/or takes a couple of hours or more daily.
2. The newly acquired technical skills by some workers make them more marketable, so they feel that they are in a better position to seek another job with better pay or better transportation facilities.
3. The declining value of the peso coupled with fast rising inflation make the frequent adjustments of the minimum wage adequate to pay for the necessities of life.[7]

To reduce the turnover rates, management has been resorting to gimmicks and creative efforts to induce workers to stay. However, so far, management has refrained from offering higher wages to keep their workers. Eventually the time may come when the cost of turnover coupled with a tight labor supply will make some *maquila* operations uneconomical.

Declining Value of the Peso

The almost daily decline in the value of the peso relative to the dollar is making the cost of Mexican labor and doing business in Mexico competitive with other cheap labor havens in spite of the high turnover rates. There is no reason to believe that the devaluation of the peso will stop abruptly or that its value relative to the dollar will reverse itself in the near future. As long as the minimum wage adjustments continue to lag behind the devaluation, the cost of labor will remain competitive thereby encouraging the *maquilas* to stay and grow.

Cost of Operations in Mexico Relative to That in the "Four Little Dragons"

The Mexican border is currently competing successfully with Hong Kong, South Korea, Singapore, and Taiwan in attracting "overseas" industrial operations. For U.S. industry, the Mexican border offers more than just cheap labor. It offers shorter logistics lines, a familiar culture, and the possibility of having their managers and their families live on American soil while conducting operations in another country. As long as labor costs remain competitive, through the declining value of the peso, and as long as labor relations remain stable, the *maquila* program will remain attractive to the United States manufacturers. The political system in Mexico has shown a great deal of stability. There is no reason to believe that the situation will change in the near future. Political instability and/or labor turmoil will drastically affect the program. Such a possibility seems to be currently remote.

Adequacy of the Mexican Infrastructure

The infrastructure in the Mexican border cities is bursting at the seams.[8] To begin with, it has never been meant to accommodate an industrial structure, let alone one that is growing by leaps and bounds, as the *maquilas* are. The problem has been exacerbated by the overflow of migrants from the hinterland. Currently, it is not unusual for power failures to occur several times a day disrupting industrial operations. Water pressure is so low sometimes that water flow is virtually disrupted at some plants at some time during working hours. Transportation is a major headache for workers who have to spend several hours every day to commute back and forth to work. A power failure on an assembly line may lower productivity, while in a semiconductor fabrication plant it can destroy an entire batch of expensive silicon wafers.

Delays in telephone communications, deep potholes in roads, slow, over-congested and aging means of transportation, lack of semidecent housing, water pump shutdowns, and brownouts, may be just irritants now, but as the pressure on the infrastructure grows through the building of more plants and the migration of more people to the border, productivity will dip to the point that industrial operations on the border may become intolerably uneconomical. When this stage is reached, which does not seem to be very far away, more *maquilas* may start to move inland away from the border. Such a move may increase the cost of operation, thereby limiting the growth of the program.

**Technology Transfer and the Integration of the *Maquila*
Program in the Mexican Industrial System**

Since the early 1970s, it has been the hope of the consecutive Mexican administrations that the *maquila* program will enhance the level and rate of technology transfer to Mexico, and raise the skill level of its work force. Lately another hope has been added, namely that the program will get integrated in the Mexican industrial system. The De La Madrid administration wants to see the *maquilas* buy most of their industrial requirements and services from Mexican industry.[9]

So far, technology transfer through the *maquila* operations has been minimal at best. The *maquilas* have been an isolated industrial island amidst the border wasteland. There has been virtually no interfacing between the *maquila* plants and the other industrial sectors in Mexico. *Maquila* management feels that Mexican industrial production is expensive, lacks quality control, and suffers from unreliable delivery schedules.

Paradoxically, if transfer of technology is optimized, the skill level of Mexican workers may be elevated to the standards accorded developed industrial societies, thereby raising the wage levels; and if the present *maquila* plants become fully integrated in the Mexican system, the industrial structure will expand in Mexico leading to extreme shortages in skilled labor and Mexico will cease to be a haven of cheap labor, and the *maquila* program will lose its raison d'être.[10]

CONCLUSIONS

In conclusion, it seems that there are strong factors indicating that the *maquila* program is still healthy and will remain so for quite a long time. There are, of course, other factors detracting from the potentialities of the program and that tend to undermine its efficiency and continued growth. However, the countervailing forces against the *maquilas* seems to be remote, at least for the time being. One can conclude that for the foreseeable future, the program will continue to grow. However, more growth will occur away from the border than near the border. For a healthy growth in plants and employment to continue, the Mexican government must maintain the prevailing political and labor stability. More positive efforts must be exerted to enhance the infrastructure and keep it operating effectively.

As for the U.S. manufacturing industry, it will continue for the foreseeable future to use overseas facilities. One cannot image the cost of United States labor to decline enough to restore the international competitiveness of American industrial production. However, automation, robotics, and the trend toward high-tech production will continue to keep a healthy proportion of U.S. manufacture at home.

NOTES

1. Table 10.1 illustrates some of the indicators of the growth for the *maquilas* according to various statistical surveys published by Mexican authorities.

Table 10.1
Selected Statistics on Maquila Plants

Year	No. of Plants	Total Employment*	Value Added**
1970	120	20,327	81
1975	454	67,214	454
1980	620	119,546	773
1985	789	217,544	1,300
1986	858	246,617	1,400

Notes: *Annual Average
         **Millions of Dollars
Source: Instituto Nacional de Estadistica e Informacion, (various publications).

Additionally,

The productivity indicator for Mexican labor in the *maquilas* increased from $10,500 in 1974 to $18,700 in 1984, while in 1986 it reached $20,600, that is, it almost doubled between 1974 and 1986.

The average annual increase in employment from 1974 to 1982 was 6.6 percent while from 1982 to 1985 it was 19 percent. In 1986 the increase was 16.9 percent. Total employment in December 1986 reached 255,000 persons in 900 plants.

The *maquila* industry in 1986 continued its ascending trend in the generation of investment, start of new plants, new employment, and enhancing regional economic development in Mexico. It generated 1,440 billion pesos in services in 1986, an increase of 10.3 percent over 1985.

The *maquila* industry holds the third position in the Mexican balance of payments directly after petroleum and tourism. However, while foreign exchange from tourism fluctuated (during 1986 and the first six months of 1987) from a low of $20 million to a high of $185 million, the monthly income from the *maquilas* held steady at between $95 and $115 million.

Mexico hosts 35 percent of all U.S. plants overseas.

2. Merrilee A. Fuller, ed., "Star Performer—Maquiladoras Do It Again," *Business Mexico*, February 1986, Bert Diamondstein of El Paso's Industrial Development Corporation noted that "everything falls on the state of the United States economy." During the United States recessions of 1974–1975 and 1980–1982 the foreign exchange generated, and number of plants and annual average number of employment in the *maquilas* declined. Not only did the annual rate of growth decline, but the actual volumes of foreign exchange and total employment declined.

3. The Committee for Production Sharing examined the impact of Tariff items 806.30 and 807.00—the enabling articles of the in-bond industry—to calculate the

number of U.S. workers directly involved in the *maquila* industry on the American side. Using as a base the U.S. Dept. of Commerce estimate that some 25,800 U.S. jobs are created for every $1 billion in U.S. exports, the Committee estimated that over 136,000 jobs were attributable in 1983 to the $4.5 billion in U.S. domestic content used in 806.3 and 807.0 production operations. The Committee also estimated that approximately two workers are involved in further processing for every one worker employed in the initial manufacture of articles and components. The number of jobs created in 1986 in this stage of U.S. production is estimated to be 208,400, making the total U.S. jobs created in the United States in 1986 as a result of their involvement in the maquila program approximately half a million jobs. The *maquilas* program also allows U.S. manufacturers to profit from the differential comparative advantage between them and Mexico by using skilled and highly technical workers on the American side while using cheap unskilled labor on the Mexican side in production sharing mode. Statement by Ralph A. Biederman, Chairman, Committee for Production Sharing presented to the Subcommittee on Economic Stabilization of the Committee on Banking, Finance and Urban Affairs, 99th U.S. Congress, 2d sess., 1986.

   4. During the past two years, a movement has begun to introduce state-of-arts technology to some *maquila* operations. At least three companies are currently actively engaged in high-tech operations in their Cd. Juarez *maquilas*. According to the Secretaria de Programacion y Presupuesto the percentage of technicians and administrative workers employed nationally by the *maquilas* has reached 18.32 percent in 1986. The percentage of the same category of workers in Cd. Juarez currently exceeds 20 percent.

   5. The latest reports by the U.S. Dept. of Commerce indicate a slight increase in manufacturing jobs, but also that the blue collar content of manufacturing cost in the United States is declining albeit the fact that the level of wages in manufacturing is still much higher than that in the service industry. However, there is a distinct trend toward keeping only highly skilled jobs at home and exporting the unskilled ones and/or the jobs that cannot be profitably automated.

   6. At the start of the *maquila* program more than 90 percent of the workers were female. For an illustration of the change in the distribution of *maquiladora* work force, see Chapter 9.

   7. The accelerated growth of the in-bond industry employment in Cd. Juarez (and invariably in most other maquila centers) has led to a high increase in turnover rates as shown in Table 10.2.

Table 10.2
Turnover Rate in Maquila Plants in Cd. Juarez

Type of employee\Year	1982	1983	1984	1985
Administrative	5.0%	4.5%	4.5%	4.6%
Technician	3.6	4.5	6.0	4.9
Worker	4.3	5.8	7.6	8.1

Source: Asociacion de Maquiladoras, 1987.

A recent study by the Secretaria de Industria y Comercio indicates that some of the technicians who leave the *maquilas* start their own businesses or work in private Mexican industrial enterprises.

In an attempt to reduce turnover rates some *maquila* managers give annual bonuses at Christmas time to workers with seniority. However, high turnover rates are increasing the cost of labor and the cost of training.

8. A survey of a sample of the *maquilas* was conducted by the Asociacion de Maquiladoras in 1984 to assess the status of infrastructure in Juarez. The results from the survey are summarized in Table 10.3.

9. Linkages between the *maquilas* and the industrial sector in Mexico's economy are extremely limited. In 1976 former president Portillo set a goal of 8 percent of value added to be produced by Mexican firms by 1982. Unfortunately, presently only about 1 or 2 percent of all inputs used by the *maquilas* are purchased from Mexican supppliers.

Maquila developer Lic. Federico Barrio stated that U.S. *maquila* managers use locally (Mexican) produced materials sparingly because they feel that Mexican suppliers cannot produce the quantity of inputs required in the necessary time frame allowed for profitable production.

According to a study titled *A Strategy for Juarez/2000* by Robert C. Haywood at the Flagstaff Institute, the highly protected Mexican manufacturing factories have been operating with high profit margins at near capacity, so the high volume, lower prices, and reliable quality controlled manufacturing supplies demanded by the *maquilas* were not lucrative or attractive business possibilities to Mexican manufacturers.

Table 10.3
Service Ratings by Maquila Locations

The Service	R A T I N G S		
	Good	Very Good	Bad-Very Bad
Telephone	21%	0%	39%
Personnel	23	4	36
Water	42	2	22
Electricity	53	0	18
Social Security	35	2	29
Telex	50	8	4
Data Transmission	50	3	11
Customs Service	44	0	8
Natural Gas	65	8	4

Note: The situation since then has deteriorated much further.
Source: Compiled by the author.

10. The latent effects of the 1983 Mexican decree covering support for the *maquila* industry, which states that the *maquilas* may sell up to 20 percent of their production in Mexico and which was later amended to allow the *maquilas* to sell 40 percent of their production locally if they are located in certain areas of Mexico, and have at least 35 percent Mexican content in their product, will encourage many U.S. firms to substantially expand their operations in Mexico, and will boost the Mexican domestic industrial sector.

PART FIVE

TRANSFER OF TECHNOLOGY: POTENTIALS AND PROBLEMS

In general, transfer of technology from industrialized countries to the developing countries has been an area of controversy and contention. Yet, in looking at the bilateral relations between the United States and Mexico, this is an area of relative calm and harmony. There seems to be a general consensus that U.S. technology has been instrumental in bridging the technological gap between Mexico and the industrialized world. More significantly, this transfer has been accomplished without an inordinate cost in economic or sociological terms. For the most part, transfer of United States technology to Mexico has been smooth, steady, and with little restructuring of the Mexican society. In Chapter 11, Loretta Fairchild and Kim Sosin report the findings of their study of technology transfer practices of 57 manufacturing firms in Mexico. The somewhat surprising conclusion of their microeconomic study is that the differences in technology acquisition and performance between domestic and transnational firms in the manufacturing sector of Mexico for the 1979–1984 period were "slight."

In a much more specific approach to the issue, Marc Scheinman examines the impact of technology transfer to a single Mexican industry—the automobile industry—and particularly on that industry's export potentials. His major contention is that exports of motor vehicles from Mexico will continue to maintain their rapid growth for the remainder of the 1980s, and, not surprisingly, the destination of most will be the United States. Scheinman's conclusion is that the very magnitude of this change in orientation from an almost exclusive concentration on domestic production to production primarily for exports will result in the further integration of the "Big-3s" auto production in North America. And it is certain that Mexico is destined to play an even more important role in the 1990s.

11

Technological Activity Comparisons across Foreign Equity Levels: Manufacturing Firms in Mexico

Loretta Fairchild and Kim Sosin

INTRODUCTION

Both sympathetic and less than sympathetic scholars of transnational firms typically argue that such firms are significantly different than, and in general more advanced than, domestically owned firms.[1] Theories of the multinational enterprise (MNE) often emphasize their advantages in, among others, acquiring technology, financing, and management expertise. According to one theory, MNEs may use to advantage the ability to internalize technological transfers. The argument is made that external markets available to domestic firms for technological ideas are scarce, expensive, and inefficient compared to internal transfers between parent and subsidiary.[2] Another analysis, product differentiation theory, emphasizes the fixed cost characteristic of research and development expenditures, which needs be done only once within an MNE, typically by the parent.[3] Both theories imply that the subsidiary's technology sources should be predominantly internal to the MNE, although external to the subsidiary, and less costly, whereas local firms must purchase information on imperfect external markets or devote resources to developing their own ideas. Although research on indigenous technological effort is now available,[4] the notion that significant indigenous activity is occuring within developing countries is rather recent.

An interesting conclusion of work on technological activity in Latin America in the early 1970s is that the differences between domestic and multinational firms are smaller than is often assumed.[5] Using a sample of manufacturing firms from Mexico, Brazil, Colombia, and Central America, the research shows few differences between foreign and local firms in performance and in implementation of new technology. The sources of new technology were rather different, however, with MNEs using more information external to the subsidiary while local firms tended to be more internally active in developing and adapting technology. The value to

129

the firm and to the country of learning by doing rather than simply purchasing or transferring technology cannot be overemphasized. This study examines these processes for Mexico in the 1980s.

After describing the sample, we compare several dimensions of performance, technology implementation, technology acquisition, and internal technological activity over the 1979–1984 period for four groups of firms: continuously locally-owned, formerly foreign but now locally-owned, minority foreign equity, and majority foreign equity.[6] Can performance differences, or the lack thereof, be explained by differences or similarities in technological behavior, or by differences in foreign connections among the ownership groups? To answer this question, we have used a rather large number of different variables because each represents a separate and important concept of performance or technology. A dichotomous variable separating the time period into the years prior to and following the Mexican crisis of 1982 is used for annual variables in the regression model because substantial differences, particularly in performance, are evident between these time periods.

THE SAMPLE

The sample consists of 57 manufacturing firms, 31 entirely Mexican-owned (*LOCAL*) and 26 with foreign equity (*FOREIGN*), of which 15 have minority foreign equity (*MINORITY FRGN*), and 11 have majority foreign equity capital (*MAJORITY FRGN*). Detailed information and data on each firm for the years 1979 to 1983 (and in some cases 1984) were acquired through lengthy personal interviews with the production or general managers. The sample is structured, with the two ownership groups chosen to be similar with respect to chief product lines and roughly similar with respect to firm size and age. Wherever possible, chief competitors are represented. Product classifications include metal products (27), chemicals (13), nonmetallic minerals (7), food and beverages (5), rubber and plastics (4) and textiles (1). Although the sample is small, the unique combination of information on methods of technology acquisition together with the detailed annual production and accounting data at the firm level permit us to study the relationship between performance and technology at a level of detail and over a period of time that have not been reported in the literature. A complete description of the variables used in data reporting for the tables of this chapter appears in the Appendix.

PERFORMANCE

We begin by considering the question of performance differences between locally-owned and multinational firms (Table 11.1). Two sets of results are shown. First, the mean values for local and foreign firms are presented, along with a test of the significance of the differences between

Table 11.1
Performance Measures: A Comparison of Foreign and Domestic Firms in Mexico

	GSALE	GFASET	GLABOR	GPRFT	GINT
Means Comparisons					
Local	-2.45	27.85	2.41	-186.05	63.35
(t) df	(-0.26)	(1.16)	(0.12)	(0.62)	(0.84)
N	128	117	140	116	109
Foreign	-3.26	52.63	2.93	-0.35	115.56
(t) df	228	118	176	124	85
N	102	87	117	85	79
Regression Analysis					
New Dom	9.90	33.89	6.60	1309.64	-10.49
(t)	(2.02)**	(1.13)	(0.97)	(-2.49)**	(-0.13)
MIN-F	1.65	8.41	-0.67	-107.33	-22.40
(t)	(0.44)	(0.35)	(-0.13)	(-0.25)	(-0.34)
MAJ-F	1.14	66.93	5.39	-134.64	153.63
(t)	(0.28)	(2.47)**	(0.97)	(-0.28)	(2.11)**
Period	-10.14	-3.63	-3.34	-192.29	-142.12
(t)	(-3.38)**	(-0.19)	(-0.81)	(-0.57)	(-2.71)**
F-Value	3.38	1.69	0.65	1.70	3.24
df	225	199	252	196	184

	GNEWEQ	PK	PEX	LPROD
Means Comparisons				
Local	512.88	0.48	4.08	0.20
(t) df	(-2.52) **	(0.74)	(-0.83)	(4.66) **
N	99	143	169	112

Table 11.1 (continued)

	GNEWEQ	PK	PEX	LPROD
Foreign	105.42	0.64	3.35	0.35
(t) df	121	245	297	122
N	82	104	135	92
Regression Analysis				
New Dom	-495.96	0.58	1.49	-0.01
(t)	(-1.84)*	(1.74)*	(0.96)	(-0.30)
MIN-F	-577.08	0.06	-0.92	0.05
(t)	(-2.65)**	(0.22)	(-0.81)	(1.34)
MAJ-F	-471.68	0.63	0.17	0.27
(t)	(-1.97)**	(2.09)**	(0.14)	(6.63)**
Period	38.81	-0.39	0.57	-0.02
(t)	(-0.22)	(-1.80)*	(0.62)	(-0.60)
F-Value	2.26	2.42	0.55	12.51
df	176	242	299	199

Notes: * Significant at 10% level.
       ** Significant at 5% level.
   The hypothesis that the variances are equal in foreign and local firms is rejected at the .05 level. In all other comparisons, the t-statistic and degrees of freedom are based upon the equal variances model.
   Sample size reflects annual observations for each firm.

these two groups. The null hypothesis for the means test is that there is no difference by ownership group. In this study, acceptance of the null is as interesting as rejection in that it shows no foreign advantage contrary to expectations in much of the literature.

The second approach shown is a regression model that allows a more complete and simultaneous comparison of the four ownership categories and tests for a difference in the dependent variable between the precrisis and crisis periods.[7] The form of the regression is:

$$Y = a_1 + a_2\,NEWDOM + a_3\,MIN-F + a_4\,MAJ-F + a_5\,PERIOD$$

where:
$NEWDOM$ = 1 for formerly foreign but now local firms, 0 otherwise, $MIN-F$ = 1 for firms with minority foreign equity, 0 otherwise, $MAJ-F$ = 1 for firms with majority foreign equity, 0 otherwise, $PERIOD$ = 1 for 1982–84, 0 for 1979–81. The basis of comparison for the ownership groups is continuously locally-owned firms, so that a positive value for a_2, a_3, or a_4 shows that one of the other three ownership groups had a higher sample value for the dependent variable.

The first six performance measures are growth rates. The average of annual growth rates for the period 1979 to 1984 for sales ($GSALE$) were positive before the crisis and become negative in 1982–1984, but were unaffected by the presence or degree of foreign ownership. However, the *NEW DOMESTIC* firms had significantly better sales growth than the *LOCAL* firms as a whole. The average of annual growth rates for fixed assets ($GFASET$) and total employment ($GLABOR$) had very similar patterns. While the positive growth rates slowed in the crisis period, they are not significantly different relative to the pre-crisis years (1979–81), perhaps because of the large variation in growth rates among firms. Performance was essentially the same for the *FOREIGN* and *LOCAL* firms. However, those with *MAJORITY FRGN* equity did have significantly faster growth of assets than the *LOCAL* firms.

Return on capital is measured by the average of annual growth rates of reported profits ($GPRFT$) and as a ratio to fixed assets (PK). While PK remained positive even during the crisis for both groups, it is stable for the *LOCAL* firms and drops dramatically for the *FOREIGN* firms as their asset accumulation continued. The year-to-year change in profits ($GPRFT$) was always negative for the *LOCAL* firms and switched from positive to negative for the *FOREIGN* firms with the crisis. Presence and degree of ownership, however, did not provide a significant cushioning factor for profit declines. Although the difference between the local and foreign ownership groups is large, the lack of significance reflects a very large profit variance among firms. However, deterioration in profits was significantly worse for the *NEW DOMESTIC* firms than the rest of the *LOCAL* firms. PK was significantly better for *MAJORITY FRGN* and *NEW DOMESTIC* than for *LOCAL* and the impact of the crisis was also significant, especially for *FOREIGN* firms.

Annual interest paid (*GINT*) grew at an average of 125 percent per year for *LOCAL* and 220 percent per year for *FOREIGN* firms before the crisis, reflecting the impact of high and variable rates, in contrast to 13 and 41 percent growth per year respectively during the crisis. However, this sharp contrast for the *FOREIGN* firms is due only to the *MAJORITY FRGN* firms. The *MINORITY FRGN* pattern is the same as *LOCAL* firms' growth of interest.

Year-to-year changes in expenditures on new machinery and equipment (*GNEWEG*) were positive throughout the period and significantly higher for the continuously *LOCAL* firms than the other three groups, with no real impact from the crisis itself. The foreign companies do export (*PEX*), substantiating Vernon's point that their activities are not confined to the local market.[8] Our data indicate, however, that it is not correct that foreign companies export a larger percentage of sales than do locally-owned firms, since the latter's average export percentages were slightly larger before the crisis. In addition, local firms were able to increase exports from 3.5 to 4.6 percent of sales during the crisis, while export percentages remained at 3 percent for the foreign firms. Finally, the productivity of labor (*LPROD*), value-added divided by labor, is an important performance measure that is significantly larger only for the *MAJORITY FRGN* firms. The crisis itself had no impact on labor productivity. Results in Table 11.1 indicate that even in a rather difficult period of rapid expansion and sudden crisis many local firms not only survived but performed in most respects as well as or better than their counterparts with foreign equity.

A very important category of firms' performance in an LDC is their level of implementation of new technology (see Table 11.2). Although this is not a precise concept we have measured several dimensions of firms' implementation of new processes. In all four measures, the local firms are performing on par with or ahead of the foreign firms. Using the production facility as it existed in 1984 at the time of the interview as the base, 25 percent of capacity was less than three years old for the *LOCAL* firms, compared to only 15 percent among the *FOREIGN* firms (*NEW*3). However, this significant difference was only present for the *MINORITY FRGN* firms. Forty-two percent of the *LOCAL* firms' production facilities were less than five years old versus 36 percent for foreign firms but none of the differences were significant for the five-year period (*NEW*5). It appears that foreign firms introduced their changes earlier, whereas the local firms changed more just before the crisis began.

The new part of production facilities, both within three years and five years, was divided into percentages that represented replacement or expansion using essentially the same technology, replacement or expansion using new technology for the same products, and replacement or expansion for production of substantially different products. About 25 percent of facilities

Table 11.2
Implementation of New Technology in Mexico

	NEW3	NEW5	NTEC3	NTEC5
Means Comparisons				
Local	24.58	41.68	23.09	31.10
(t) df	$(1.75)^{u*}$	(−0.73)	(0.17)	(−0.04)
N	31	31	22	30
Foreign	14.75	35.98	25.00	30.65
t (df)	51	54	38	51
N	26	25	18	23
Regression Analysis				
New Dom.	−8.37	21.07	−6.28	−7.00
t (df)	(−0.83)	(1.63)	(−0.28)	(−0.37)
MIN-F	−13.30	−7.30	1.55	3.27
t (df)	$(-1.84)^{*}$	(−0.79)	(0.11)	(0.23)
MAJ-F	−8.93	6.90	0.43	−8.50
(t) df	(−1.11)	(0.65)	(0.03)	(−0.55)
F-Value	1.24	1.57	0.04	0.20
(t) df	53	52	36	49

Notes: *Significant at 10% level.
     **Significant at 5% level.
   ^{u}The hypothesis that the *variances* are equal in foreign and local firms is rejected at the .05 level. In all other comparisons, the t-statistic and degrees of freedom are based upon the equal variances model.

new within three years and 30 percent new within five years (*NTEC*3 and *NTEC*5) were made solely to introduce new technology, apart from product changes. Presence or degree of foreign ownership had no impact.

EXTERNAL SOURCES OF TECHNOLOGY

Although the performance results are mixed, locally-owned firms appear to be competing successfully with firms that have direct access to foreign technology. Are they using other ways to acquire modern foreign technology, via licensing, technical assistance contracts or use of foreign consultants, administrators, engineers and equipment, which allow them to perform comparably?

A major source of external technology is the purchase of foreign-made equipment (see Table 11.3). Only 59 percent of *LOCAL* firms' equipment was foreign (as an average for the period 1979–84) compared to 74 percent for *FOREIGN* firms, which is a significant difference (*PEQF*). It is of interest that while the *NEW DOMESTIC* firms used significantly less foreign equipment than the continuously *LOCAL* firms, and the *MAJORITY FRGN* firms used significantly more, the *MINORITY FRGN* firms used as little foreign equipment as the LOCAL Firms. Both *MAJORITY FRGN* and *MINORITY FRGN* firms received significantly more of their equipment

Table 11.3
External Sources of Technology for Mexico

	PEQF	PFEQ^P	TA/SALES	CVE	PFLICPAT^C
Means Comparisons					
Local	59.25	2.00	0.63	5.20	0.06
(t) df^S	(4.71)**	(6.50)^{u**}	(2.24)^{u**}	(2.26)^{u**}	(2.43)^{u**}
N	165	159	127	30	31
Foreign	73.59	25.34	1.11	25.84	0.32
(t) df^S	316	148	228	25	35
N	153	136	106	25	25
Regression Analysis					
New Dom	−23.61	−2.59	1.61	1.00	0.76
(t)	(−4.91)**	(−0.51)	(4.92)**	(0.07)	(1.00)
MIN-F	0.11	9.48	0.62	19.67	1.65
(t)	(0.03)	(2.40)**	(2.34)**	(1.90)*	(2.94)**
MAJ-F	21.47	39.07	1.26	22.60	0.45
(t)	(5.63)**	(9.25)**	(4.35)**	(1.91)*	(0.64)
Period	−0.83	0.23	0.10		
(t)	(−0.29)	(0.07)	(0.49)		
F-Value	19.16	23.90	8.51	1.97	11.23
df	313	290	223	51	51

Table 11.3 (continued)

Means Comparisons	LICPAT	CNT	PFTA^c	NTA
Local	0.18	0.52	0.19	0.32
(t) df	(1.28)^u	(2.76)**	(3.38)**	(1.11)^u
N	31	31	31	31
Foreign	10.46	1.33	0.60	4.66
(t) df	24	53	54	24
N	25	24	25	25
Regression Analysis				
New Dom	0.81	0.60	3E-16	-0.30
(t)	(0.07)	(1.25)	(5E-16)	(-0.05)
MIN-F	17.35	1.31	1.40	7.05
(t)	(1.99)*	(3.74)**	(3.09)**	(1.66)*
MAJ-F	0.08	0.40	0.97	0.12
(t)	(0.01)	(1.02)	(1.94)*	(0.02)
F-Value	1.53	4.71	12.11	1.08
df	52	51	51	52

Notes: ^{c} The prefix PF indicates proportion of firms giving an affirmative response. The regression results are maximum likelihood estimates from a probit model and the "F-value" row is the likelihood ration.

For all other footnotes, see Table 11.1.

from the parent or group, than recent and continually *LOCAL* firms, but getting machinery from the parent was much more important for the *MAJORITY* than *MINORITY FRGN* firms (*PFEQP*). The average number of visits by outside engineering consultants (*CVE*) followed exactly the same pattern as PFEQP. In addition, there was no difference in the use of consultants before and during the crisis.

Foreign engineers on staff represented only a miniscule fraction of total engineers for all firms and there were no differences by ownership. Foreign licenses or patents were used by only 6 percent of *LOCAL* firms (*PFLICPAT*). This difference was significant for *MINORITY* FRGN but not for *MAJORITY FRGN*, indicating perhaps that the use of formal rather than informal contracts for the transferal of technology is more common for the former. These results also hold for the number of licenses and patents held by each firm (*LICPAT*).

Considering as a unit the number of technical contracts of any sort (*CNT*), use by *MINORITY FRGN* firms was significantly higher than for *LOCAL* firms, but this was not true for the other two groups. The final three measures of external technology sources compare firms' technical assistance contracts. Significantly more *FOREIGN* firms in both equity groups had such contracts (*PFTA*) (60 versus 19 percent). However, the number of such contracts held by each firm (*NTA*) was significantly greater only for the *MINORITY FRGN* firms. The peso amount of annual technical assistance fees as a percent of sales (*TA/SALES*) was also significantly higher for both groups of *FOREIGN* and for the *NEW DOMESTIC* firms.

The *MINORITY FRGN* firms were very active in seeking diverse external sources of technology, some apart from the parent. On the other hand, the *MAJORITY FRGN* firms transferred technology from the parent, using relatively few formal contracts. Overall the relative use of formal foreign technical arrangements by all *LOCAL* firms is quite low and therefore not particularly helpful in explaining *LOCAL* firms' ability to compete successfully.

INTERNAL TECHNOLOGICAL ACTIVITY

The extent of innovative activity or research on process technology can be evaluated in various ways (see Table 11.4). The term "research" as used here indicates innovative activities of an applied nature, designed to change products or processes, as opposed to ongoing normal operations for production and quality control. It is meant to imply specific formal efforts to advance the "achievement distribution" toward the "innovation possibility frontier," rather than implying advancement of the "scientific frontier."

Sixty-three to 73 percent of firms in both groups did research on production process innovation (*RDPC*84) since 1978 and 46 percent of all firms did research on adaptation of materials (*RDMAT*84) in the same period, with no differences among ownership groups. Apparently firms were forced to augment their programs for adapting domestic materials when imports became difficult to acquire in the crisis. An indirect measure of research effort is labor hours per week by engineers devoted to such activity, divided by total labor hours. A comparison of engineers' time devoted to process innovation (*PRCDEV*), materials adaptation (*MATDEV*), and development of new products (*PRDDEV*), each as a percentage of total labor hours, showed *LOCAL* firms on par with all the *FOREIGN* firms. The *NEW DOMESTIC* firms were significantly higher in all three categories, perhaps from a desire to compensate for foreign technology previously generated from the parent. Expenditures on research and development as a percent of sales were not significantly different for *MAJORITY FRGN* compared to *LOCAL* firms, although *MINORITY FRGN* firms spent significantly more on their own R&D (*RD/SALES*).

A firm's own research efforts might be undertaken in a variety of locations, for example, principally within the firm, in a joint research effort with other local affiliates, or subcontracting to a local private or government research laboratory. *LOCAL* firms did significantly more of their research within Mexico either within the firm itself or in conjunction with its local affiliates (*PRDMEX*), than did either group of foreign firms (92 versus 41 percent). However, this variable indicates that foreign firms were also technologically active within Mexico, not relying totally on the parent or other international affiliates.

TECHNOLOGICAL OUTPUT

The argument might be made that, while firms are going through the motions of technical activity, few innovative results have emerged. However, *LOCAL* firms had registered their own patents on process innovation, both during the period 1978–1980 and 1981–1984. All patents included in the study, whether for processes, products, or trademarks are the firm's own. Reregistry of patents brought from another firm was explicitly excluded. *FOREIGN* firms did not register any patents during either period. Patents do not entirely reflect a firm's innovative activity, however, because many firms refuse to register a patent as this would in fact allow competitors access to their developments. Furthermore, if they do not plan to market the new designs or machines, they prefer secrecy to a patent which might be very difficult to protect. Firms also reported the number of specific, "patentable" process innovations they had developed each period. They had to be very explicit about the innovation, in terms of exactly what it was for, who developed it, and when it was introduced for it to be included. *FOREIGN* firms had twice as many "patentable" process innovations in the 1978–1980 period as *LOCAL* firms but the number increased markedly in the 1981–1984 period and was very similar for both groups of firms (*IDPC*80 and *IDPC*84). Perhaps the crisis itself stimulated this additional innovative effort, as adaptation to more local materials was necessary. (See Table 11.5)

Another result of innovative technological activity is that firms create some of their own machinery. *PFDESIGN* indicates the percentage of firms that designed or built any of their own machinery (including specific sizeable modifications of machines purchased elsewhere). Nearly 80 percent of all firms had done so, with no variation by ownership group. Firms also ranked the importance of the machinery they had developed to the overall production process (*IMPDSGN*).

Firms were asked to rank in order of importance the reasons they designed or built their own machinery instead of buying. Among the reasons ranked first or second, cost considerations were most important for 60 percent of the responses. The need for an item too specialized to buy anywhere on world markets was a distant second, at 14 percent of the responses, and inability to import was third at 12 percent. Eleven percent were seeking a lower production level than could be obtained with standard equipment, but no firms were seeking to utilize more of Mexico's abundant labor and 14 percent of responses (mostly as the second ranked reason) were doing

Table 11.4
Internal Sources of Technology for Mexico—Activities

	RDPC84^c	RDMAT84^c	PRCDEV	MATDEV
Means Comparisons				
Local	0.63	0.47	9E-3	8E-3
(t) df	(0.77)	(-0.04)	(-0.06)^u	(-0.73)^u
N	30	30	29	29
Foreign	0.73	0.46	9E-3	5E-3
(t) DF	54	54	48	46
N	26	26	26	26
Regression Analysis				
New Dorm	-0.39	0.16	0.02	0.02
(t)	(-0.68)	(0.29)	(2.38)**	(3.37)**
MIN-F	0.45	0.42	4E-3	3E-3
(t)	(0.99)	(0.99)	(0.82)	(0.89)
MAJ-F	-0.04	-0.44	2E-3	-2E-3
(t)	(-3E-90)	(-0.91)	(0.33)	(-0.39)
F-Value	2.07	2.90	1.94	4.38
df	51	51	51	51

their own, designing to use less labor. This probably reflects the Mexican entrepreneur's conviction that labor in Mexico should not be considered inexpensive because of low productivity and the time and trouble involved in handling personnel difficulties. These choices were essentially the same, regardless of ownership group.

Firms were also asked if the crisis had affected their efforts in designing their own machinery. The *LOCAL* firms split evenly, with half becoming more active, perhaps to compensate for inability to import. However, 73 percent of *MINORITY FRGN*, compared to only 30 percent of *MAJORITY FRGN* firms, became more active in building their own machinery with the crisis.

Technological output follows the pattern established by technological effort, as *LOCAL* firms' results from internal efforts equaled those of *FOREIGN* firms in all categories. However, it should be noted that *FOREIGN* firms also exhibited more internal local activity and output than is generally presumed.

Table 11.4 (continued)

	PRDDEV	RD/SALES	PRDMEX
Means Comparisons			
Local	0.01	0.39	92.12
(t) df^s	$(-2.10)^{u**}$	$(2.44)^u$	$(-5.50)^{u**}$
N	29	53	26
Foreign	4E-3	5.10	41.21
(t) df	32	48	37
N	26	49	24
Regression Analysis			
New Dom	0.03	0.25	-15.00
(t) df	(3.44)**	(0.093)	(-0.93)
MIN-F	-5E-3	9.42	-52.21
(t)	(-0.91)	(3.93)**	(-4.67)**
MAJ-F	-3E-3	0.71	-56.00
(t)	(-0.56)	(0.31)	(-4.49)**
Period		-1.01	
(t)		(-0.57)	
F-Value	5.54	4.67	10.54
df	51	97	46

Note: For all footnotes, see Tables 11.1 and 11.3.

FORMS OF TECHNOLOGY ACQUISITION

Firms were asked to designate the forms in which they acquired their technology or technical knowledge, assigning 100 percent of such acquisitions among:

1. machinery or materials purchases
2. designs, blue prints, including foreign contracts
3. development by the firm, including hiring knowledgeable professionals and R&D programs, and
4. *other*.

All *LOCAL* firms received the least of their technology in the form of designs and blue prints, with most of their acquisitions split evenly between

Table 11.5
Implementation of New Technology

	IDPC80	IDPC84	PFDESIGN	IMPDSGN
Means Comparisons				
Local	.45	2.26	0.77	.52
(t) df	(0.82)	(-0.05)	(0.30)	(0.45)
N	29	31	31	31
Foreign	.92	2.20	0.81	.58
t (df)	51	54	55	55
N	24	25	26	26
Regression Analysis				
New Dom.	-0.36	-0.94	-0.38	5E-17
t (df)	(-0.37)	(-0.51)	(-0.63)	(8E-17)
MIN-F	0.86	0.92	5.39	0.43
t (df)	(1.19)	(0.67)	(4E-3)	1.02
MAJ-F	-0.16	-1.71	-0.70	-0.11
(t) df	(-0.21)	(-1.16)	(-1.47)	(-0.25)
F-Value	0.74	0.94	10.83	1.50
(t) df	49	52	52	52

Note: ᵘThe hypothesis that the *variances* are equal in foreign and local firms is rejected at the .05 level. In all other comparisons, the t-statistic and degrees of freedom are based upon the equal variances model.

their own development and machinery purchases. *MINORITY FRGN* firms got the least in the form of machinery and placed the most emphasis on their own development. *MAJORITY FRGN* had the opposite pattern, with machinery acquisition primary and their own development least significant. This probably reflects the degree of conformity to parent firms' technologies. The *MINORITY FRGN* relative emphasis on equipment development affirms the finding described above of their increased activity in machinery development with the onset of the crisis.

Sixty-seven percent of all firms made at least minor changes in the foreign technology they acquired. About 40 percent of *LOCAL* firms made only minor adaptations and 40 percent used the foreign technology with no changes.

In the other three groups, however, twice as many firms made minor changes than those who changed nothing. Only two or three firms in each category made major adaptations in their foreign technology acquisitions. With regard to why firms made adaptations in their foreign technology (combining first and second rankings), 47 percent of the responses were adaptations to different raw materials, and 23 percent of responses were adaptations to a smaller market. Only 5 percent of responses were attempting to use more labor and 17 percent preferred to use less labor than the foreign capital/labor mix. The dominance of the response of raw materials adaptation probably reflects Mexican long-standing import substitution policies. However, the other reasons reflect differences in the Mexican economy relative to those of its technology sources. The reported tendency to reduce the use of labor is not desirable for job creation efforts in Mexico.

CONCLUSION

Based on results from this sample, the differences in technology acquisition and performance between domestic and transnational firms in the manufacturing sector of Mexico over the 1979–1984 period were slight. Furthermore, although the Mexican crisis had an impact on both ownership groups' performance, it was of minor importance to their technology behavior, perhaps forcing some redesigning of machinery to deal with difficulties in importing traditional machines and materials.

While in general *NEW DOMESTIC* firms were similar to the continuously *LOCAL*, their engineers devoted significantly more time to innovation involving processes, products, and materials. Although *MINORITY FRGN* firms used as little foreign equipment as *LOCAL* firms, they were the most active ownership group in seeking diverse external disembodied technology, going beyond their parent in some of their formal foreign contracts. On the other hand, firms with *MAJORITY FRGN* equity were more likely to internalize technology within their international affiliates, with less use of other sources including their own innovation.

The following further points emerge from the analysis. First, these foreign firms do not rely exclusively on foreign affiliates for technical information. Second, the local firms do engage in internal innovative activities, certainly at levels comparable and occasionally above foreign firms. Third, although much of the activity by both groups of firms is adaptation to fit raw materials availability, it is important to note that more sophisticated approaches to innovation are not uncommon. For example, many of these firms have active R&D departments involved in changing the design of technology and building their own equipment. Athough some firms preferred to use less labor than that embodied in the foreign designs, the design changes also took the appropriate and expected form of adjusting the technology of production to a smaller market.

NOTES

1. For some examples of this argument, see Ghayur Alam, and John Langrish, "Non-Multinational Firms and Transfer of Technology to LDCs," *World Development*, Vol. 9, No. 4, 1981, pp. 383–387; Thomas J. Biersteker, *Distortion or Development? Contending Perspectives on the Multinational Corporation* (Cambridge, MA: MIT Press, 1978); Albert O. Hirschman, et al., *Toward a New Strategy for Development* (New York: Pergamon Press, 1979); Stephen J. Kobrin, "Multinational Corporations, Socio-cultural Dependence, and Industrialization: Need Satisfaction or Want Creation?" *Journal of Developing Areas*, Vol. 13, No. 2, January 1979, pp. 109–125; Sanjaya Lall, "Is 'Dependence' A Useful Concept in Analyzing Underdevelopment?" *World Development*, Vol. 3, No. 11, 1975, pp. 799–810; Vincent A. Mahler, *Dependency Approaches to International Political Economy: A Cross-national Study* (New York: Columbia University Press, 1980); J. B. Nugent, and P. A. Yotopoulos, "What Has Orthodox Development Economics Learned from Recent Experience?" *World Development*, Vol. 7, No. 6, June 1979, pp. 541–554; Daniel Lloyd Spencer, *Technology Gap in Perspective Strategy of International Technology Transfer*, (New York: Sparton Books, 1970); Melville J. Ulmer, "Multinational Corporations and Third World Capitalism," *Journal of Economic Issues*, Vol. 14, No. 2, June 1980, pp. 452–471; Constantine V. Vaitsos, *Intercountry Income Distribution and Transnational Enterprises* (Oxford: Clarendon Press, 1974); Raymond Vernon, "The Economic Consequences of U.S. Foreign Direct Investment," *The Economic and Political Consequences of Multinational Enterprise: An Anthology* (Boston: Division of Research, Harvard Business School, 1972).

2. See, for example, M. Casson, *Alternatives to the Multinational Enterprise* (London: Macmillan Press, 1979); John H. Dunning, "Toward an Eclectic Theory of International Production: Some Empirical Tests," *Journal of International Business Studies*, Spring/Summer 1980, pp. 9–31; S. Hymer, *The International Operations of National Firms: A Study of Direct Foreign Investment* (Cambridge, MA: MIT Press, 1976); Alan M. Rugman, ed., *New Theories of the Multinational Enterprise* (New York: St. Martin's Press, 1982).

3. P. R. Krugman, "The 'New Theories' of International Trade and the Multinational Enterprise," in *The Multinational Corporations in the 1980s*, ed. C. P. Kindleberger and D. B. Audretsch (Cambridge, MA: MIT Press, 1983).

4. Daniel Chudnovsky, and Masafumi Nagao, *Capital Goods Production in the Third World: An Economic Study of Technology Acquisition* (New York: St. Martin's Press, 1983); C. J. Dahlman, and L. E. Westphal, "Technological Effort in Industrial Development—An Interpretative Survey of Recent Research," in *The Economics of New Technology in Developing Countries*, ed. F. Stewart and J. James (London: Frances Printer, 1982); L. G. Fairchild, "Performance and Technology of U.S. and National Firms in Mexico," *Journal of Development Studies*, October 1977; L. G. Fairchild, and K. Sosin, "Evaluating Differences in Technological Activity between Transnational and Domestic Firms in Latin America," *Journal of Development Studies*, July 1986, pp. 697–708; Pradip K. Ghosh, ed., *Appropriate Technology in Third World Development*, International Development Resource Books, No. 14, (Westport, CT: Greenwood Press, 1984); Jorge Katz, "Creacion de Technologia en el Sector Manufacturero Argentino," *El Trimestre Economico*, January–March 1978, pp. 167–190; Sanjaya Lall, "Determinants of Research and Development in an LDC: The Indian Engineering

Industry," *Economic Letters*, 1983, pp. 379–383; Sanjaya Lall, *Developing Countries in the International Economy* (London: Macmillan Press Ltd., 1981); Vernon W. Ruttan, and Yujiro Hayami, "Toward a Theory of Induced Institutional Innovation," *Journal of Development Studies*, pp. 203–223; S. Teitel, "Toward an Understanding of Technical Change in Semi-Industrialized Countries," *Research Policy*, 1981, pp. 127–147; S. Teitel, "Creation of Technology within Latin America," *The Annals of the American Academy of Political and Social Science*, 1981, pp. 136–150; S. Teitel, "Technology Creation in Semi-Industrial Economies," *Journal of Development Economics*, September/October 1984, pp. 39–61.

5. L. G. Fairchild, and K. Sosin, "Manufacturing Firms in Mexico's Financial Crisis: Determinants of Severity and Response," *Mexican Studies/Estudios Mexicanos*, Vol. 3, No. 1, 1987.

6. The changes to 100 percent Mexican for the formerly foreign firms took place between 1972 and 1983, with most occurring between 1975–1980.

7. Both scale and age variables were included in the original regressions but were consistently insignificant throughout the study. Given the need to preserve degrees of freedom, these variables were omitted from the final model.

8. Raymond Vernon, *Storm over the Multinationals: the Real Issues* (Cambridge, MA: Harvard University Press, 1977).

APPENDIX

All data were adjusted to 1979 pesos. The following describes the variables used, in order of their appearance in the tables. Annual variables are for the period 1979–1983 for all firms, with some cases for 1984.

Variables appearing in Table 11.1:

GSALE	Annual growth rates of net sales
GFASET	Annual growth rates of net fixed assets at historical cost, adjusted to 1979 prices
GLABOR	Annual growth rates of total labor hours per year
GPRFT	Annual growth rates of gross profit, before taxes and dividends
GINT	Annual growth rates of annual interest expense
GNEWEQ	Annual growth rates of expenditures on new machinery and equipment
PK	Annual observations of ratios of gross profit (before taxes and dividends) to net fixed assets
PEX	Percent of annual sales exported
LPROD	Value added divided by labor hours per year

Variables appearing in Table 11.2:

NEW3	Percent of 1984 production facilities installed within the previous three years
NEW5	Percent of 1984 production facilities installed within the previous five years

NTEC3   Percent of production facilities new within three years which em-
                bodied new technology, for the production of the same products
NTEC5   Percent of production facilities new within five years which em-
                bodied new technology, for production of the same products

Variables appearing in Tables 11.3:

PEQF   Percent of value of installed machinery that was of foreign origin
PFEQP   Percent of equipment imports from the parent or group
CVE   Total number of visits by consulting engineers (production or in-
                dustrial) from outside the firm for all years
PFLICPAT   Percent of firms using any foreign licenses and/or patents as of
                1984
LICPAT   Number of foreign licenses and/or patents held as of 1984
CNT   Number of technical contracts held by the firm as of 1984 (in-
                cluding one for patents, licenses, technical assistance or
                trademarks)
PFTA   Percent of firms using a foreign technical assistance contract as of
                1984
NTA   Number of foreign technical assistance contracts in use as of 1984
TA/SALES   Annual observations of expenditures for technical assistance con-
                tracts divided by net sales

Variables appearing in Table 11.4:

RDPC84   Percent of firms that put formal, regular attention (that is, at least
                part-time labor hours allocated) on developing changes in
                methods and processes, since 1978
RDMAT84   Percent of firms that put formal, regular attention (that is, at least
                part-time labor hours allocated) on adapting raw materials, since
                1978
PRCDEV   Ratio of number of labor hours per week engineers spent on
                developing new production processes, divided by total labor
                hours per week
MATDEV   Ratio of number of labor hours per week engineers spent on
                adaptation of raw materials, divided by total labor hours per
                week
PRDDEV   Ratio of number of labor hours per week engineers devoted to
                development of new products, divided by total labor hours per
                week
RD/SALES   Average of annual observations of expenditures on research
                divided by net sales. Sample size reflects annual observations for
                each firm. The number of firms represented is relatively low
                because many firms keep no separate account on research ac-
                tivities, which are often part-time efforts by engineering staff who
                also work on production or quality control.

PRDMEX   Percent of all research and development efforts conducted in Mexico (including research by affiliates and on contract)

Variables appearing in Table 11.5:

*IDPC*80   Number of "patentable" inventions for processes developed by the firm (but not registered) in the period 1978 to 1980

*IDPC*84   Number of "patentable" inventions for processes developed by the firm (but not registered) since 1980

PFDESGN   Percent of firms that had built or designed any of its own machinery, including major modifications of purchased processes

IMPDSGN   Degree of importance to production of the machinery and equipment developed by the firm

12

Mexico's Growing Role in the Integration of the North American Automotive Industry

Marc Scheinman

INTRODUCTION

In the 1990s Mexican decision makers will look back on the 1980s as the period in which they began to restructure their economy, from one that was highly protectionist and inward-looking, to one that was more market-oriented, competitive in international markets, and also more flexible, with regard to the implementation of foreign direct investment regulations. These same individuals, in government and private industry, will remember the 1980s as a series of roller coaster rides in which Mexico was first catapulted to unprecedented levels of growth, that averaged 8.4 percent from 1978 to 1981, before plummeting severely, for most of the remainder of the decade.[1] By sharp contrast, in the last five years, 1982–1986, gross domestic product (GDP) has increased by only 0.67 percent, annually, on average.[2]

If the 1980s began with Mexico as a favorite among international creditors and foreign investors, then they would conclude less happily, with Mexico becoming the second most heavily indebted developing country, after Brazil, with inflation rates that frequently surpassed 100 percent, annually. Declining international oil prices, mounting government deficits, and inflation spurred a reexamination of Mexico in which international lenders and foreign investors subsequently reduced their Mexican exposures dramatically, as the secondary commercial bank markets consistently discounted the value of Mexican debt and the likelihood that it would be repaid.

When American executives, particularly those responsible for managing subsidiaries of the Big-3 U.S. auto manufacturers in Mexico—Ford, Chrysler, and General Motors—review the 1980s they are certain to conclude that it was during this very troubled period that their Mexican production facilities were expanded vastly. The facilities were transformed until they achieved world-class status, in terms of increased productivity and quality, at significantly lower costs. For these executives, especially in the area of finished vehicles, the transformation of the 1980s will also be remembered as the first era in which production for export replaced the traditional emphasis on the domestic market, which by the middle and late 1980s was in a state of depression.

To return to the present, it is the major thesis of this chapter that motor vehicle exports from Mexico will continue their explosive growth for the remainder of the decade and their major destination will be the United States. The very magnitude of this change in orientation, from an almost exclusive concentration on domestic production to production primarily for export, will result in the further integration of the U.S. Big-3's auto production in North America. And it is certain that Mexico is destined to play an even more important role in such plans for the 1990s. In order to evaluate these developments this chapter focuses on two distinct five-year periods, 1977–1981 and 1982–1986, before making projections for the future.

PERIOD I (1977–1981)

The Background

When José Lopez Portillo assumed the Mexican presidency in 1977 he arrived at a delicate moment, politically and economically. Politically, his predecessor, Luis Echeverria, was considered a leftist with a zeal for taunting the foreign business community. In fact, it was under his leadership that the "Mexicanization Laws" (of 1973) were formalized and actually enforced. These laws stipulated that in all but the rarest circumstances and consonant with the national interest, foreign businesses would be restricted to minority control (maximum of 49 percent), while minimum Mexican interest in such businesses was set at 51 percent. Of course, those foreign businesses that were established prior to 1973 were not subject to such restrictions. Echeverria's nationalistic policies left the Mexican economy in a depressed state.

In contrast to Echeverria, many observers, both Mexican and American, viewed Lopez Portillo as "the businessman's candidate" who would restore stability. Luckily, for Lopez Portillo and Mexico, the enormous oil reserves that had recently been discovered provided the basis for a new era of unprecedented growth. One key indicator of this growth was the spectacular development of the Mexican automotive industry that was crucial to Mexico not only for purely economic reasons, but for psychological ones, too. For cars, with their heavy capital investments and high technology manufacturing, symbolized modernization and the contemporary industrial society.

The "Boom" in Mexican Auto Production/Sales

The boom in Mexican auto production coincided with one of the deepest postwar recessions in the United States subsequent to the Iranian/energy crisis of 1979. From 1980 to 1982 U.S. motor vehicle production and sales reached their lowest mark in two decades.[3] In contrast to the depressed U.S. market, sales of Chrysler, Ford, General Motors, Volkswagen, Nissan, and Renault reached all-time highs in Mexico during these years. From 1977 to 1981 Mexican vehicle sales in the domestic market increased by 97 percent, from 289,247 to 571,013[4] while, during the same period, exports increased 23 percent, from 11,743 to 14,428.[5] Overall Mexican production, domestic plus exports, increased 113 percent.[6] A closer understanding of the trends embodied in these figures can be gleaned from analyzing Table 12.1.

The two most significant trends revealed from Table 12.1 are:

1. Mexico's domestic market for motor vehicles accounted for no less than 93 percent of total vehicle production during the 1977–1981 period, thereby indicating that the boom, which saw production and sales double within the five year span, was overwhelmingly driven by production for the Mexican market, since export production never exceeded 7 percent (1978) of total production output.

2. On the other hand, while export sales increased in unit terms, by 23 percent, from 1977 to 1981, these sales actually *declined* by 43 percent when examined as a ratio of total production.

It is clear that the rapid expansion in vehicle production is directly related to Mexican economic growth. However, it would be useful to specify further the relationship between domestic and export production and to examine who the major exporters are, as well as the destinations of their exports, during Period I (1977–1981).

Once the Mexican boom gathered momentum, the relative importance of exports declined significantly. For example, 1978 marked a watershed; in this year of recovery and growth, Mexican vehicle production reached a new peak of 384,128.[7] Yet, this figure surpassed the previous high of 1975 by only about 23,000 vehicles, which indicates that 1978 was mostly a recovery year following two deeply recessive years; it was a prelude to take-off, for both domestic and export growth. During that year exports

Table 12.1
Mexican Vehicle Production, Sales, and Exports: 1977–1981

YEAR	TOTAL PRODUCTION	DOMESTIC SALES	EXPORTS
1977	289,247	280,813	11,743
1978	384,123	361,028	25,828
1979	444,426	425,232	24,756
1980	490,006	464,411	18,245
1981	597,118	571,013	14,428

Source: Asociacion Mexicana De La Industria Automotriz, A.C. (AMIA), *La Industria Automotriz En Cifras*, (Mexico City: 1986)

increased by 14,000 vehicles (120 percent) and comprised a record of almost 7 percent of total production, while overall production increased by 104,010 (37 percent).[8] However, once the boom was clearly underway in 1979 exports began to decline. At the end of Period I in 1981 exports were only about 2 percent of total production; in other words, exports had declined by 64 percent when analyzed as a ratio of total production (from 6.7 percent in 1978 to 2.4 percent in 1981); in fact, exports also declined in absolute or unit terms in 1979, 1980, and 1981.[9]

Not so ironically, in 1981, at the end of Period I, exports were at a five-year low, but domestic sales and total production reached unprecedented levels reflecting the tremendous expansion in the Mexican economy. To date, Mexico has yet to duplicate the almost 600,000 vehicles produced in 1981. If exports of vehicles declined in relative importance as the Mexican domestic economy expanded, it is still important to note that automotive exports fluctuated between 12,000 and 26,000. During the 1977–1981 period, Volkswagen and Nissan were the two most important exporters, accounting for 93–95 percent of total exports.[10] Volkswagen alone frequently accounted for almost 75 percent of exports, while third-ranked Chrysler's exports never exceeded 7 percent.[11] All of Volkswagen's exports were sent to Germany; Nissan's were divided between Central and South America; and Chrysler's were destined to Latin America and later Saudi Arabia. Just as significant is the complete *absence* of the United States as a destination for Mexican produced vehicles.

During 1981 despite some disturbing signals in the form of increasingly high rates of inflation and a decline in international oil prices, Mexico was considered a model developing country by the foreign investment and banking community, largely as a result of its huge oil reserves. One key indicator of this "success" story was the unprecedented boom in automotive sales, an expansion that symbolized a growth in stature as well as economic standard of living.

By the end of 1982, only one year after reaching unprecedented heights, the Mexican economy suddenly went into reverse as inflation neared 100 percent, oil prices continued to decline, and in August Mexico's leaders announced that they could no longer pay back the interest on their foreign debt, which had zoomed to $80-plus billion, without massive aid or financial restructuring from the international banking community. Instead of the impressive growth figures that characterized Period I, particularly the 1979–1981 period, Mexico's economy contracted, and grew negatively in 1982 and 1983. After accounting for inflation real GDP declined by almost 6 percent in 1982 and 1983; in per capita terms the drop amounted to 11 percent.[12] Given the sensitivity of automotive vehicle production and sales to inflation and the performance of the economy in general it is hardly surprising that 1982 marked the beginning of a deep recession that has persisted throughout Period II (1982–1986), a period in which the Mexican auto industry was being restructured and increasingly integrated within the production schedules of U.S. manufacturers.

PERIOD II (1982-1986): RESTRUCTURING THE AUTOMOBILE INDUSTRY

The year 1982 saw the beginning of radical change in Mexican auto industry history, an era of explosive export growth in which exports to the United States became dominant. During this period, Chrysler and General Motors have replaced Volkswagen and Nissan as the major automobile exporters. At the very same time, domestic sales have dropped dramatically, as inflation averaged 81 percent or three and one-half times more than the 23 percent average for the earlier 1977-1981 period.[13]

In 1986 exports reached an all-time high of 72,429, compared with *only* 15,819 vehicles in 1982, the first period of Period II.[14] During this period, exports increased almost 358 percent. However, during the same period, domestic sales dropped 45 percent, from 466,663 vehicles in 1982 to 258,835 in 1986.[15] Overall production (domestic plus exports) declined 28 percent, from 472,637 in 1982 to 341,052 in 1986.[16] These depressed figures effectively have set the Mexican automobile industry back more than a decade. In 1973 overall production totalled 285,513 vehicles, but the next year rebounded to 350,755 units and did not go below about 325,000 until the recession year of 1977 in which only 280,813[17] units were produced. (See Table 12.2 for complete Period II figures).

"Recession" in Mexico and the "Boom" in Auto Exports

If the boom in Mexican auto sales coincided with a deep recession in U.S. vehicle production and sales, especially in 1980, 1981, 1982, then Period II is characterized by precisely the opposite relationship. Since 1983 the United States auto industry has recovered strongly, while the general economy has also grown consistently, and at times vigorously. Mexican development, in sharp contrast, has sputtered and is enmeshed in a period of contraction. This reversal in domestic circumstances has provided the foundation for

Table 12.2
Mexican Vehicle Production, Sales, and Exports: 1982-1986

YEAR	TOTAL PRODUCTION	DOMESTIC SALES	EXPORTS
1982	472,637	466,663	15,819
1983	285,485	272,815	22,456
1984	357,998	330,287	33,635
1985	458,680	391,649	58,423
1986	341,052	258,835	72,429

Source: AMIA, *La Industria Automotriz Terminal En 1986*, (Mexico City: Enero, 1987)

profoundly restructuring the Mexican auto industry and integrating it increasingly with U.S. production and the American market.

The major reasons underlying the American auto industry's dramatic recovery include: massive investments in new plant and equipment amounting to $55 billion between 1982 and 1986, or about the same amount invested in the previous ten years; increased outsourcing of finished vehicles and original equipment components used in the assembly of new automobiles; increased productivity with correspondingly lower employment (reduced costs); and the imposition of voluntary restraint agreements against Japanese imports.[18] To compete more effectively against lower priced imports U.S. manufacturers rallied behind three key objectives: increased quality, increased productivity, and reduced costs. One of the most important strategies in achieving this trinity of objectives was to turn overseas—internationalization—to take advantage of much lower production costs; and, in the case of Mexico, domestic plant capacity that would otherwise have remained idle. For example, already existing abundant sources of comparatively cheap, efficient, and effective labor could be employed producing completed vehicles for export at the same quality standards required by consumers in the United States.

The downturn in the Mexican economy occurred at virtually the same moment that Detroit began to implement its internationalization strategy. One important result of the new strategy was to increase dramatically U.S. automobile investment in Mexico, to use Mexico as an export platform for finished vehicles destined for the United States. Although Mexico had been an increasingly important source of U.S. automotive parts imports, particularly engines, since 1976 (imports increased from $419 million in 1981 to $1.2 billion in 1983 alone),[19] its role as an exporter of completed vehicles was virtually nonexistent because about 95 percent of all Mexican production was absorbed by the domestic market, which until 1982 had grown explosively. Under such growth conditions the Mexican economy inflated. As a result, the peso and Mexican labor were overvalued, factors which discouraged exports.

By 1983 all of these conditions changed. The year 1983 was another watershed year for Mexico and for the United States. Just as the American motor vehicle industry recovered and began to earn record profits, as inflation was brought under control, and the price of oil continued to drop steeply, the Mexican automobile industry entered a deep recession that forced Mexican government officials and U.S. and Mexican auto executives to make difficult decisions about what suddenly appeared as a highly uncertain future for the Mexican motor vehicle industry, particularly for the domestic market.

By 1983 it was clear to Mexico's new president, Miguel De La Madrid, that new, far-reaching programs would have to be implemented if Mexico were to recover. A new emphasis was placed on encouraging export growth and the earning of foreign exchange in order to pay for crucial imports and the interest on the foreign debt, and to create more competitive businesses as the basis for future growth, instead of relying so heavily on crude oil exports. Within this new framework of thinking, amidst dramatically changed domestic and international conditions, the auto industry was to play a key role.

The Mexican auto industry has always been very visible because it is, for all intents and purposes, foreign-owned. Since 1962 the Mexican government began to increasingly regulate the conditions under which these foreign-owned companies operate. The regulations were enforced through the implementation of three auto decrees (1962, 1972, and 1977) whose major objectives were to increase the share of domestic materials and components utilized in the construction of motor vehicles from about 15 percent to about 60 percent;[20] ensure majority ownership (60 percent) for Mexican parts manufacturers; and to balance the rising trade deficit in automotive products, particularly parts (this deficit worsened during the boom because of the inability of domestic suppliers to meet the growing demand). These three decrees were perfectly consistent with the Mexicanization Laws; they were nationalistic and aimed at protecting and sharing in the profitability of an increasingly burgeoning domestic market. Under these conditions, regulation of the auto industry was confined largely to domestic production, while exports to offset the growing trade balance in automotive products was effectively restricted to parts, not complete vehicles.

With the collapse of the domestic market and the desperate need for foreign exchange, in 1983 the De La Madrid government proclaimed a fourth auto decree. Its two chief objectives were to have vehicle assemblers balance their foreign exchange transactions on a "model year" basis and to increase local content requirements: 60 percent for cars (up from 55 percent) and 65–70 percent for light trucks (up from 60 percent) and higher for other commercial motor vehicles.[21] The U.S. auto manufacturers' response to the decree was to embark on massive export development programs. This involved billions of dollars of new investments in plant construction and modernization that enabled Chrysler, Ford, and General Motors to produce "world class" vehicles, primarily for sale in the United States.

In return for Ford's half-billion-dollar commitment to build its new plant in Hermosillo, with a production capacity of 130,000 vehicles, 80 percent of which are to be exported to the United States, the Mexican government relaxed its national integration ratio to 30 percent instead of the purposed 60 percent.[22] Similar arrangements have been granted to Chrysler for its extensive export program in Toluca, where it now manufactures almost 30,000 Ram Chargers and K-cars. A further encouragement for exports and movement away from the nationalistic "Mexicanization" Laws of the previous decade has been the open solicitation of foreign manufacturers, particularly Americans to establish plants that assemble U.S. manufactured components for sale as finished products in the United States. These plants, *maquiladoras*, permit foreigners to maintain 100 percent control. Following the new auto decree these plants have grown extremely fast, while some of the most rapid growth is accounted for by *maquiladoras* devoted to automotive assembly operations. Currently, General Motors has 23 *maquiladoras* and Ford has four; Chrysler is now considering involvement in such a program.

Although it is certainly difficult to overestimate the significance of the 1983 auto decree on exports, there were two other factors that coincided with the decree and also played a crucial role in the investment decisions of Chrysler, General Motors, and Ford. These key variables were considerations of net price (production costs) and quality. By 1983 the business exchange rate was 120 pesos per U.S. dollar, compared with 25 pesos per dollar in 1981. As a result Mexican production costs in 1985 were only 14 percent as high as comparable figures in the U.S. automotive industry. In terms of quality, the United States companies in Mexico were convinced that they could meet their own standards if they were to invest sufficient funds in state-of-the-art technology; the relaxation of minimum local content ratios would also guarantee quality and further reduce costs.

Given the coincidence of the three key factors, foreign auto producers in Mexico initiated a new era of explosive export growth to compensate for the collapse of the domestic market. In spite of such growth, amounting to 356 percent during the 1982–1986 period, the auto producers lost approximately $1.5 billion in roughly the same time.[23] In a highly volatile context, such as Mexico's, it would prove to be very difficult to balance domestic and export production.

Recent Trends in Exports to the United States: 1984–1986

The years 1984 and 1985 were mini-recovery years for domestic auto sales in Mexico, as inflation seemed to stabilize around 60 percent, but the 391,649 vehicles sold in 1985 were still 31 percent below 1981's record high.[24] More importantly 1984 and 1985 marked the first two years in which U.S. manufacturers established a dominant export position and the United States, as opposed to Europe (West Germany) became the primary destination of exports from Mexico.

In 1983 exports of complete vehicles to the United States were minimal (203), most of which were heavy trucks from Kenworth. These numbers constituted only about 1 percent of all vehicles exported from Mexico. However, two years later, at the end of 1985 (subsequent to the 1983 auto decree) exports to the United States comprised about 84 percent of all Mexican exports. And the composition of the exports changed, too. Lightweight trucks and passenger cars accounted for 99 percent of the units exported, as General Motors began shipping its El Caminos and Caballeros and Chrysler its K-cars. The year 1986 ended with Chrysler accounting for 60 percent (43,689 units) and General Motors for 26 percent (18,672).[25]

By contrast, Nissan placed a distant third with a 13 percent share (9,124 units) and Volkswagen had less than 1 percent.[26] These figures represent a dramatic reversal of export leadership. As recently as 1984 Volkswagen accounted for 45 percent (15,171 units) of all Mexican exports, more than both Chrysler and General Motors combined. Perhaps most significant in the new American dominance is Chrysler's remarkable growth rate in exports; since 1984 it has achieved an annual growth rate of 178 percent.[27] This growth is the result of exports of Ram Chargers from the new Laga Alberto plant in addition to K-cars. And now, with the recent completion of Ford's Hermosillo plant, exports to the United States will continue to grow at unprecedented rates, up to 130,000 per year. And recently General Motors has announced that soon it will export 100,000 completed vehicles from Mexico.

The latest vehicle import figures from the U.S. international trade administration indicate that over the two-year period from November 1984 to October 1986, growth in value of Mexican vehicles imported into the United States increased almost twice as fast as units imported and that passenger cars have become much more important than lightweight truck imports. For example in the November 1984 to October 1985 time frame 37,912 vehicles were imported from Mexico at a total value of approximately $265 million with lightweight trucks accounting for about twice as many units and slightly more than twice the value of passenger cars. During the subsequent period (November 1985–October 1986) 55,199 vehicles were imported, an increase of 46 percent over the previous year.[28] Most important still is the 86 percent growth value of these imports to $493 million. In contrast to the preceding year, passenger car imports almost tripled in units, but more than tripled in value, to $342 million. As 1986 drew to an end, passenger cars comprised 63 percent of all vehicles imported from Mexico and 69 percent of total imported in dollar terms.

CONCLUSION: PERIOD III (1987–1991): THE OUTLOOK FOR THE FUTURE AND BEYOND

With the recent fall 1986 release of the Tracer, from the plant in Hermosillo, Ford executives are now predicting confidently that exports of these cars will reach 130,000 in 1988, most of which will be destined for the U.S. market.[29] This represents the entire installed capacity of the new plant at Hermosillo, which began in 1984 and was built at an estimated cost of $500 million. When Ford achieves its objectives for the Tracer over the next two years, it will replace Chrysler as the leading auto exporter.

Chrysler executives appear equally bullish, with respect to their Mexican operations, where they have recently added production of the Chrysler LeBaron to their line and are now planning to add two more new models, Dodge Sundance and Plymouth Shadow. Like the Tracer, these cars are targeted for the U.S. market. Chrysler officials believe that exports of the two new models will eventually reach 25,000–50,000 vehicles. Unlike the Tracer, both the Sundance and Shadow are intended to complement U.S.

production capacity, which by itself, is unable to meet demand for these models in the American market. Tracers, however, are produced entirely outside of the United States.

General Motors' plans remain the least clear. A recent reorganization that now places Mexican production under the umbrella of Chevrolet-Pontiac/Canada (CPC) indicates that important changes that are likely to increase production of Mexican vehicles for the export market are being put into place. Such changes have not only been rumored in the press, but are reflected by General Motors de Mexico's executives who have already announced that in 1988 General Motors will export 100,000 finished vehicles from Mexico, an increase of 435.6 percent over 1986's export figure of 18,672.

Each of the Big-3 U.S. automakers has announced plans for explosive export growth in 1988, which have been recorded in Mexico's official gazette or chronicle, *Diario Oficial*. Ford projects exports of 130,000, while both Chrysler and General Motors predict exports of 100,000 vehicles. The significance of these figures can hardly be overestimated, given the recent collapse in Mexico's domestic market. In fact these projections indicate that the 360,000 units to be exported by the Big-3 in 1988 make it very likely that that year will mark the first in which exports will surpass sales of vehicles produced for the domestic market.

Predictions for the local Mexican market are not nearly so bright. With inflation continuing to run at a very high rate, economists believe that this situation will put increasing pressure on the automakers to request further price increases to offset similar rises in their expenses. Such price increases can hardly help boost domestic sales, since the Mexican car-buying public, particularly the purchasers of the smallest cars, the *populares* like the Volkswagen sedan (Beetle), have already absorbed serious losses in purchasing power.

Industry analysts' predictions range from 0–7 percent annual growth in domestic sales. However, even if we accept the most optimistic figure, which is not likely, domestic sales would be only 276,953 vehicles this year, which would approximate low levels of sales in 1977 (280,813) and 1983 (272,815), the year that initiated the current recession.

Yet, whether we project an optimistic 7 percent rate of growth, or no increase at all in domestic sales, the total sales—domestic plus exports—of vehicles produced in Mexico during 1987–1988 will set a new record in 1988 and will surpass the previous high of 597,118 vehicles, established in 1981, by as much as 20 percent. And this achievement will be even greater if Volkswagen, once again, resumes vigorous exports and Nissan, too, continues to expand export production. Both of these developments appear likely since these two foreign-owned companies have embarked on major investment programs during the past year and in the absence of a revived domestic market for their lower-end, cheaper-priced vehicles the export market is the logical focus for the near future.

The year 1988, therefore, will be a watershed year for the automotive industry in Mexico since record sales will be achieved at a moment when the domestic market is still relatively depressed, as is the rest of the economy. This achievement will have an extraordinary significance, because it will mark the first time that the automotive industry in Mexico will have been driven primarily by export sales. This new emphasis on production for export markets, especially in the United States, is helping to transform Mexican operations to world-class status.

It appears that export sales will continue to drive auto manufacturing in Mexico since industry experts envision 1992 as the earliest date at which domestic sales return to their historic high of 571,013 vehicles, established in 1981. Without such a resumption of strong, local demand, exports will have to be promoted by Mexican government incentives to the foreign-owned automakers, in the form of continued lower local content requirements and the reduction of tariffs on imported parts. Because the automotive industry is so crucial to Mexico's overall plans to increase exports, especially in the manufacturing sector, it is almost certain that the government will furnish these incentives. One clear indication that supports this contention is the recent government announcement that beginning in 1988 tariffs on imported parts will be reduced by 10 percent, from 40 to 30 percent. The additional imports required for further export expansion will be obtained at a cheaper price, which can also increase overall competition in the Mexican automotive parts industry, which traditionally has been heavily protected by the government. Ironically, Mexican decision makers in the 1990s may well look back on the troubled 1980s as the time in which their otherwise slow industrial recovery was led by explosive export growth in the automotive industry, and that such an achievement was made possible by increased cooperation between the government and foreign-owned companies, especially American ones.

Increasing exports from Mexico into the American market are likely to continue at an accelerated pace for other reasons, too, namely the persistent internationalization of the automotive industry and the rationalization of North American vehicle and parts manufacturers. In an effort to avoid growing protectionist sentiments in the U.S. Congress and the possibility of new quotas on imported cars, many foreign-owned firms, particularly Japanese and Korean ones, are adding significantly to their production capacities in the United States and Canada, which they use as export bases to the U.S. market. In the United States alone, foreign automakers are adding capacity at a rate that will augment vehicle production by between 1.5 and 2.0 million units, by 1990. At the same time, the U.S. International Trade Commission and private industry analysts forecast growth rates of less than 1 percent annually, for the duration of the decade. Such sluggish growth combined with the additional production capacity will only put greater pressure on U.S. manufacturers to remain cost competitive, as new entries from Korea, Brazil, Taiwan, and Yugoslavia increasingly flood the

American market. One effective strategy for meeting this new combination of forces is for the Big-3 U.S. manufacturers to increase the number of captive imports from countries like Mexico, countries in which massive investments have transformed production to world-class status, in terms of increased quality, increased productivity, and reduced costs.

Given the recent achievements in productivity in Mexico it appears very likely that the Big-3 will increase the integration of Mexican operations into their North American marketing plans. Such an integration will include the production of the most sophisticated parts, such as drivetrains and motors, as well as finished vehicles. It is also very likely that Mexico's growing importance will have major consequences for U.S. subsidiaries in Canada as evidenced by the reorganization of Chevrolet-Pontiac/Canada. One result is already clear; as in the United States, Mexican automotive production will become increasingly rationalized with Canadian marketing plans and in the near future we will have a much more integrated North American automotive industry, at least as far as the Big-3 are concerned.

NOTES

1. Leopoldo Solis, and Ernesto Zedillo, "The Foreign Debt of Mexico," *International Debt and The Developing Countries* (Washington, D.C.: World Bank, 1985), p. 260.

2. Inter-American Development Bank, *Annual Report: 1986*, Washington, D.C.: IDB, p. 2.

3. Vehicle production in 1980 totalled 8,010,374. This was down from 11,391,867 in 1979; 1981 figures were lower still at 7,981,167; and 1982 figures were the lowest at 6,876,034. *Automotive News (1986 Market Data Book Issue)*, Detroit, MI: 1986, p. 3.

4. Asociacion Mexicana De La Industria Automotriz, A.C. (AMIA), *La Industria Automotriz En Cifras* (Mexico City: MX, 1986), p. 105.

5. AMIA, p. 159.

6. AMIA, p. 53.

7. AMIA, p. 53.

8. See Table 12.1.

9. See Table 12.1.

10. Secretaria de Programacion y Presupuesto (SPP), *La Industria Automotriz En Mexico* (Mexico City: MX, 1981), p. 130; and SPP, *La Industria Automotriz En Mexico* (Mexico City: MX, 1984), p. 116.

11. SPP, *La Industria*, 1981, 1984.

12. American Chamber of Commerce of Mexico (AMCHAM), "The Mexican Economy: 1985 Results and Prospects for 1986," *Business Mexico*, February 1986, p. 26.

13. Various issues of *Business Mexico*.

14. AMIA, *"La Industria Automotriz Terminal En 1986,"* Mexico City: Enero, 1987, p. 35.

15. AMIA, "La Industria," p. 3.

16. AMIA, "La Industria," p. 31.

17. *Automotive News (1986 Market Data)*, p. 3.

18. See, especially, United States International Trade Commission (USITC), "The Internationalization of the Automobile Industry and Its Effects on the U.S. Automobile Industry," *USITC Publication 1712*, (Washington, D.C.: USITC June 1985).

19. USITC, "The Internationalization of the Automobile Industry," p. 79.

20. Stephen Downer, "Ford in Hermosillo," *Automotive News*, November 24, 1986, p. 2.

21. *USITC Publication 1712*; and "Prospects for the Mexican Automotive Industry in the Late 1980s," *International Motor Business* (London: Economist Publications, April 1986), pp. 3–20.

22. USITC, "Prospects for the Mexican Automotive Industry," pp. 3–20.

23. Stephen Downer, "Mexican Auto Industry Banking on Export Boom," *Automotive News*, February 9, 1987, p. 2.

24. See Tables 12.1 and 12.2.

25. AMIA, "La Industria Automotriz Terminal," pp. 33, 35.

26. AMIA, "La Industria Automotriz Terminal," pp. 33, 35.

27. AMIA, "La Industria Automotriz Terminal," pp. 33, 35.

28. U.S. International Trade Commission, *The U.S. Automobile Industry: Monthly Report on Selected Economic Indicators* (Washington, D.C.: USITC, December 1986), pp. 2–3. All statistical information in this section of the chapter is from this report.

29. Special thanks for their help and insights must be given to the Ford and Chrysler executives in Mexico City and to the U.S. Department of Commerce officials, especially Dick Benson.

PART SIX

ENERGY: COMMON OBJECTIVES AND COMMON PROBLEMS

Two important events during the last ten years have caused major changes in the North American energy picture. First, in the late 1960s the United States became a net importer of oil. Secondly, shortly after that, in the early 1970s Mexico became a major oil producer. This combination also changed the economic relations between the two countries. The United States, by far the largest consumer of oil in the world, found a new, closer, and much more reliable source of supply. Mexico, on the other hand, found a very large market for its newly found—or rediscovered—exportable product. This combination has great potentials to benefit both countries, and has thus created a commonality of interest not often seen in bilateral relations between the two neighboring countries.

More than any other commodity, oil is an international product. Every country's oil policies must take into account policies of other countries. The United States and Mexico, despite their relative isolation from other producing and consuming regions have to function within the general framework of international oil markets, and are affected by events in these markets. In the first of three chapters in Part Six, David Hawk presents an analytical evaluation of the policies managing—or mismanaging—the energy picture for the United States, the world's largest consumer of petroleum products. His emphasis is on the role of myths, particularly the myth that the United States has an infinite supply of energy resources, in governing what America does and how it does it.

In Chapter 14, José Barrera-Flores looks at the other side of the picture, that is, the producing side. Mexico is a major producer and exporter of oil and thus subject to the market's volatility. Specifically, the author analyzes the effect of the instability of the international oil market on Mexico during 1986. Particularly important is his presentation of policy changes which became necessary to combat the drop in oil prices, and the ultimate impact of these contracting policies on the Mexican economy.

Finally, in Chapter 15, Farhad Simyar extends the hypothesis of Chapter 14 to other countries. He provides an analysis of the impact of changes in oil prices on the global energy picture. He portrays the "winners" and "losers" of oil price changes and concludes that contrary to common belief, the main "winner" of the last major price increase was not OPEC or any individual OPEC country; rather it was the industrialized West, particularly the United Kingdom, which was able to accelerate the costly and previously uneconomical exploration and drilling of its North Sea oil, thus becoming a major oil producer. He also argues that the "shortage" that preceded the last major oil increase was not caused by OPEC producers nor by the Iranian revolution. Rather it was the consuming nations and *their* multinational companies that perpetrated the shortfall to make price escalations possible.

13

Powering the American Eagle: The U.S. Energy Myth and Its Probable Consequences

David L. Hawk

INTRODUCTION

The role of myths in governing what America does and how it does it provides the central theme of this chapter. Emphasis is on a particular American myth and how it has led to serious economic and environmental problems within the nation and with its trading partners. The myth is that the United States has infinite energy and material resources for industrial production.

Problems with U.S. industrial production cost and quality stem from a myth about resources. Production inefficiencies, low product qualities, and growing environmental externalities all somehow relate back to an absence of concern for efficient use of valuable material and energy resources. Except for narrow measures of labor productivity, Americans have yet to develop a concern for improving all dimensions of production efficiency.

The value system that organizes and manages U.S. production presumes material and energy resources as infinite inputs of uniform quality. Improving the use efficiency of these valuable and scarce resources will probably require change in America's economic values and the myth that organizes them: the myth of the autonomous American Eagle.

MYTHS: WHAT ARE THEY?

The contents of this chapter presume socioeconomic myths as helpful means to examine and improve economic purposes, motivations, and actions. Myths are not presumed to be necessarily good or bad. They are presumed to need periodic inspection, recognition for what they are, and receptivity to improvement. That the United States needs sustainable improvement in what it does and how it does it is a given. One means to accomplish this may be via upgrading the myth that guides its economic decisions.

Myths provide essential underpinnings to most socioeconomic and political activity. They are ambiguous and powerful. They are not amenable to traditional analysis methods. Digital distinctions like real or imaginary, good or bad do not open up a myth. Myths are more like a virtual point in mathematics; difficult to actually see, but for all practical purposes there and very useful.

Experience in industrial work settings illustrates that improving tangible actions requires improving the factors that motivate the actions. These factors often exist in a complex hierarchy that begins with myths and ends with some action, or inaction. Considerable work in U.S. companies by Hasan Ozbekhan, Eric Trist, and Russell Ackoff of the Wharton School of Finance illustrates the critical importance of accessing the underlying motivations prior to attempting to improve the manifestations. Where factors of motivation appear weak, the goals that guide purposeful action are probably also weak. Where goals and purposes of an industrial organization are found to lack focus or relevance, then a broad-based search for a new mission must begin. This is often called corporate futures planning, organizational ecology, or idealized design. Common to all these approaches is the need to access the myths that give collective meaning to what an economic organization is, does, and how effectively it does it. A myth is similar to Plato's concept of the idea or the ideal, except that it is more operational. The contents of this chapter relate to this body of knowledge, but differ in that the subject is a nation of companies and citizens, not a single company.

The concept of this chapter was initiated with a concern about the mission, motivations, and actions of the U.S. economy. A case is presented that U.S. difficulties result from trouble with its sponsoring myth. The myth has structured the nation's perspective toward its resources, or those in other countries which the U.S. has access to, and how they are to be used. Serious difficulties do exist with regard to industrial production. These may in part relate to basic resources and their use. It is clear that radical changes are taking place and the United States must in some way respond. It must correct its myth, its measures of progress, or its national economic position.

The myth of General Motors as the largest and most profitable auto company in the world, and a flagship North American Corporation, exemplifies the problem analyzed herein. G.M. has suffered serious setbacks. Its purposes, motivations, and actions are in doubt. So too is the national context of G.M. Both the company and the nation were built on a definition of efficiency and a set of environmental assumptions that are no longer valid or appropriate. It may seem a bit too poetic but history clearly illustrates that when an organization's myth dies the organization dies. It is proposed that the United States is an organization and that its organizing myth is in trouble. These suppositions are examined in the next three sections. Suggestions are made in the final section as to what might be done to improve the situation.

THE IMPORTANCE OF MYTHS

Myths run throughout societies. They organize societies. They provide the basis for a social infrastructure connecting humans to ideas about the state of the world, the state of their nation, and their state of mind. The resulting cultural fabric supports what a society is and where it is headed. A myth holding that chances for a Christian and Islamic afterlife are improved by dying in fierce battles encourages wars to be especially gruesome. A myth that missiles keep peace supports a logical framework where more peace can be purchased through more missiles. A myth that work is important gets us up in the morning. We need to better understand our myths so that we may better manage them. Myths are important in guiding all types of socio-organizational activity. Myths encourage education, innovation, consumption, and lawfulness. Myths unify separate realities. Myths even offer an ethical touchstone for individuals in a quandary about what to do, and what to refrain from doing. Myths are critical to religious, political, and economic activity. They may be even more important in complex modern societies than they were in prehistoric settings. Modern individuals appear dangerously fragmented and disassociated, and in need of meaningful connections.

Organizing myths continually change and evolve through decay, disintegration, renewal, and adaptation. The rate of change varies with the myth. Myths that hold empires and nations together are generally more enduring than those that support architectural, culinary, or clothing styles. Myths tend to be ambiguously defined. As such, they can attract and hold a large variety of interpretations and reinterpretations. Some tangible evidence of a myth's relevance is helpful, but can be changed to fit the needs of circumstance. A family in the 1960s could illustrate American well-being by having opposing symbols of Cadillac excess and Volkswagen economy sitting side-by-side in a driveway. In the 1970s, both became foreign. By the 1980s, both were foreign, but once again more expensive and less efficient. Economic myths can support especially strange forms of logic and human behaviors. A myth that international economic competition is fair when you sell more than you buy, and unfair when you buy more than you sell, encourages perverse types of discussions about trade.

Myths can also serve as dividers. Different myths allow for differences of culture, perception, and organization. This can be beneficial, as in the difference between oriental and occidental cultural traditions, or harmful, as in the bitter differences between Marxian and capitalistic economic analysis. Some myths are specifically designed to emphasize boundaries and their maintenance. Others emphasize the beneficial exchanges that differences make possible. A myth can give purpose to a social group and mobilize its membership. Aspirations, dreams, or fears set in motion by a myth can release and organize human energies and capabilities. When and where these binding agents disappear, organizations soon follow. As was stated at the outset, when an organization's myth dies the organization follows. New myths can of course be found, or created, but when an organization's myth is changed, so too is the intrinsic nature of the organization.

THE AMERICAN MYTH: WHAT IS ITS BASIS?

Much American literature references the "Myth of the Frontier" and gives it a leading role in bringing development to a wild land, rich with virtually limitless material and energy resources. The shortage was seen in the form of people needed to exploit the natural resources. "Frontier" men and women were imported and organized via a pioneering myth. Vast material resources were turned into products and distributed to world markets. Abundant energy reserves were critical to each stage of U.S. industrial production. Wood, water, coal, oil, natural gas, and then uranium became critical to growing energy needs associated with the transforming of raw materials into finished products, and the distribution of those products to local and world markets.

The quality of U.S. products steadily increased through an increase in the number of transformations of raw materials entering the industrial process. Growing inputs of energy was the key. Declining relative inputs of labor and its role was one result. The basic measure of success, productivity of labor, showed this trend to be desirable. Iron ore was transformed into pig iron, into wrought iron, into low-strength steel, into high-strength steel, and then into an array of final products like core-ten steel. At each stage an increased input of energy and capital was required and a decreased input of human labor resulted. Signs began to emerge in the 1950s that energy resources might prove to be a limiting factor, but nuclear material was raised as an energy source that would support the escalation process infinitely. Electricity made with nuclear power plants was to become so cheap that it wouldn't pay to meter its use. Waste and garbage was to become completely recyclable and thus another nonproblem. By the 1960s both dreams were in doubt.

It is now accepted that certain critical material resources are very limited and that economical energy resources are quite limited. Material substitution, seen as an important way to short-circuit the problem, is now seen as a difficulty strategy. Substitution tends to be energy intensive. The myth of unlimited American resources lacks its essential manifestations. It is essentially dead. People waiting for energy prices to decline and for industrial production to pick up no longer see themselves as the critical economic resource. Except for books like Kahn and Simon's *The Resourceful Earth*, population growth is perceived as more of a global problem than a global solution. Written as a direct response against the Carter presidency's pessimistic *The Year 2000 Report*, this overly optimistic thesis seems to only continue America's underlying dilemmas. Meanwhile the evidence supporting the central organizing myth of the United States, that a nation with unlimited natural resources, continues to dry up while pollution piles up. The American Eagle, symbol of a rich and proud nation, is now as endangered as is the myth it stimulated.

The pioneering spirit behind the myth of the unfettered eagle soaring above the limitations of the land-locked has supported an array of economic beliefs and practices. These are clearly seen in Adam Smith's *Wealth of Nations*. The relationship between America's central myth and the economic principles in Smith's book is predictable. The book and the nation emerged at about the same time. To be sure, many of the ideas in *Wealth of Nations* are stimulating, but the world of 1987 is a very different place than the world of 1787. Human motivations may not have changed much in 200 years, but numbers of humans and the settings in which they "each try to maximize their own narrow self-interests" have changed markedly. The quantity and quality of natural resources have significantly declined while humans with wants and desires have exponentially expanded. Via worldwide television and telecommunications, U.S. versions of dreams, wants, and consumption habits have become a global norm.

Just as myths evolve, so too do economic ideas and practices. Toynbee described this via the shifting economic dominance and relevance of nations in his book *The Rise and Fall of Nations*. Spengler did likewise in his focus on the underlying phenomena involved in the *Decline of the West*. Braudel clarified the material, energy, and technological forces at work in both phenomena in his three-part series on *Civilization & Capitalism 15th–18th Century*. These works offer some advice about the American energy myth and its probable consequences. They also give grounds for some optimism in the human capabilities in creatively redefining and reorganizing socioeconomic action. This is where new forms of economic exchange evolve and connect diverse sets of people with diverse values, needs, and resources and can lead to mutual improvement of all participants.

A means to study a myth's affect and effects is to look at the differences in its economic results and consequences. Hasan Ozbekhan has illustrated the important difference between results, which are those things you seek to achieve, and consequences, which are those things that confront you once your intentions are realized. Even where consequences are not bad, their unexpected nature causes them to destabilize the intended results. John Brunner, in his book, *The Compleat Traveller in Black*, outlines the critical importance of this distinction in human affairs. The "traveller" would go around and initiate great distress in various communities and give them their poorly considered wants and allow them to realize their ambitions.

INSIDE THE AMERICAN MYTH: WHAT ARE ITS VALUES?

Many current U.S. economic problems may result from its founding myth: a belief that America was a nation of entrepreneurial pioneers that were given a frontier rich with unlimited natural resources and a manifest destiny to exploit them via maximization of many individual satisfactions. Symbolized by the high-flying, autonomous eagle, the myth of America has made the United States one of the most powerful forces in the modern world. Recently, the nation has begun to lose this economic and political dominance.

There are two contrasting ways of arguing about the decline and how best to reverse it; it is also possible to accept it as predetermined. The first position is the most politically popular. It proposes that the "eagle" has been shackled and restrained by too much regulation of economic development and has tolerated too much harassment from its international enemies. The obvious strategy to rectify this is to set the eagle free, so that it may once again fly high and rediscover its greatness. Deregulation and military strength are the two operational tactics for achieving this end.

The second argument, one that is seldom heard from politicians who want to be elected, is that fundamental flaws were built into the initial American myth, causing it to be inconsistent with reality. Parts of the 1980 presidential election addressed this via debate about *The Year 2000 Report* and why Americans needed to change or not change. One side of this debate turned out to be very indigestible and unpopular. The same dilemmas still exist for the next general election, except that they may have grown larger. Instead of giving the eagle great doses of capital injections or fanning its posterior to get it airborne, the strategy behind this argument is to seek a new national myth, and build a new production consensus around it. Based on current evidence, the new myth must be stimulating, robust, and appreciative of current international economic and resource problems. It must clearly address long-term global population/political/pollution realities.

America's resource myth was initiated and supported by immigrants finding bountiful resources near the ocean upon arrival. Rich forests and thick topsoil were everywhere. Resources appeared to be so plentiful that a perception emerged that they could be used and abused in any manner desired. Settlers presumed resources to be infinitely available. Whenever and wherever problems emerged the people could simply move, and take their guiding myth with them. Once horizontal mobility became a problem, a second great myth was adopted: that new technologies would be invented to allow Americans to resolve, sidestep or ignore whatever resource problems they had created or might encounter. Widespread development and use of high-rise architecture in the United States is one manifestation of this dream. Even though skyscraper development was first conceived in Europe, it found a very sympathetic context in the United States. Via technological development, the frontier definition of progress could continue unabated.

The myth of technological avoidance linked back to support the earlier resource myth. America became technologically sophisticated in a very short time. Present evidence points out that it may have been largely due to the arrival of a great influx of diverse, highly-motivated, and well-trained foreign nationals. With the support of these intellectual resources Americans came to assume that they were and would always be the world's undisputed leaders of "smart" technologies. Even the term smart came to be used in a peculiarly American way. It came to be associated with being able to get something from nothing, and at very little initial cost; that is, getting someone else to pay for lunch. The June 1981 issue of *Fortune* magazine clearly illustrates the momentum of this continuing desire to be successful through being smart. They set out to translate 30 years of European experience in improving quality of working life and quality of production into a value system that Americans could relate to. They chose the unfortunate phrase of "Working Smart" as an American replacement for European "Working Quality."

Narrow measures of economic efficiency and national development were derived to support an agenda for development which did not have to pay attention to natural resources and could place an emphasis on labor reduction, technological change, and smart strategies. These measures became basic to American approaches to industrialization; approaches that now are at the center of current resource dilemmas involving shortages, misuse, and abuse.

National problem-solving through movement had ceased to be an option by the twentieth century. Space travel was the only refuge for human flight from humanly generated troubles. By the 1960s, Americans began to look back on what was left in the wake of their rapid economic development. Tentative speculation began as to what growing externalities meant for their children's future. Abandoned urban centers, vacant factories, redundant social groups, acidic lakes, despoiled forests, rural wastelands, garbage sites, toxic waste dumps, and polluted watersheds spotted the nation's historic beauty. The founding American myth, and its measures, appeared ripe for a very intense and critical evaluation.

Americans' first response was to try to outlaw the consequences of the results of their economic development via extensive social welfare programs and pollution control laws. By the 1980s it was obvious that the causes of these serious problems had yet to be addressed. The underlying operating assumptions and their supporting myth were untouched. The problem becomes more serious as other nations adopt variations of the American myth for their own national economic development.

Present knowledge points out that the nation and the eagle that guides it depend on the healthfulness of the political, economic, and natural environments in which they operate. It has become very dangerous to continue to perceive either as an autonomous entity with no context. Pollution abundance and energy shortages have caused Americans to experience first indications of their interdependencies with others. Energy shortages provided some of the most tangible evidence that something was wrong with the nation's myth. Even if energy were unlimited, the bottomless oil wells and infinite uranium mines were often under the control of other nations, that were sometimes unfriendly and often very entrepreneurial in their own right; that is, they had also read Adam Smith.

Regardless of this initial learning, two levels of disagreement about energy and material resources continue. The first level is whether or not energy and material resource limits are an important issue to a nation. The second is whether the importance is due to limits or is arranged by sinister national and/or corporate forces. Once limits are assumed to be important, there is general agreement as to the economic consequences of shortages in these essential industrial resoures, regardless of whether the limits are "real" or "fabricated." The oil shortages of 1973 and 1974 helped U.S. citizens learn this. The debate continues as to what or who was responsible. Current U.S. dependence for almost 40 percent of its petroleum needs, and 90 percent of U.S. strategic metal needs obtained from outside national borders provides the probable basis for future U.S. learning.

Even assuming limits are not a problem, or a problem that can be managed, there exist serious dangers in the way in which U.S. citizens and companies make use of resources. Environmental degradation and the health dangers that accompany it are growing. Finding sufficient sites for garbage and controlling ocean dumping are only the most recent chapters in this unfolding story. Pollution residues are as limited or as unlimited as the resources whose refinement and use produce them. To avoid some of the socioeconomic dramas, dramatic changes are needed in how Americans perceive themselves and their natural resources. The United States finds itself in an interdependent global context where human time and energy are plentiful, energy and material resources are limited, uneconomical and/or unevenly distributed. A new, more robust myth is needed.

POWERING THE AMERICAN EAGLE: HOW WILL IT LAND?

America was shocked in 1974 to find out that energy was important to economic organization and that our link to it had become very fragile. By 1981, the nation, and its chosen political leaders, had learned little more than how to ignore the education of eight years prior. One of those that had been very concerned in 1974, M. A. Adelman of M.I.T., recently warned that once again: "We could have a crisis just as phony as the others, and just as painful, if we do things which are as foolish as what we did before with price and allocation controls. I'm afraid that's going to happen again."[1]

The United States, the world's leading energy consumer, is distinctly not its leading producer and is producing less with time. Oil and natural gas are the main sources of energy in industrial economies, thus quantities of reserves of both is an important issue. So too is their national location. Table 13.1 provides the distribution of proven oil and gas reserves as of 1987. It gives an overview of the potential dangers for a nation, like the

United States, whose economic systems depend on other nations for about 40 percent of energy requirements.

The underlying dilemma for the United States only begins in this table. The small percentage of U.S. oil and gas reserves, relative to its consumption, is indeed quite significant (4 percent world reserves versus 33 percent of world consumption), but the difference is even greater if the high cost and low qualitative potential of U.S. crude oil is factored into the equation. This is easily done by giving a factor to the cost effectiveness of each barrel to perform work. This then includes the qualitative potential of the resource. This allows for an important distinction between high and low quality resources and recognizes that economic resources are always heterogeneous. This may ultimately prove to be the most important variable in determining economic efficiencies that underlie international trade. Table 13.2 gives a numeric indication of this point.

America's resource dilemma is further exacerbated when the information from the Tables 13.1 and 13.2 is combined. Saudi oil and gas end up with 60 times the potential to perform economic work as that of U.S. oil and gas, that is, it has 60 times the economic value. This is due to qualitative and accessibility differences in the raw material. Each has a different thermodynamic potential to perform economic work due to the quantity of

Table 13.1
Total Known Gas and Oil Reserves in the World

MILLION

NATION	BARRELS OF OIL/GAS	% OF WORLD
Saudi Arabia	171,000	24.5%
Kuwait	92,000	13.0%
Soviet Union	61,000	8.7%
Mexico	49,000	7.0%
Iran	48,000	6.9%
Iraq	44,000	6.3%
United Arab Emerates	33,000	4.7%
United States	28,000	4.0%
Venezuela	26,000	3.7%
United Kingdom	13,000	2.0%
Norway	11,000	1.6%
Others	126,000	17.7%

Source: American Petroleum Institute, Washington, D.C., 1987.

Table 13.2
Relative Thermodynamic Potential of Different Types of Crude Oil

NATION	PRODUCTION COST/BARREL
Saudi Arabia	$ 0.50
United Kingdom/Norway	$18.00
Marginal U.S. Producers	$30.00

Source: American Petroleum Institute, Washington, D.C., 1987.

work that must first be invested. Discovered in 1851, this type of difference was key to development of the engines of industrial revolution. A resource with high potential meant that little work needed to be performed on the resource prior to it being able to add economic value. Relating this traditional engineering knowledge to current economic analysis needs requires further interpretation and experimentation. It needs to be applied to an array of operating facilities so that its role in measuring new kinds of efficiency can be assessed. It may prove to be what is needed to avoid some serious crises that are looming on our horizon. As Robert Hirsh recently expressed the concern in Science Magazine:

The National Dilemma. . . . It is clear that there are a number of options that could stop the current slide into extreme national dependence on foreign oil. However, because none are simple, because people are generally happy with lower energy prices, and because the country tends to be short-term oriented, there appears to be a low probability of action before that problem becomes severe. It is for these reasons that a future energy crisis seems likely, probably sometime in the early to mid-1990s, when oil dependence is above 50% and OPEC has regained control of world oil markets.[2]

Part of this may be the result of the historic U.S. perspective on resources and their use; that is, the U.S. energy myth. As Hirsh continues: ". . . the U.S. government and the oil and gas industries are oriented toward the short-term and the cheap answers to problems that need time, money, and sophisticated solutions."[3]

TOWARD A NEW NATIONAL RESOURCE MYTH

Whatever else it needs, a more robust myth will require finding or designing a new set of American values and a revaluation of America's mission in the world. A change in our trading relationships will certainly occur in the near future, and it may not be in support of our standard of living. Historical records paint a pessimistic scenario for any nation that needs to change as much and as rapidly as the United States. The record of empires like those of Egypt, Persia, Greece, Rome, France, England, and Germany show this. What should America do as its eagle comes in for a landing? One approach is to carefully look at our trading partners to try to see why they are so much more successful in international trade.

The argument that keeps Americans from doing this is that our trading partners are unfair. Much public information says that our trading partners are successful because they have been very good at using public funds to support industrial interests. Public resources are unfairly used to support prices and to discourage consumption of foreign products. The predictable conclusion is that these countries must be pressured into having a "free economy," where the market price approximates the actual cost of production.

There is considerable evidence that government "interference" occurs, and that it occurs in all nations. In the neglected international trading areas of food and shelter products there are obvious examples of heavy direct subsidies by governments. The United States is itself heavily emerged in subsidizing production in these two areas. Food and buildings are important and growing sectors of national and international accounts, yet U.S. agriculture concerns receive about $30 billion per year directly in subsidies. The building industry receives even more support via liberal tax deduction policies. Neither subsidy is necessarily wrong, but exists. The hypocrisy keeps the discussion from getting into and focusing on underlying inefficiencies of production. These inefficiencies may be directly tied to resource use and abuse.

Another approach to our trading dilemma is that our trading partners are simply more efficient at producing quality goods. While the evidence is not yet clear, there are strong signs that U.S. industry is inefficient in the design, organization, and management of production activities. The analytical dilemma is that these forms of inefficiency are not traditionally measured nor discussed. They simply don't show up in traditional accounting practices of short-term, bottom-line, or financially-oriented production. The United States, with its rich raw material base, may have become spoiled and as a consequence be stuck with inefficient approaches and practices. An easy way to study this would be to compare our use of material and energy resources with trading partners like Japan and Korea, which import many of the resources needed in production. Initial study shows that they get about 25 percent more product and produce about 40 percent less waste from comparable U.S. resource inputs.

The United States continues to measure efficiency via its frontier ethic, as if people's time is the scarce resource, and materials and energy are without real limits. If a man-day can be saved by wasting a ton of material, traditional calculations will generally support doing it. Equally as serious is the attitude toward product quality that is initiated and/or supported by the resource attitude. If 100 man-days can be saved by allowing 10 percent of the products to go out with defects, it is assumed to be a good short-term business decision. Advertising studies support this logic. They show that consumers don't recognize or appreciate quality anyway. If it can be produced a good salesperson will find a buyer for it. Quality of design and production are secondary to financial and accounting concerns. As long as

U.S. car companies could generate a startling new product facade each year, it was assumed smart to retain the same basic mechanical and ergonomic design for 30 years.

The dilemma for the United States is that its chief trading partners failed to believe this. They read different books and found alternative, more efficient myths. Honda's 1974 studies told them that quality and efficiency was very important in the minds of U.S. consumers. It was found that consumers also liked the two characteristics of quality and efficiency to be complementary, not in opposition. Hondas are now very important to U.S. consumers.

Traditional measures of productivity and economic succcess have somehow led us astray. Our national productivity measures appear to tell us that we are more or less okay, yet there is a lot of unsold product sitting around, and next door is a lot of by-product waste. This is like the man with his head in an oven and his feet in an icebox, and with a mean temperature of 98.6 degrees. From the average number, he appears to be quite healthy.

The United States has adopted one of many ways to do business. It is time to experiment with some of the alternatives to business as usual in U.S. industry. This objective has been the central subject matter of several recent National Science Foundation Workshops. In one in particular, the contents showed a close relation to problems in North American economies. Even though the central subject matter was building economics, the important issues were resources and international production.

SECOND LAW ECONOMICS: WHAT WAS THE FIRST LAW?

Held at the New Jersey Institute of Technology over Memorial Day Weekend in 1985, the Building Economics meeting was to be a critical examination of the national and emerging international building industries, where they were going, and what were their analytical needs. Representatives from seven nations attended the meeting. An array of dilemmas, later found to be common to almost all economic sectors, were initially discussed. These included the predictable issues of techniques for industrial production, influence of government regulation on product design and production efficiency, policies for encouraging innovative technologies, techniques of input-output analysis, relevance of utility theory, use of computers in the industry, and role of international tariffs and duties. The less predictable issues of resource use and abuse, and the inefficiencies that this supports emerged in the discussion. The detailed contents of the meeting can be examined in the final report of the workshop.[4]

The interesting point for this chapter is that after two days of discussion, the participants became frustrated with the cyclical arguments of the issues being important yet the researchers had little analytical power to predict or analyze them. From this comment it was noted that many of the industry's problems somehow related to material and energy use and abuse. Within parts of the industry, materials accounted for 80 percent of product cost leaving the factory. In the part of the industry responsible for building operations, it was noted that three years of energy operating costs can exceed the initial capital cost of the building. But somehow the primary methods of evaluating the effectiveness of the industry and its products were productivity increases through reduction of labor and reduction of cost of the product in anyway allowable within the limits of building laws.

The participants felt that if resource issues could be included in the analysis of what constitutes a high-quality, efficient product, then many seemingly intractable issues could be managed. A Japanese representative presented a paper on how some aspects of this agenda were already being researched and taught in their universities, and experimented with by their industry. While the results had not been very satisfactory, he felt it was a beginning. A more comprehensive schema was required.

Nicholas Georgescu-Roegen, Professor Emeritus of Vanderbilt University, participated in the last two days of the meeting. He provided a great deal of mythical and analytical insight into problems in economic analysis and how these might be avoided or resolved via the opportunities in starting a new area of analysis like building economics. He argued that this area did not have to be constrained by the shortcomings built into classical economic theory. Between his mathematics and myths was a strong optimism in the potentials awaiting the economizing of U.S. industry. He pointed out why products of the building industry were an especially interesting place to begin experimentation with economizing.

The building industry is the nation's largest single user of material and energy supplies; in addition, many of the nation's pollutants and wastes result from the making of buildings and products for buildings. There is great inefficiency and waste in both of these areas of production. If, as mentioned above, 80 percent of a product's cost comes from materials, then saving material at the expense of labor may prove to be a profitable venture. It can also encourage higher quality of the product. Japanese home manufacturing industries have already discovered this idea. Resource considerations have become central considerations for their relatively efficient, high-quality production.

This approach requires a different form of evaluation and methods of measurement. Some U.S. construction industry companies are laughing at these types of concerns and the companies that are trying to develop them. Their argument is that the building industry is and always will be a locally-based and controlled industry. This may be similar to the U.S. auto companies poking fun at those well-made, efficient little foreign cars in 1972.

Central to the resource approach to economic analysis of production is the concept of entropy and its role in the economic process. Georgescu-Roegen books describe the how and why of classical economics ignoring the entropy process in its analysis. The entropy law points out how materials and energy are and should be seen as the basis of it all. In quality design they have always been critical. The information in the previous table is one example of entropy analysis. A barrel of oil that is a mile underground, and filled with sulfur, is not as valuable as one that is near the surface and in an almost pure state. Another example is seen in the dilemma encountered in calculating the heating efficiency of a new heating technology. It was found to be 110 percent efficient by traditional methods. Some thought that a perpetual motion machine had finally been discovered. Others thought something was seriously wrong with the method of analysis. Regardless, the company used the analysis to market the product, which turned out to be less efficient then a foreign product. When entropy measures were used to evaluate the same device, measures that took into account the quality of the natural gas fuel going into the process, it was found to be only 6 percent efficient and not a good long-term investment for building heating. These measures need a great deal more work before they can be applied generally to industrial production in North America, but they do at least offer hopeful signs that economic improvement is possible.

CONCLUSIONS

The theoretical work behind the materials and energy approach to efficiency is usually rejected as too "crackpot" or pessimistic for American tastes to ever adopt. It is considered more in line with European pessimism and/or oriental mysticism, but incompatible with American optimism. Regardless, it deserves some serious attention in the United States. The first stage of this would be experiments with a different attitude and measures of industrial efficiency. This could lead to changes in many aspects of measures used to evaluate industrial production.

For example, U.S. industry often uses oil and gas to produce very tightly controlled quantities of specialized heat required in process. Often this fuel is first transformed into electricity, then the electric power is turned into heat energy. This is embarassing on two fronts. It is about as efficient as taking the power from a waterfall and first turning it into heat energy prior to letting it act as mechanical energy to drive the turbines. There would be significant loss in each transformation. It is also much more polluting in that it generates considerably more heat and particle wastes via the additional transformations. This logic of production efficiency persists. Perhaps it is due to presumptions that electricity is easier to work with and thus will save worker time.

A much more robust myth is needed for the United States. It has been argued that a materials and energy resource efficiency approach is one viable alternative worth some experimentation. Under the title of Second Law Economics, economics that appreciates the Second Law of Thermodynamics, this approach could illustrate that doing the right thing is also the profitable thing, especially over the long term. It is a context building and not a context using approach. When the context is in motion, as it appears to be now, this could be the appropriate strategy for the next several decades.

NOTES

1. *Insight*, February 23, 1987.
2. Robert Hirsh, "Impending United States Energy Crisis," *Science*, March 20, 1987.
3. Hirsh, "Impending United States Energy Crisis."
4. David L. Hawk, ed., *Building Economics Research Agenda* (Washington, D.C.: National Technical Service, 1986).

14

Impact of the International Oil Market on the Mexican Economy

José G. Barrera-Flores

INTRODUCTION

During the past several years the Mexican economy has faced many difficulties in its attempt to achieve growth and stability, which have led to a severe economic crisis. While the explanations as to the origin of this crisis and possible solutions differ widely, there would appear to be a consensus with respect to the extreme dependency of the economy upon oil exports. The instability of the international oil market since 1981 has had negative effects upon the growth of the Mexican economy, while the fall in the international crude oil prices and the decrease in the world market share during 1986 demonstrate the high level of petrolization and fragility of the economy.

Within a framework of structural economic problems, the loss of approximately $8.5 billion in oil exports in 1986 and the lack of foreign financial resources served merely to worsen the country's economic crisis. In this context the purpose of this chapter is to analyze the effects of the evolution of the international oil market on the Mexican economy, with particular emphasis on the balance of payments and public finance. At the same time, the chapter summarizes the main economic strategies implemented by the government in order to minimize the effects of the oil shock.

MEXICAN OIL EXPORTS AND THE INTERNATIONAL OIL MARKET

The third international oil market crisis developed during 1986, creating an additional problem for oil-exporting countries. While the previous crises (1973-1974 and 1979-1980) eventually ended with substantial increases in crude oil prices, and a strengthening of the Organization of the Petroleum Exporting Countries (OPEC), the third crisis proved different. In the first quarter of 1986 the international crude oil price plummeted amidst a climate of great market instability, worsening the interal and external disequilibria faced by oil-exporting countries.

The principal cause of the third oil crisis was OPEC's decision to increase its participation in the international market, primarily in response to the greater shares being captured in recent years by non-OPEC producers. This decision, made at an OPEC meeting in December 1985, marked a radical change in OPEC strategy. Since 1981 the policy of the Organization had been to defend oil prices by means of production cuts even when this meant a loss in its market share.

The combination of the excess supply of world oil generated by this new policy, along with several million barrels per day (MMBD) of idle capacity created a price war among oil-exporting countries.[1] This served only to further destabilize the market and cause prices to fall. The price crash was so pronounced that in a matter of a few short months the average price of 13 selected export crudes fell from $26 dollars per barrel in December 1985 to less than $10 per barrel in July 1986.[2]

Within this arena of uncertainty, and as a measure of prevention against the repercussions the fall in prices could have, the Mexican authorities modified their pricing policy in order to ensure that Mexican oil remained competitive in the world market.

In the second quarter of 1986 OPEC decided to change its strategy again primarily as a result of the reduction in its oil export revenues. OPEC returned to its policy of establishing individual production quotas, with the objective of obtaining market stability and higher oil prices. This measure represented production cuts of more than 3.0 MMBD in September in comparison to August, and was strengthened by the support it soon received from other oil-exporting countries. Mexico was among the nations to support this strategy, with an actual cut of 10 percent (from 1.50 to 1.35 MMBD). This new policy of the oil exporters caused international crude prices to recuperate in the final months of the year, to almost $15 per barrel in December.

Throughout this situation, many oil-exporting countries were seriously affected, not only because of loss of foreign exchange but due to their reduced world market participation. In the Mexican case, its crude oil sales, which had been estimated for programming and budgeting of the public sector at 1.5 MMBD, with an average price of $22.60 per barrel fell to 1.282 MMBD, with an average price of $11.82.[3] In other words, Mexican crude oil exports dropped from an estimated level of 12.4 billion to a mere $5.58 billion. At the same time, given the link that exists between crude oil prices and those of petroleum-based products, Mexican exports of these goods were reduced from an expected value of $1.3 billion to only $640 million.

Total oil export revenues generated in 1986 were $6.171 billion, representing a net reduction of $7.5 billion in comparison with the year's estimate and a reduction of $8.5 billion with respect to 1985. The value of this reduction represented more than 5 percent of the gross domestic product of Mexico, which illustrates the magnitude of the oil shock on the Mexican economy.

MEXICAN ECONOMIC POLICY

Throughout 1986 Mexican authorities responded to the instability in the international oil market with economic policies designed to absorb the oil shock. With this in mind, on February 21, 1986, the federal government announced ten measures designed primarily to minimize the external effects on public finance and balance of payments, to obtain financial resources from the banking system in order to finance the public deficit, and to maintain exchange rate stability.[4]

With respect to the public finance sector, the government carried out expenditure cuts, primarily in investment projects, and increased government income by means of a more flexible tariff and pricing policy for goods and services produced by the public sector. At the same time, a tight credit policy was announced, restricting the availability of financial resources to the private sector. Similarly, interest rates were raised, with the purpose of increasing financial savings by offering positive real interest rates. This measure was implemented in conjunction with a foreign exchange policy designed to reduce capital flight. Finally, the Mexican peso was devalued with respect to the U.S. dollar with the purpose of strengthening nonpetroleum exports and fostering more efficient import substitution. This economic policy called for a substantial increase in the exchange rate of the Mexican peso with respect to the U.S. dollar throughout 1986.

A few months later, on June 23, 1986, an Integral Stability and Growth Program (ISGP) was announced, with objectives similar to those established in the February proclamation, but with the distinguishing feature of a formal recognition of the need to reduce the net transfer of resources to foreign creditors, as well as the urgent need to protect the worker's real wages.[5] With respect to resource transfers, the Mexican external debt was restructured with extentions on maturity, and a reduction of the rate spread was achieved. As far as purchasing power is concerned, increases in the nominal minimum wage were awarded at a rate almost equalling that of inflation.

The ISG program can be seen as the preparation for a new agreement between Mexico and the International Monetary Fund (IMF), which became public on July 23, 1987.[6] Although the agreement does maintain the basic spirit of IMF programs, two important changes proposed by the Mexican government were included. First, the need to use the operational deficit (which excludes the effect of inflation of debt servicing), instead of the financial deficit as an indicator for evaluating public finance was accepted. Secondly, both sides recognized that the growth and development of the Mexican economy depend upon the behavior of the international oil market.

This latter point had never appeared in any IMF agreement, and would allow the Mexican authorities to obtain contingency credits from international financial institutions should the price of crude fall below the $9.00 per barrel.

ECONOMIC AND FINANCIAL RESULTS

The economic outcome for the Mexican economy during 1986 without doubt depended upon many variables. However, it would appear that the interaction of three fundamental factors can be singled out: the prevailing economic structure; the direct and indirect effects of the oil shock along with the lack of external financial resources; and, the economic policy strategy followed by the authorities.

Concerning the foreign sector, as a result of the aforementioned elements the *balance of payments* in 1986 registered a severe drop in oil exports, some $8.5 billion less than 1985. The plummeting oil exports broke the rather precarious external balance that had been observed since 1982, and its repercussions were soon felt by the rest of the economy. This restricted availability of oil resources forced the financial authorities to accelerate the rate of devaluation of the peso to a yearly rate of 148 percent. This rate represented a depreciation of the peso by 20 percent in real terms.

Among other factors, the increased price of the U.S. currency caused a reduction in the imports of goods and nonfactorial services of some 11.9 percent. This meant a decrease in imports of these types of products from $18.5 billion in 1985 to $16.3 billion in 1986.

At the same time, the exchange rate policy made Mexican nonpetroleum products more competitive in world markets. Exports of these goods grew by some 40 percent over 1985, increasing from $7.0 billion in 1985 to $9.8 billion in 1986, a record figure in the economic history of the country. However, due to the high rate of devaluation in real terms, the generation of foreign exchange from nonfactorial services (in-bond industries, transportation, tourism, border transactions, and other services) grew only a mere 0.3 percent, from $5.945 billion in 1985 to $5.965 billion in 1986.

Primarily as a result of these factors, the 1986 account showed a negative balance of $1.297 billion, after having reported positive results during 1982-1985. In 1985 alone, the surplus was $1.237 billion. Deficit financing registered in 1986 was covered primarily by the capital account surplus, which was in turn partially the result of the return of Mexican capital from abroad. This surplus in the capital account allowed at the same time an increase in the reserves of the Central Bank, a paradoxical result in a country suffering from a severe external shock.

On the other hand, Mexican *public finance* was seriously affected by the decreased income from the oil sector, given the direct relation that exists between federal government income and oil exports from Petroleos Mexicanos (PEMEX, the state-run oil company).[7] The financial deficit of the public sector in 1986 rose to 12.6 trillion pesos, an increase of 36 percent in real terms in comparison to 1985, and representing 16.1 percent of the GDP. Perhaps one of the most important factors in explaining this result is that the income of the federal government derived from oil activity decreased some 35 percent in real terms. This in turn is explained mainly by the fact that PEMEX paid 48 percent less taxes.

Another factor which helps explain the high public sector deficit in 1986 is the growth of interest payments on the public debt, a consequence of high interest rates and steeper foreign exchange rates due to the spiraling inflation. The interest payments during 1986 grew over 15 percent in real terms.

As a result of the positive real returns offered by the *financial system,* as well as a coherent management of both interest rate and foreign exchange policies, the financial sector slightly improved its performance. The higher return on national financial instruments with respect to external ones not only eliminated capital flight, but also allowed for the return of some Mexican capital from abroad. The final destination of a good part of this capital explains the tremendous growth experienced by the Mexican stock market during the year. This latter point illustrates the paradox of a troubled economy and the rapid expansion of the stock market.

The increase in the cost of the American dollar, the high public sector deficit, and the elevated levels of domestic interest rates, among other factors, were translated into a high rate of *inflation.* The consumer price index registered a growth of some 105.7 percent in 1986, after having shown levels of 60 percent and 63 percent in 1984 and 1985, respectively.

In this context of multiple conditioning factors, the *gross domestic product* of Mexico showed a drop of 3.8 percent placing the economy at a level of production smaller than that of 1981, and in terms of income per capita, at lower levels than those registered in 1979.

CONCLUSIONS

The behavior of the international oil market aggravated the economic situation of oil-exporting nations, and Mexico was no exception, suffering in 1986 one of the most difficult years in its economic history.

Although in 1986 economic disaster was narrowly avoided, in spite of predictions by various sources to the contrary, the strategy of economic policy, aimed at absorbing the oil shock, allowed for a reduction of the negative effects, even though the magnitude of the problems surpassed the corrective capacity of the policies.

Perhaps the most damaging effect of the crisis was observed in public finance, where due to its strong reliance upon oil exports, along with its vulnerability in the face of high inflation, a substantial increase in the public sector deficit was registered. At the same time, the current account of the balance of payments showed a high deficit, although much less than had been predicted.

The experience of the Mexican economy during 1986 served to emphasize the degree of dependence that the country has upon the exports of a single product: oil. At the same time, the crisis brought to light the fragility of the balance of payments and public finance in the face of an unfavorable international oil market. Even when it was possible to partially absorb the impact of the external shock, its effects hampered the search solutions to the social and economic problems that were already afflicting the country.

NOTES

1. By comparison, various sources estimate the present idle world capacity at 11-12 billion barrels per day.

2. The 13 selected export crude oils are: Brent, Forcados, Suez Blend, Urales, Dubai, West Texas Intermediate. West Texas Sour, Alaskan North Slope, Iran Light, Iran Heavy, Bonny Light, Isthmus, and Maya.

3. The average 1986 prices were $13.46 per barrel for Isthmus and $10.55 per barrel for Maya. Their participation in the value of exports was 50.5 percent and 49.5 percent respectively, while in volume the numbers were 44.4 percent and 55.5 percent respectively.

4. See Miguel De La Madrid, "Mensaje a la Nacion," *Excelsior,* February 22, 1986.

5. See Federal Government, "Programa de Aliento y Crecimiento," *El Mercado de Valores,* June 30, 1986.

6. See Federal Government, "Carta de Intencion al Fondo Monetario Internacional," *Excelsior,* July 25, 1986.

7. According to the fiscal regime of PEMEX, income earned through foreign sale of crude oil is transferred to the federal government by means of the payment of exploitation rights. The income of the federal government in 1986 programmed for this concept represents 37.9 percent of total budgeted income.

15

Winners and Losers of the Oil Price Roller-Coaster

Farhad Simyar

SCOPE

The purpose of this chapter is to study the impact of oil price changes with particular reference to crude oil price increase of 1978-79 in the international oil market. More specifically, the chapter will attempt to determine the major winners and losers of oil price fluctuations. Several major countries or groups of countries as well as some industries in the United States are studied here to determine the impact of such price changes.

In order to examine this phenomenon, the chapter first looks at the historical oil prices after the formation of OPEC. Next, it reviews briefly the 1978-79 crisis, checking the role of OPEC and the role of Iran. Finally, the paper examines the nature of the superpowers', as well as the major oil companies' involvement, both direct and indirect, in order to ascertain the real beneficiaries of this crisis.

INTRODUCTION

The year 1973 witnessed two very well publicized developments, both of which were blamed for the subsequent oil shortages: the Arab-Israeli October "Yom-Kippur" war leading to the subsequent threat of Arab oil embargo, and the resulting quadrupling of oil prices by December 1973. There is much evidence that neither the threat of an embargo nor the quadrupling of oil prices was instrumental in creating *real* shortages in the West, yet the myth persists that OPEC was the responsible party.[1] Regarding the embargo, studies show that the Arab countries were not in a position to effectively enforce an embargo and that there was "no coherent and systematic planning either in terms of the embargo or in the conditions of its lifting."[2] However, with the unintentional or maybe even, according to some sources, intentional help of the major oil companies, the threat of the embargo triggered panic and hoarding which resulted in oil shortages in many parts of the world. It should be noted that throughout the 1960s, that is, for the first ten years of OPEC's life, the posted price of oil remained constant and its actual market price was even lower.

The next crisis and one that, in most circles, was blamed to have caused a phenomenal price increase, was the Iranian revolution of 1978-1979. The Iranian revolution was to a large extent an internal matter and one that not only was not supported by the majority of OPEC members, but in fact it was opposed by most Arab members of OPEC, in particular Saudi Arabia, and Iraq, two of OPEC's major producers. OPEC had, thus, no role in the threat or actual creation of any worldwide oil shortage.

During the early part or 1978, most OPEC members reduced their production over that of 1977 due to sluggish demand, which was mostly caused by new or increased production and competition by non-OPEC countries. For example, Saudi Arabia's production for the first ten months of 1978 was down by 15 percent to a daily average of 8 million barrels per day. However, for the last two months of the year, in order to offset Iranian cutbacks, the daily average was raised to 11 million barrels per day, not to mention similar reactions from other OPEC members. The Iranian cutback for 1978 was a mere 27 million tons (less than 1 percent of world production), while only the new or increased production from Mexican, North Sea, and North Slope fields was 70 million tons, more than enough to offset the Iranian shortfall. Thus, not only was there no significant change in OPEC's oil production during 1978 and 1979, but there was actually an increase in the total world production during the same period.

WINNERS AND LOSERS

The oil price increases that resulted from the 1973 and 1979 crisis had a beneficial effect on the major oil companies as well as on the economy of several non-OPEC producing countries, as will be discussed later in this chapter. At this point, however, it should be pointed out that, in the eyes of many, OPEC was held responsible for both the shortages and the subsequent price increases. It is, at best, doubtful that OPEC was the responsible party. As mentioned before, several studies show that in 1973 OPEC was not solely responsible for the oil shortages and the subsequent price increases and that the major oil companies were also involved in that exercise and benefited the most.[3]

In 1979, on the other hand, the picture is even clearer: OPEC had virtually no direct responsibility in the price increases. As indicated earlier, the total OPEC production in 1978-1979 did not change significantly, while the total world production actually increased. As for the sharp and rapid increase in the price of oil, OPEC was in fact a follower, insofar that it followed, often timidly, the price increases of the Rotterdam spot market.[4] (See also Chart 15.1.) Furthermore, the Saudis, as the major OPEC producer, "resolutely kept their prices down, and the first sign of rising prices [early in 1979] came not from OPEC but from the British oilfields in the North Sea."[5]

Chart 15.1
Spot versus OPEC Oil Prices

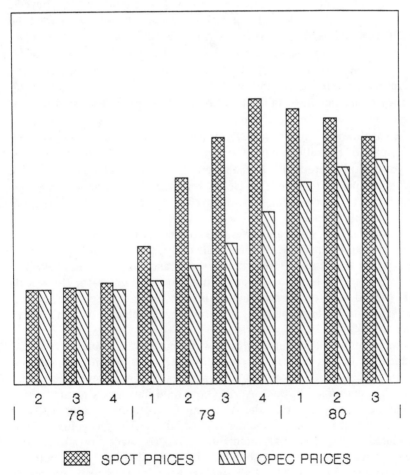

Source: PIW, October 20, 1980.

Some have argued that the dramatic increase in the spot market prices in 1978-1979 were due to the world market anticipating an Iranian triggered and OPEC created shortage or price increase, or both. The issue of an Iranian induced shortage has been demonstrated to have been a myth in view of the increase in the total world production of oil. As for OPEC initiating a price increase, it should be remembered that the Iranian revolution was treated by the rest of OPEC members as strictly an internal matter, and none of those members declared any intention of siding with Khomeini's regime against the West. In fact most indications at the time, reinforced by subsequent events, pointed to the fact that most OPEC members (with the possible exception of Libya) were against and extremely harassed by the radicalism and fanaticism represented by Khomeini's regime and, as such, would certainly not have supported any Khomeini initiated oil boycott against the West.[6] Besides, Khomeini's new regime desperately needed the revenue from oil exports to get Iran's strike-riddled economy moving again and was, thus, in no position to continue stopping the flow of Iranian oil. It is possible that the above facts may not have been quite so obvious to the general public or to the lay observer. However, any expert analyst in the oil industry could not have failed to recognize the above developments nor have failed to see their significance.[7]

The gasoline shortages were never proved to be the result of a conspiracy on the part of the oil companies, or on the part of the Carter administration, or both; but gradually, over the rest of 1978 and 1979, a retrospective picture was pieced together that clearly revealed actions resembling a conspiracy. For the oil companies and their refiners and dealers, the motivation was obvious: big bucks.

Meanwhile, U.S. companies were up to their own strategy. They began drawing down inventories. By the middle of 1978, the nation's gasoline inventory was at its lowest level in three years, and the companies held it at that level—a level too low to permit any extra demands—for the rest of 1978. (Asked later to comment on this drawdown, Energy Secretary Schlesinger said with his usual passion, "That was regrettable. It was an error in judgment.")[8]

Coincidental with the refinery drop was a cutback in domestic crude oil production. Just as the Iranian revolution began, crude oil production in the United States suddenly went into its sharpest decline in seven years. And the decline continued through April. One would have never learned about the cutback, however, from the American Petroleum Institute. Statistics released by that lobbying group nicely covered up what was going on. But Associated Press reporters, finding that "API's projections have consistently overstated domestic production in recent months," went on to dig up the true production data, and concluded that "the virtually unnoticed and still unexplained domestic dropoff plus changes in American refinery operations cost the United States more gasoline than the widely blamed cutback in Iranian imports.'' Oil company brass said the decline was because of "extreme cold weather" and "heavy rains," which caused pumps to break down and interfered with trucking from remote wells. But Associated Press reporters went back to the weather records and found that in the seven U.S. oil-producing areas that accounted for three-fourths of all production only three had had cold weather or heavy rains. In short, the domestic production cutback seemed to have been planned.[9]

No sooner had the Iranian fuss gotten underway than Schlesinger began making his dire warnings, which had the effect—some believed it was the effect he desired—of frightening many industries and businesses into stockpiling oil and drawing down franatically on the already barely adequate stock of gasoline, thereby helping to create the very shortage they were mistakenly trying to escape.

Although in fact the United States was importing more oil in January and February during the Iranian shutdown than it had imported during the same period in 1978, major oil importers pretended that the Iranian "shortage" Schlesinger kept talking about was real. It was the excuse they gave for slashing the amount of gasoline they supplied to their retail dealers. But General Accounting Office (GAO) investigators, looking into the economic effects of the Iranian cutoff, reported on March 5, 1979, that the companies that depended on Iranian oil for only 2 to 4 percent of their supply were curtailing gasoline sales to their dealers by 10 to 15 percent. (Actually, some of these companies were cutting dealer supplies by as much as 30 percent.) The GAO sleuths called it "puzzling."[10]

Not only was more crude oil imported during the two months of the Iranian shutdown, more was imported—9 percent more—during the whole first six months of 1979 than had been imported during the same period of 1978; indeed, some companies were importing a great deal more: Gulf up 23.5 percent for the first six months, Mobil up 17.9 percent, Exxon up 15.5 percent. It was certainly a strange "shortage."[11]

Nationwide demand for gasoline was up only 3 percent. (The statistics showing the abundance of imports were not released until August, long after the gas lines had disappeared.) No industry spokesman could explain. "Where did the oil go? You've got me bothered by the fact that I don't have a satisfactory answer to the question," said Anthony L. Seaver, Exxon International's manager of planning.[12]

One place that a considerable amount of oil from some sources did go was back overseas. A CIA study showed that in the first five months of the year, at a time when the U.S. administration was deploring the oil scarcity, U.S. companies exported more oil than they had in either of those glut years 1977 and 1978. In 1977, exports had ranged from only 192,000 to 288,000 barrels daily; yet in 1979, during the alleged U.S. pinch, the companies were sending out of the country from 329,000 barrels daily in January to 445,000 barrels daily in both April and May, according to the CIA.[13]

Many observers both in and out of government were convinced that oil supplies were being withheld from the market to promote tighter market conditions and higher prices. Alfred F. Dougherty, Jr., director of the Foreign Trade Commission's (FTC) Bureau of Competition, was one who publicly made that accusation.[14]

Indeed, for the first five months of 1979, refineries ran at an average of only 85.8 percent capacity, compared to an average of 91.2 percent during the last six months of 1978. Some experts believed that if refineries had operated at just 90 percent of capacity up to the start of the vacation season, there would have been no gasoline shortage.[15]

Schlesinger did not help matters by urging the oil companies in April to decrease gasoline production and turn to the production of home heating oil to ensure enough for the following winter. It was a bubble-headed suggestion that only added to the suspicion that the Department of Energy secretary had something in mind other than making life easy for motorists. "It doesn't make sense," commented Lawrence Goldstein, senior economist of the Petroleum Industry Research Foundation, "to maximize middle distillate (including heating oil) production at the outset of the driving season."

From the moment the shortages began to appear, there were suspicions—and evidence, in some cases—that the oil companies were, one way or another, holding back their supplies until prices were forced up. The first sharp shortage of gasoline occurred in California in late April, with nine counties—where 10 million of the state's 15 million drivers lived—turning to odd-even gasoline rationing: the state that only a few months earlier was turning away the 400,000-barrel-a-day glut of the Alaska pipeline? How in the world could California have developed a shortage so fast? "I wish I knew," a federal official told the *New York Times*. Suspicions of industry hoarding were so strong in California that Carter ordered an investigation in May; in August the Department of Energy (DOE) said it could find no evidence of dirty work.[16]

Then, just as swiftly, the California shortage disappeared and the District of Columbia area was mysteriously afflicted. In June, with long lines at the pump because gas supplies to area service stations had been cut back by 25 to 30 percent, a DOE audit showed that in fact the major oil company storage tanks in the area had received 5 percent more gasoline than during the same period in 1978.

When the mysterious shortages moved into the New York-New England area, new questions were raised, and never answered. When, on July 2, the Italian-manned tanker Texaco Hannover pulled up to Texaco's Eagle Point refinery (the company's third-largest refinery), at Westville, New Jersey, to deliver 750,000 barrels of crude oil, it was instructed to wait at the dock for three days to unload the cargo, because the refinery's storage tanks were filled to the brim with 1.8 million barrels of crude oil. Additionally, Al Grospiron, president of the Oil Workers Union that represented seamen on Mobil tankers, charged that Mobil's storage tanks were filled, up and down the East Coast. A tanker seaman told House Commerce Committee staff members investigating the gasoline shortages, "We knew that the tanks were full, and we'd go into town [New York City] and see the gas stations closed, and people told us there was no fuel."[17]

Grospiron also made the interesting accusation of "hoarding on the high seas." He charged that for several weeks during the gas crisis Mobil's tankers were under orders to reduce speed, drifting along for nine days between Beaumont, Texas, and Boston, a trip that ordinarily required no more than five days. Tankers that normally would have loaded in 16 hours, said Grospiron, were taking up to four days to fill their tanks.

All the causes of the gasoline shortage and price escalations were never uncovered, and such uncovering as did occur was usually months late in coming, and then hedged and smothered in bureaucratese.[18]

So far, this chapter has attempted to show that Iran and OPEC were not the major instruments or beneficiaries in the market to change oil prices, even though they have frequently been portrayed as such. The next question that arises is who were the actors and beneficiaries of oil price increase?

As mentioned earlier, the evidence presented is of a circumstantial nature. Based on this evidence, we will try to show that among the major beneficiaries were, in fact, the major oil companies. However, whether they were the principal actors or merely fortunate bystanders cannot be established at this stage.

Other beneficiaries include the home countries of the major oil companies; the oil producing countries (both OPEC members and non-OPEC countries); and the international banking community.

The Oil Companies

From numerous aspects, the major oil companies, also affectionately known as the Seven Sisters, were the major winners of the oil crises, particularly those that obtained significant increases in the price of oil.

The most spectacular gain was by far the dramatic rise in the Seven Sisters' sales which was not accompanied by a proportional increase in costs. This resulted in a dramatic increase in profits and return on equity, not to mention comparable increases in stock prices. (See Charts 15.2 and 15.3.) The dramatic rise in profits enabled the majors to not only pay high dividends, but also to invest heavily in capital assets and R&D activities and still be able to end up with substantial higher retained earnings.

It is interesting to note that in order to maintain the same debt-to-equity ratio, along with increase in owner's equity, the gap between total assets and total owners' equity of the major oil companies had been steadily widening. This put a strain on the money market that not only contributed heavily to the rise in interest rates, but along with high inflation, resulted in an additional incentive for the oil companies to keep oil prices high. In this way they would continue to maintain a high profitability so as to remain in a strong position to service their debts.

Another interesting point is that most of the capital expenditure (including R&D) was channeled into North America and Western Europe, to further

Chart 15.2
Net Profits of the 7 Sisters and 26 Major Oil Companies

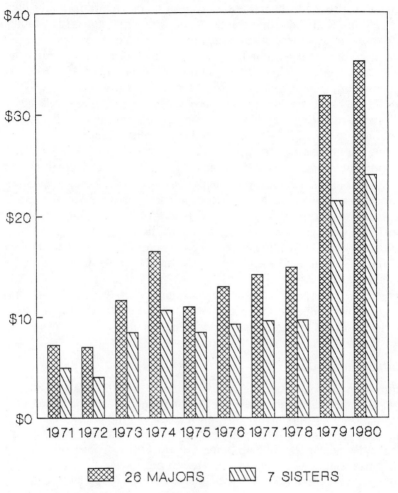

Source: PIW, October 20, 1980

research on alternative sources of energy as well as exploring the previously uneconomical and more expensive oilfields, while the source of crude oil of the major companies was from the OPEC countries. It is again interesting to note that in 1979 the Middle East, which supplied some 48 percent of the world crude oil, received only about 0.6 percent of the oil companies' investments, whereas the African states that supplied only 10 percent of the world crude oil received 3 percent of that investment.

Chart 15.3
Average Return on Equity and Book Value of the 7 Sisters and 26 Major Oil Companies

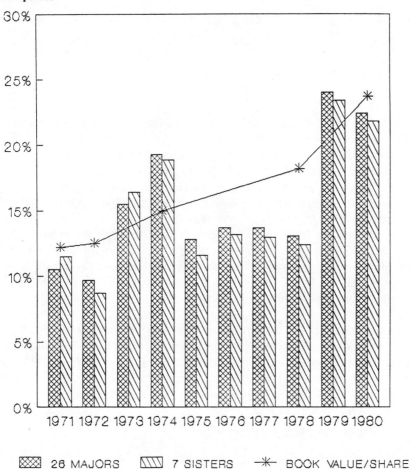

Source: PIW, October 20, 1980.

As is evident from the statements of major oil companies, the capital expenditure of the companies resulted in the transformation of the resources (crude oil) from the Middle East partially to capital assets and R&D in the West, with Western consumers footing the bill in the form of higher prices. This transformation is, of course, not a new phenomenon and has existed for many years.[19] However, the order of its magnitude increased dramatically and in proportion to the increase in the price of oil.

The Home Countries of the Majors

The home countries of the majors consist of the United States, United Kingdom, and the Netherlands, all of which are, to varying degrees, also non-OPEC oil producers and will therefore be discussed under a subsequent heading below.

Oil Producing Countries

OPEC Members

Although, at first glance, OPEC members seem to have gained the most from the increases of the oil prices, it soon becomes apparent that OPEC members gained the least from the increases. The first major increase in 1973 did indeed result in a windfall gain of the order of billions of dollars to these countries. Eventually, however, much of these gains was considerably offset by the rampant inflation that occurred in the Western industrialized countries.[20] This inflation was particularly harmful to OPEC countries since most of the latter embarked on massive development projects that were being implemented by Western contractors or which needed Western manufactured goods and services, or both. Furthermore, as mentioned in an earlier section, OPEC countries benefited very little from the huge sums of money that were spent mainly by the majors in oil-related expansion and R&D activities.

Finally, many OPEC countries suffered noneconomic damages too. In some instances, the very rapid pace of development not only strained the countries' weak and fragile infrastructure beyond capacity, but also inflicted severe damages to the countries' social fabric. Some examples can be observed in a most dramatic way in the aftermath of the Iranian revolution and to a lesser degree in Nigeria.

Non-OPEC Oil Producers

The major non-OPEC oil producers consist of: North America (United States, Mexico, and Canada); Latin America; Western Europe; and Communist bloc countries. The countries that benefited most from the developments resulting from the oil price increases and which will be discussed in this chapter are the United States, U.S.S.R., and the U.K.[21] The most obvious benefit gained by the aforementioned countries was the fact that the previously uneconomical fields such as those in North Slope (Alaska), North Sea, and Siberia, just to mention one example for each country, became commercially viable. In the North Slope and the North Sea oilfields (discovered in the 1960s) oil production was costing from 10 to 20 times as much as comparable capacity in the Middle East. The cost of extracting liquid fuels from alternative sources such as oil shales, heavy oils, tar sands, and coal was also high and was rising steeply. For example, the estimated cost of producing one barrel of oil from the above fields was about $4 to $6 prior to the 1973–1974 price increase when the market price was about $2 whereas in 1977, it had risen to $17–$24 while the market price was only $12. As another example, to develop an on-shore oil field in the Middle East in 1977 required an investment of between $100–$200 for each barrel a day. To develop the same capacity in the North Sea required $3,000 or more per barrel in the same year.[22]

A quick look at the number of wells drilled in two countries, United States and United Kingdom, will further support this argument. (See Table 15.1.)

It should be noted that the significant increase in the number of wells drilled occurred in spite of the sky-rocketing drilling costs, particularly on off-shore wells. Another benefit, and one that was not limited to the United States and United Kingdom, but applied to all the Western industrial countries, was the governments' share of the oil companies' windfall profits in the form of taxes.

It would again be interesting to compare the total taxes paid by the oil companies covered by the Chase Manhattan studies with the OPEC surpluses. (See Table 15.2.)

In addition, of the final sales price of petroleum products in Western Europe, the governments' take in the form of taxes is higher than either OPEC's or the oil companies' costs and profits. For instance the average Western European government share of the final sale price of gasoline in 1980 was 52 percent versus the oil companies' share of 17 percent and OPEC's 31 percent (the latter two including both costs *and* profits), with the French government maintaining the highest intake ratio of 65 percent of the retail value.

As mentioned earlier, the home countries of the major oil companies are also themselves non-OPEC oil producers. Thus the offshoot of the benefits gained by the said companies affects directly their home countries too.

Table 15.1
Total Wells Completed or Drilled

A: U.S.A. (Total Wells Completed)

1972	1975	1978	1981
28,755	39,097	48,513	80,500

B: UK (Total Wells Drilled)

1967–1974	1975–1979
161	254

Source: *Basic Petroleum Data Book*, Vol. I, No. 3, Washington, D.C.: American Petroleum Institute, 1983; and BP Briefing Paper: "U.K. North Sea Oil," March 1980.

Table 15.2
A Comparison of OPEC Surplus and Tax Payments by Major Oil Companies, 1972–1980 (billion dollars)

	1972	1974	1980
OPEC surplus	3	68	116
Total taxes paid by 26 major oil companies to their respective governments	38	67	129
Total capital expenditures by 26 major oil companies	13	23	56

Source: Chase Manhattan study of 26 oil companies, 1981.

Therefore, the non-OPEC oil producers benefited directly from profits and dividends of the oil companies in the form of a boost to their stock market, increased exports, heavy investments in R&D and capital expenditure which have already been discussed in an earlier section.

It should be pointed out that the increase in the oil prices did have adverse effects on some sectors of the non-OPEC oil producers, notably on the automobile industry. However, the cost-benefit analysis of all the non-oil industries is beyond the scope of this chapter.

In the COMECON countries, the U.S.S.R., as the major oil producer, experienced both economic and political benefits. From the economic point of view, similar to the case of the Western oil producers, oil fields that were hitherto uneconomical became commercially viable. In addition, oil exports to Western countries became a major source of hard currency for the U.S.S.R., accounting for over half of its hard currency earning in 1980.[23]

Politically, the oil crises helped the U.S.S.R. tighten its grip on the other COMECON countries. In 1980 the U.S.S.R. exported 22 percent of its oil production, two-thirds of which went to COMECON countries at 40 percent of OPEC prices. Thus, not only did the oil price increases help the U.S.S.R. increase its hard currency intake, but also made the COMECON countries more dependent on the U.S.S.R., and therefore politically, as well as economically, inseparable.

International Banking Community

Much of the revenue earned by OPEC eventually found its way back to the Western countries, mostly to the United States and United Kingdom, both as a direct result of the massive development projects undertaken by

OPEC countries as well as through other types of investment. For example, as of the end of 1979, OPEC had invested some $56 billion in the United Kingdom, and $55 billion in the United States. The distribution of this investment is illustrated in Table 15.3.

CONCLUSIONS

The preceding analysis attempted to show several points: Contrary to popular belief, Iran and OPEC were not the culprits in 1978–1979 oil price increase, neither the sole nor even the principal beneficiary of the price change. Most of the benefits were accrued to the West; and the United Kingdom, in particular, gained a great deal. The latter was able to accelerate the costly and previously uneconomical exploration and drilling of its North Sea oil, and it also benefited from a great deal of investment by the OPEC countries.

Another point that this chapter tried to make was that, again contrary to popular belief, neither Iran nor other OPEC members were directly responsible for the oil shortages in 1979. In 1973, it was not so much the politically inspired oil embargo that created worldwide shortages, but the fact that the United States had become a net importer of oil, from the net exporter that it used to be.

The 1979 Iranian revolution was an internal affair and in any case the cutback in Iran's output was both temporary and not large enough to cause severe shortages, especially in the United States. It should also be noted that around that time Saudi Arabia had increased its oil production and that OPEC as a whole made only slight increases in the price of its oil. The spotmarket, however, showed very large increases and OPEC had no choice than to follow the trend set by the spotmarket. This trend thus encouraged OPEC to cancel its long-term contracts and sell on the spotmarket instead.

Table 15.3
Distribution of Investment by OPEC Countries

In U.S.		In U.K.	
Bank Deposits	26%	Eurodollar & other deposits	80%
Corp. stocks & bonds	24%	Bank sterling deposits	7%
Real estate & other	22%	Real estate & other	5%
Gov. bonds & notes	15%	Corp. stocks & bonds	4%
Treasury bills	12%	Gov. bonds & notes	3%
		Treasury bills	1%

Source: *Business Week*, October 6, 1980.

Table 15.4
Partial Distribution of World Oil Production

	U.K.	Saudi Arabia	Total OPEC
1980	2.6%	16.0%	44.0%
1981	3.1%	17.0%	39.5%

Source: BP Statistical Review of World Oil Industry, 1980 and 1981.

A final point supporting the assertion that Iran or OPEC did not have a very significant role in determining oil prices is the price trend during the oil glut of late 1981 and 1982. By 1981, several OPEC countries (such as Nigeria, Iran, and Iraq) were experiencing a tremendous need for hard currency. This need was made all the more pressing by the fact that Iran as well as many OPEC members had, by 1981, lost their earlier surpluses and were now experiencing deficits. Consequently, these countries were trying to effectively lower the official OPEC price, but this did not occur until the U.K. lowered the price of its North Sea oil. Thus, it was a non-OPEC producer, and one with a small production (compared to OPEC) that finally determined the lower official OPEC price. (See Table 15.4.)

Needless to say notwithstanding its small annual production, Great Britain can still exercise a tremendous influence using its political clout as well as its membership as a home country in the Seven Sisters' Club. Finally, although some observers have suggested that OPEC was deliberately created to act as a "scapegoat" for the Seven Sisters, this author cannot support this argument for lack of concrete data, even though OPEC or some of its members seem to have frequently acted in the interest of the Seven Sisters.[24] However, the chapter has shown that non-OPEC producers in the East or West as well as oil services industry and banking industry benefited or lost as the oil price roller-coaster rolled up and down on the charts within the past 15 years.

NOTES

1. John M. Blair, *The Control of Oil* (New York: Pantheon Books, 1976).

2. Benjamin Shwadran, *Middle East Oil: Issues and Problems* (Cambridge, MA: Schenkman Publishing Co., 1977).

3. See, for example, Blair, *The Control of Oil*; and Shwadran, *Middle East Oil*.

4. F. Simyar, and K. Argheyd, "OPEC: Market Dominant or Subservient," *International Journal of Management*, Vol. 4, No. 1, March 1987, pp. 105–117.

5. Anthony Sampson, *The Seven Sisters* (New York: Bantam Books, 1981), p. 386.

6. In June 1978, Ali Attiga, secretary general of the Organization of Arab Petroleum Exporting Countries, told a group of European businessmen that they need not worry: "there would be no more shocking upward movement of Arab oil

prices for at least the next ten years. He talked as though the marketplace had tamed OPEC." (*OPEC Bulletin*, 1981.)

7. On February 13, 1979, Senator Henry M. Jackson, chairman of the Senate Committee on Energy and National Resources, wrote to the Comptroller General of the U.S. General Accounting Office, asking, "how will the halt in Iranian oil production affect U.S. oil supply?" In his reply, the Comptroller General stated that "the apparent net shortfall to the U.S. as a result of the Iranian cutoff appears to be rather small, . . . about 3 percent of U.S. consumption. [This] shortfall would not critically affect the United States." He then noted that "some major oil companies have announced curtailments of gasoline sales to their customers in the 10 to 15 percent range while our figures indicate that many of these same companies are dependent upon Iranian oil for only 2 to 4 percent of supply." (U.S. Congress Hearing, 1979.)

8. Robert Sherrill, *The Oil Follies of 1970–1980* (New York: Doubleday Company, 1983).

9. Sherrill, *The Oil Follies.*

10. "Iran and World Oil Supply," *Senate Hearing Before the Committee on Energy and Natural Resources* (Publication Number 96-4, Volumes 1–3), Washington, D.C.: United States Government Printing Office, March 12, 1979.

11. "Iran and World Oil Supply."

12. Sherrill, *The Oil Follies.*

13. Sherrill, *The Oil Follies.*

14. "Iran and World Oil Supply."

15. "Iran and World Oil Supply."

16. Sherrill, *The Oil Follies.*

17. Sherrill, *The Oil Follies.*

18. In mid-September, the Department of Energy ended its preliminary investigation of the hoarding charges with the conclusion that industry was innocent. It could hardly have come to any other conclusion, for the investigation was based entirely on information supplied by the suspects themselves. DOE continued to use the Iranian cutoff as the (discredited) cause for the shortages.

19. *Financial Analysis of a Group of Petroleum Companies*, New York: The Chase Manhattan Bank, 1980.

20. According to OECD and IMF reports, in 1974 OPEC had a surplus of $68 billion that by 1977 dropped to almost zero. In 1980 this surplus had once again increased, reaching $116 billion.

21. Other countries such as Mexico, Argentina, Norway, the Netherlands, and a few others also benefited from the oil price increases. However, in the case of Mexico, most of the oil-related activities were performed by either the U.S.- or U.K.-based majors and in any case, the U.S., U.S.S.R., and U.K. were deemed to be the major determinants of oil (and frequently non-oil) policies in the world.

22. *OPEC Information Booklet*, Vienna: OPEC, 1984.

23. "Russia can get by with a little help from its enemies," *The Economist*, May 8, 1981, p. 97.

24. Particularly the role of the Khomeini regime during and in the aftermath of the Iranian revolution seems to have directly benefited the Seven Sisters and later on, arms manufacturers and dealers.

Bibliography

Alam, Ghayur, and John Langrish. "Non-Multinational Firms and Transfer of Technology to LDCs," *World Development*, Vol. 9, No. 4, 1981, pp. 383–387.

American Chamber of Commerce of Mexico, A.C. *Mexico Economic Fact Sheet*, 1984-1985.

"ASPA Opposes Immigration Bill," *Resource*, October 1985, p. 1.

Aspe, Pedro. "Charting Mexico's Economic Progress," *The Wall Street Journal*, August 8, 1987.

Automotive News, 1986 Market Data Book.

Banco de Mexico. *Indicadores Economicos*, 1982-1987, various issues.

_____. *Informe Anual, 1986*, pp. 108–113.

Biersteker, Thomas J. *Distortion or Development? Contending Perspectives on the Multinational Corporation*. Cambridge, MA: MIT Press, 1978

Blair, John M. *The Control of Oil*. New York: Pantheon Books, 1976.

Borjas, G. J. and M. Tienda. "The Economic Consequences of Immigration," *Science*, February 6, 1987, pp. 645–651.

Branson, William. "Asset Markets and Relative Price in Exchange Rate Determination," *Sozialwissenschafter Annalen*, 1977, pp. 69–89.

Brunner, John. *The Compleat Traveller in Black*. New York: Bluejay Books, 1986.

Buiter, W. H., and T. N. Srinivasan. "Rewarding the Profligate and Punishing the Prudent and Poor: Some Recent Proposals for Debt Relief," *World Development*, March 1987, pp. 411–418.

Casson, M. *Alternatives to the Multinational Enterprise*. London: Macmillian Press, 1979.

Castaneda, Jorge. "Mexico's Coming Challenges," *Foreign Policy*, Fall 1986, pp. 120–160.

Cesareo, Morales. "El Comienzo de una Nueva Etapa de las Relaciones Economicas entre Mexico y Estados Unidos," In *Mexico Ante la Crisis*. Vol. I, edited by Pablo Gonzalez-Casanova, and Hector Aguilar-Camin. Mexico City: Siglo XXI, 1985, pp. 64–88.

Charira, Ricardo. "Symbiosis Along 1936 Miles," *Forbes*, June 17, 1985, p. 29.

Chudnovsky, Daniel, and Masafumi Nagao. *Capital Goods Production in the Third World: An Economic Study of Technology Acquisition.* New York: St. Martin's Press, 1983.

Cornelius, Wayne. "The Political Economy of Mexico Under De La Madrid: Austerity, Routinized Crisis, and Nascent Recovery," *Mexican Studies,* Winter 1985, pp. 1–28.

Crawley, Eduardo. "Mexico," *The Latin America and Caribbean Review.* 8th ed. Saffron Walden, Essex: World of Information, 1987, pp. 95–96.

Dahlman, C. J., and L. E. Westphal. "Technological Effort in Industrial Development: An Interpretative Survey of Recent Research," In *The Economics of New Technology in Developing Countries,* edited by F. Stewart, and J. James. London: Frances Printer, 1982.

"Debating Immigration Reform," *America,* June 16, 1984, p. 449.

Decree for the Development and Operation of the In-Bond Industry. Translated by the American Embassy, Mexico City: Government of Mexico, 1983.

Diamondstein, Bert. "Star Performer: Maquiladoras Do it Again," *Business Mexico,* February 1986.

Dornbusch, Rudiger. "Exchange Rate Economics: Where Do We Stand?" *Brookings Papers on Economic Activity,* Number 1, 1980, pp. 143–194.

———. "Expectations and Exchange Rate Dynamics," *Journal of Political Economy,* Vol. 84, No. 6, December 1976, pp. 1161–1176.

Downer, Stephen. "Ford in Hermosillo," *Automotive News,* November 24, 1986, p. 2.

———. "Mexican Auto Industry Banking on Export Boom," *Automotive News,* February 9, 1987, p. 2.

Doyle, Lawrence, et al. *Manufacturing Process and Materials for Engineers.* New York: Prentice-Hall, 1969.

Dunning, John H., "Toward an Eclectic Theory of International Production: Some Empirical Tests," *Journal of International Business Studies,* Spring/Summer 1980, pp. 9–31.

El Financiero (various issues).

Ethier, Wilfred J., "Illegal Immigration: The Host-Country Problem," *American Economic Review,* Vol. 76, No. 1, March 1986, pp. 56–71.

Fairchild, L. G., "Performance and Technology of U.S. and National Firms in Mexico," *Journal of Development Studies,* October 1977.

———. "Evaluating Differences in Technological Activity between Transnational and Domestic Firms in Latin America," *Journal of Development Studies,* July, 1986, pp. 697–708.

Fairchild, L. G., and K. Sosin. "Manufacturing Firms in Mexico's Financial Crisis: Determinants of Severity and Response," *Mexican Studies/Estudios Mexicanos,* Vol. III, No. 1, 1987.

Financial Analysis of a Group of Petroleum Companies. New York: The Chase Manhattan Bank, 1980.

FitzGerald, E. V. K. "A Note on Capital Accumulation in Mexico: The Budget Deficit and Investment in Finance," *Development and Change,* July 1980, pp. 391–417.

———. "Looney and Frederiksen on Mexican Fiscal Policy: A Reply," *World Development,* March 1987, pp. 405–406.

_____ . "The Fiscal Deficit and Development Finance: A Note on the Accumulation Balance in Mexico," *Working Paper No. 35,* Cambridge: Cambridge University Center of Latin American Studies, 1979.

Frankel, Jeffrey. "Monetary and Portfolio-Balance Models of Exchange Rate Determination," In *Economic Interdependence and Flexible Exchange Rates,* edited by J. Bhandari and B. Putman. Cambridge, MA: MIT Press, 1983.

Frenkel, Jacob A. "A Monetary Approach to the Exchange Rate: Doctrinal Aspects and Empirical Evidence," *Scandinavian Journal of Economics,* Vol. 78, No. 2, May 1976, pp. 200–224.

Garcia, D. "Across the River—Into the Jail," *Newsweek,* July 7, 1982, p. 35.

Gardner, David. "Bankers Rush for Mexican Equity," *Financial Times,* June 2, 1987.

_____ . "Mexico Looks to IMF for Appreciation of Its Efforts," *Financial Times,* July 1, 1986.

_____ . "Youth and Ability Win Day for Salinas," *Financial Times,* October 6, 1987, p. 6.

Georgescu-Roegen, Nicholas. *The Entropy Law and The Economic Process.* Cambridge, MA: Harvard University Press, 1971.

_____ . *Energy and Economic Myths.* New York: Pergamon Press, 1976.

Ghosh, Pradip K. *Appropriate Technology in Third World Development,* International Development Resource Books, no. 14. Westport, CT: Greenwood Press, 1984.

Gilbreath, Kent. "A Businessman's Guide to the Mexican Economy," *Columbia Journal of World Business,* Summer 1986, pp. 3–14.

Greenwood, M., and J. McDowell. "The Factor Market Consequences of U.S. Immigration," *Journal of Economic Literature,* Vol. 24, No. 4, December 1986, pp. 1738–1772.

Harth, Eric. *Windows On the Mind.* New York: Quill Press, 1983.

Hawk, David L., ed., *Building Economics Research Agenda.* Washington, D.C.: National Technical Information Service, 1986.

"Hearings on United States-Mexico Economic Relations" (98-1297), Subcommittee of the Committee on Appropriations, United States Senate, Washington, D.C.: U.S. Government Printing Office, 1985.

"Heels Dragged on Local Debt Swap," *Latin America Weekly Report,* July 16, 1987, p. 4.

Hirschman, Albert O., et al. *Toward a New Strategy for Development,* New York: Pergamon Press, 1979.

Hirsh, Robert. "Impending United States Energy Crisis," *Science,* March 20, 1987.

"How Debt Swaps Work," *Journal of Commerce,* December 16, 1986.

Howard, Donald. "The Unwelcome Immigrants," *Newsweek,* January 23, 1984, p. 36.

Hume, Ellen. "Immigration-Control Measures Spawn Alliances That Encompass Diverse Political and Social Camps,"*The Wall Street Journal,* August 28, 1985, p. 21.

Hymer, S. *The International Operations of National Firms: A Study of Direct Foreign Investment.* Cambridge, MA: MIT Press, 1976.

"Imagen de la Industria Maquiladora," *Desarrollo Economico del Estado de Chihuahua,* A.C., 1983 and 1985.

"Immigration: How It's Affecting Us," *Atlantic,* November 1983, p. 47.

La Industria Automotriz En Cifras. Mexico City: Asociacion Mexicana De La Industria Automotriz, A.C. (AMIA), 1986, p. 105.

La Industria Automotriz En Mexico. Mexico City: Secretaria de Programacion y Presupuesto (SPP), 1981, p. 130.

La Industria Automotriz En Mexico. Mexico City: Secretaria de Programacion y Presupuesto (SPP), 1984, p. 116.

La Industria Automotriz Terminal En 1986. Mexico City: Enero, 1987, p. 35.

Inter-American Development Bank. *Annual Report: 1986.* Washington, D.C.: IDB, p. 2.

"The Internationalization of the Automobile Industry and Its Effects on the U.S. Automobile Industry," *USITC Publication 1712,* Washington, D.C.: United States International Trade Commission, June 1985.

Jackson, David. "Making the Great Escape," *Time,* September 13, 1982, p. 73.

Johnson, Harry G. "The Monetary Approach to the Balance of Payments." In *Further Essays in Monetary Economics,* edited by H. Johnson. Cambridge, MA: Harvard University Press, 1973.

Kaletsky, Anatole. *The Costs of Default.* New York: The Twentieth Century Fund, 1985.

Katz, Jorge. "Creacion de Technologia en el Sector Manufacturero Argentino, *El Trimestre Economico,* January-March 1978, pp. 167–190.

Kaufmann, Walter. *Discovering the Mind.* Vol. I-III, New York: McGraw-Hill, 1980.

Keen, Judy. "4M Would Get Amnesty," *USA Today,* October 17, 1986, p. 5A.

Khan, Herman, and Julian Simon. *The Resourceful Earth.* New York: Basic Books, 1984.

Kobrin, Stephen J. "Multinational Corporations, Socio-cultural Dependence, and Industrialization: Need Satisfaction or Want Creation?" *Journal of Developing Areas,* Vol. 13, No. 2, January 1979, pp. 109–125.

Kouri, Pentti J. K. "The Exchange Rate and the Balance of Payments in the Short Run and in the Long Run: A Monetary Approach," *Scandinavian Journal of Economics,* Vol. 78, No. 2, May 1976, pp. 280–304.

Koyck, L. M. *Distributed Laggs and Investment Analysis.* Amsterdam: North Holland, 1954.

Krugman, P. R. "The 'New Theories' of International Trade and the Multinational Enterprise," In *The Multinational Corporations in the 1980s,* edited by C. P. Kindleberger and D. B. Audretsch. Cambridge, MA: MIT Press, 1983.

Lall, Sanjaya. "Determinants of Research and Development in an LDC: The Indian Engineering Industry," *Economic Letters,* 1983, pp. 379–383.

_____ . *Developing Countries in the International Economy,* London: Macmillan Press, 1981.

_____ . "Is 'Dependence' A Useful Concept in Analyzing Underdevelopment?" *World Development,* Vol. 3, No. 11, 1975, pp. 799–810.

Lekachman, Robert. *The Varieties of Economics.* Vol. 1-2, Gloucester, MA: Peter Smith Publishing, 1977.

Looney, Robert E. *Economic Policy Making in Mexico: Factors Underlying the 1982 Crisis,* Durham, NC: Duke University Press, 1985.

_____ . *Mexico's Economy: A Policy Analysis with Forecasts to 1990.* Boulder, CO: Westview Press, 1978.

_____ . "Mexican Optimism and Economic Reality: An Analysis of the Industrial Development Plan," *Rivista Internazionale di Scienze Economiche & Commerciali*, May 1984.

_____ . "The Mexican Oil Syndrome: Current Vulnerability and Longer Term Viability," *OPEC Review*, Winter 1985.

_____ . "Scope for Policy in an Oil Based Economy: Mexican Stabilization Policies in the 1970s," *Socio-economic Planning Sciences*, 1987.

_____ . "Mexican Economic Performance During the Echeverria Administration: Bad Luck or Poor Planning?" *Bulletin of Latin American Research*, May 1983.

_____ . Mechanisms of Mexican Economic Growth: The Role of Deteriorating Sources of Growth in the Current Economic Crisis," *Journal of Social, Political and Economic Studies*, Spring 1987.

_____ . "The Regional Impact of Infrastructure Investment in Mexico," *Regional Studies*, No. 4, 1981, pp. 285–296.

_____ . "Consequences of Military and Civilian Rule in Argentina: An Analysis of Central Government Budgetary Trade-Offs, 1961-1982," *Comparative Political Studies*, April 1987, pp. 34–46.

_____ . "Feasibility of Alternative IMF-Type Stabilization Programs in Mexico, 1983-1987," *Journal of Policy Modeling*, October 1983.

Looney, Robert E., and P. C. Frederiksen. "Fiscal Policy in Mexico: The FitzGerald Thesis Reexamined," *World Development*, March 1987, pp. 399–404.

MacEwan, Arthur. "Latin America: Why Not Default?" *Monthly Review*, September 1986, pp. 1–13.

Mahler, Vincent A. *Dependency Approaches to International Political Economy: A Cross-national Study*. New York: Columbia University Press, 1980.

Mares, David. "Mexico's Challenges," *Third World Quarterly*, July 1987, p. 795.

Marquez, Travier. "La Economica Mexicana en 1977 y su Futuro," Madrid, October 1977 (mimeo).

"The Mexican Economy: 1985 Results and Prospects for 1986," *Business Mexico*, February 1986, p. 26.

"Mexico," *Latin America Weekly Review*, October 2, 1986, pp. 2–5.

Morales Castaneda, Raul. "El Sector Externo y la Crisis Economica Actual en Mexico: Una Perspectiva Historica," *Analisis Economico*, Atzcapotzalco: UAM, pp. 227–321.

Murphy, John, and John Pardeck, eds. *Technology and Human Productivity*. New York: Quorum Books, 1986.

Nugent, J. B., and P. A. Yotopoulos. "What Has Orthodox Development Economics Learned from Recent Experience?" *World Development*, Vol. 7, No. 6, June 1979, pp. 541–554.

OECD Economic Outlook, 1986.

OPEC Bulletin, 1981.

OPEC Information Booklet, Vienna: OPEC, 1984.

Opie, Redvers. *Mexican Industrialization and Petroleum*. Mexico City: ECANAL, August 1979.

Orme, William. "Debt-Equity Swaps as a Passing Mexican Fancy," *Journal of Commerce*, December 16, 1986.

_____ . "Swaps Spur Foreign Investment in Mexico," *Financial Times*, January 5, 1987.

208   Bibliography

_____ . "Tax Evasion Takes its Toll of Mexico's Revenue," *Financial Times*, August 21, 1987, p. 4.

Ortiz, Edgar. "Mexico's Financial Crisis: Origins and Perspectives." In *Mexico's Economic Policy: Past, Present and Future,* edited by William E. Cole. Knoxville: University of Tennessee, 1987.

_____ . "Estabilizacion y Cambio Estructural," *Economics and Finance: Current Issues in the North American and Caribbean Countries.* Mexico City: CIDE, 1987.

_____ . "Crisis y Deuda Externa. Limitaciones de las Politicas de Estabilizacion y Alternativas para el Desarrollo y la Renegociacion del Endeudamiento," Simposio Internacional, Crisis y Deuda Externa: Los Puntos de Vista de Mexico y Estados Unidos, Mexico, FCPS/UNAM, May 1986.

Pear, Robert. "Senate Gets New Version of Immigration Bill," *The New York Times,* May 24, 1985, p. 91.

Peters, Tom. *A Passion for Excellence.* New York: Random House, 1985.

Pine, Art. "Mexico-IMF Reach Tentative Agreement on Economic Restructuring Framework," *The Wall Street Journal,* July 15, 1986.

Pool, John C., and Steve Stamos. *The ABC's of International Finance.* Lexington, MA: Lexington Books, 1987, p. 113.

Programa Nacional de Fomento Industrial y Comercio Exterior, 1984-1988, Mexico City: Poder Ejecutive Federal, 1984.

"Prospects for The Mexican Automotive Industry in the Late 1980s," *International Motor Business,* London: Economist Publications, April 1986, pp. 3-20.

Rao, Potluri, and Roger Miller, *Applied Econometrics.* Belmont, CA: Wadsworth Press, 1970, Chap. 7.

Rohter, Larry. "Waiting Game Is Over in Mexico As Presidential Choice Is Named," *New York Times,* October 5, 1987, p. 1.

Ruffie, Jacques. *The Population Alternative: A New Look at Competition and the Species.* New York: Pantheon Books, 1986.

Rugman, Alan M., ed. *New Theories of the Multinational Enterprise.* New York: St. Martin's Press, 1982.

Russell, George. "Trying to Stem the Illegal Tide," *Time,* July 8, 1985, p. 50

"Russia Can Get By with a Little Help from Its Enemies," *The Economist,* May 8, 1981, p. 97.

Ruttan, Vernon W., and Yujiro Hayami. "Toward a Theory of Induced Institutional Innovation," *Journal of Development Studies,* pp. 203-223

Sampson, Anthony. *The Seven Sisters.* New York: Bantam Books, 1981, p. 386.

"The Saudis and the Cartel," *Insight,* Washington, D.C.: *Washington Times Magazine,* February 23, 1987, p. 38.

Sawyer, W. Charles, and Richard L. Sprinkle. "The Effects of the Mexican Economic Crisis on Trade and Employment in the United States," *Journal of Borderland Studies,* Vol. 1, No. 2, Fall 1986, pp. 66-74.

Scheinman, Marc. "Mexico's Explosive Growth in the Automotive Exports." In *North American Economies in the 1990s.* Vol. II, edited by Khosrow Fatemi. Laredo, TX: Laredo State University, pp. 767-785.

Secretaria de Hacienda y Credito Publico, "Estrategia del Financiamiento del Desarollo," *El Mercado de Valores,* Ano XLVI, No. 52, Diciembre 29, 1986, pp. 1214-1232

Sherrill, Robert, *The Oil Follies of 1970-1980,* New York: Doubleday Company, 1983.

Shwadran, Benjamin. *Middle East Oil: Issues and Problems.* Cambridge, MA: Schenkman Publishing Co., 1977.

Simyar, F., and K. Argheyd. "OPEC: Market Dominant or Subservient." *International Journal of Management.* Vol. IV, No. 1, March 1987, pp. 105–117.

Sind, Yoram J. *Product Policy: Concepts, Methods and Strategy.* Reading, MA: Addison-Wesley Publishers, 1982.

Solis, Leopoldo. *Economic Policy Reform in Mexico.* New York: Pergamon Press, 1981.

Solis, Leopoldo and Ernesto Zedillo. "The Foreign Debt of Mexico," *International Debt and The Developing Countries.* Washington, D.C.: World Bank, 1985, p. 260.

Spencer, Daniel Lloyd. *Technology Gap in Perspective Strategy of International Technology Transfer.* New York: Sparton Books, 1970.

Stockton, William. "Mexico's New Bid to Stem Capital Flight," *New York Times,* July 28, 1986.

Studdard, Ellwyn R. "Identifying Legal Mexican Workers in the U.S. Borderlands: Perceptions & Deceptions in the Legal Analysis of Border Migration," *Southwest Journal of Business and Economics,* Summer 1986, p. 14.

Swardson, Anne. "Banks Agree To Lend Mexico As Much as $7.7 Billion," *Washington Post,* March 21, 1987.

Sylos-Labini, Paolo. *The Forces of Economic Growth and Decline.* Cambridge, MA: MIT Press, 1984.

Teitel, S. "Creation of Technology within Latin America," *The Annals of the American Academy of Political and Social Science,* 1981, pp. 136–150.

_____ . "Technology Creation in Semi-Industrial Economies," *Journal of Development Economics,* September/October 1984, pp. 39–61.

_____ . "Toward an Understanding of Technical Change in Semi-Industrialized Countries," *Research Policy,* 1981, pp. 127–147.

Thurow, Lester. *Investment in Human Capital.* Belmont, CA: Wadsworth Publishing Company, 1970.

The U.S. Automobile Industry: Monthly Report on Selected Economic Indicators, Washington, D.C.: U.S. International Trade Commission, December 1986, pp. 2–3.

Ulmer, Melville J. "Multinational Corporations and Third World Capitalism," *Journal of Economic Issues,* Vol. 14, No. 2, June 1980, pp. 452–471.

Vaitsos, Constantine V. *Intercountry Income Distribution and Transnational Enterprises.* Oxford: Clarendon Press, 1974.

Velez, Alex, and Ronald M. Ayers. "Toward More Effective Planning for Risk by Businesses: Applications to the U.S.-Mexican Border," *The Southwest Journal of Business and Economics,* Vol. III, No. 1, Fall 1985, pp. 1–10.

Vernon, Raymond. "The Economic Consequences of U.S. Foreign Direct Investment," *The Economic and Political Consequences of Multinational Enterprise: An Anthology.* Boston: Division of Research, Harvard Business School, 1972.

_____ . *Storm over the Multinationals: the Real Issues.* Cambridge, MA: Harvard University Press, 1977.

World Economic Outlook: 1986.
Youngquist, Walter. *Investing in Natural Resources.* Homewood, IL: Dow Jones-
   Irwin, 1980.

Index

Ackoff, Russell, 166
Adelman, M. A., 172
Africa, 194
agriculture, 65, 67–68, 70, 105
Alaska, 196
American Civil Liberties Union, 70
American Farm Bureau, 70
American Petroleum Institute, 190–91
American Society for Personnel Administrators, 70–71
Anti-Drug Abuse Act [United States, 1986], 97, 101
Arab countries. *See* OPEC; *name of specific country*
assest model of exchange rates, 17, 53–59
Associated Press, 190–91
automotive industry: between 1977 and 1981, 150–52; between 1982 and 1986, 153–57; costs, 160; employment, 154; and energy resources, 154, 177, 198; expansion of the, 149–50; exports of the, 49–50, 128, 149–64, 153–60; future of the, 157–60; and inflation, 152, 153, 154, 156, 158; investments in the, 24, 154, 155–56, 158, 160; and *maquiladoras*, 155–56; and prices, 154, 156, 158; production, 128, 150–52, 153, 157–58, 159, 160; and quality, 156, 160; recession in the, 154; restructuring of the, 152, 153–57;

sales, 43, 150–52, 153, 156, 158, 159; and technology transfer, 128, 149–64
Ayers, Ronald M., 78

Baker [James] Plan, 26, 32, 38
banking system, 26, 43, 149, 152, 183–84, 193, 198–99, 200. *See also name of specific bank or funding institution*
Belgium, 116
Bell Helicopter Company, 92–93
Belssaso, Guido, 91
Blatchford, Joseph, 70
Border Industrialization Program, 105
Border Patrol, 65, 66
border region: development/economy of the, 11–12, 62, 75, 105–6, 115; infrastructure of the, 120, 121; and the interdependence of Mexico and the United States, 62; and the Mexican economy, 77–80; overview of, 11–12; and political risk, 76, 77–82; and population growth, 11–12; social unrest in the, 105; U.S.-Mexican trade relations, 91–101; *See also* drug trafficking; illegal aliens; immigration; labor; *maquiladoras*
Bracero Program, 105, 115
Bradley Plan, 32
Brazil, 129–30, 149, 159–60
Britain. *See* United Kingdom

211

basis/values of American energy, 168–72; function of, 165–66; importance of, 167–68

Narcotics Control Trade Act [United States], 100
National Aeronautics and Space Administration, 92
National Association of Agricultural Employers, 70
National Development Plan [Mexico, 1983–88], 22
National Drug Enforcement Policy Board [United States], 99
National Industrialization and Foreign Trade Program [Mexico, 1984–1988], 41–42
nationalism, 23–24, 38, 150, 155
National Labor Relations Board [United States], 70
National Science Foundation [United States], 176
Nayarit, Mexico, 100
Netherlands, 196
New Jersey Institute of Technology, 176–78
Nigeria, 196, 200
Nissan Corporation, 151, 152, 153, 156–57, 158
Nogales, Mexico, 65, 67
nonmetallic minerals industry, 130–43
North American Corporation, 166
Nuevo Laredo, Mexico, 65, 118

oil: consumption, 164, 165–78; embargo, 187–88, 199; quality, 173–74, 175–76; shortages, 164, 172, 187–200; spot market, 189, 190, 199. See also oil companies; oil exports; oil income; oil market; oil policies; oil prices; oil production
oil companies: 187–88, 193–96, 200. See also name of specific company
oil exports: amount of, 181; decline in, 43, 184; and GATT, 46; and inflation, 185; and the international oil market, 181–83; of Iran, 190; Mexican, 5, 31–32, 181–86; and oil prices, 45, 46; patterns of, 46;

revenues from, 5, 182–83; to U.S., 8–9, 164, 191; U.S. taxes on, 46. See also oil market
oil income, Mexican, 5, 8, 9, 21, 26, 182–83
oil market: and the automotive industry, 154, 198; and the costs of extracting oil, 196–97; crude, 190–91; and debt issues, 17, 19, 22, 25, 26, 47, 53–59, 152, 193; decline in, 26, 46, 152, 164, 181–86, 188, 190–91, 192; and exchange rates, 53–59; increase in the, 188; and inflation, 58, 193; instability of the, 164, 181–86; and interest rates, 54–59, 193; internationalization of the, 164, 181–86; investments in the, 193–94, 198–99; and the Mexican economy, 5, 6, 8, 9, 21, 31–32, 47, 106, 150, 164, 181–86; myths about the, 164, 165, 168–78, 187–200; overview of the, 8–9; productivity in the, 176; and research and development, 193–94; and subsidies, 175; and taxes, 46, 197; and the United States, 6, 9, 46, 164, 165–78, 172–74, 175, 190–91, 192. See also oil; oil companies; oil exports; oil income, Mexican; oil market; oil policies; oil prices; oil production; OPEC; name of specific country
oil policies: mismanagement of, 164, 165–78. See also oil; oil companies; oil exports; oil income, Mexican; oil market; oil prices; oil production
oil prices: and debt issues, 17, 22, 26, 53–59; decline in, 26, 46, 152, 164, 181–86; and exchange rates, 53–59; and exports, 5, 43, 46; and foreign reserves, 19; increase in, 38; and inflation, 58; and interest rates, 54–59, 193; and the Mexican economy, 106, 164, 181–86; and oil production, 182, 200; roller coaster, 187–200; and taxes, 197; and the world's energy picture, 164, 187–200
oil production: crude, 190–91; decline in, 188, 190–91, 192; increase in, 188; instability of, 164, 181–86;

South America, 152
Soviet Union, 196, 198
Special Drawing Rights [SDRs], 10
spending [Mexico], 19, 21, 24, 26,
    27–32, 134, 138, 183
standard of living, 75, 152
subsidies: and the debt issues, 22, 23,
    24, 26; oil, 175; in the United
    States, 175
swap/debt capitalization, 6, 16, 19–20,
    23–24, 32, 41

Taiwan, 116, 120, 159–60
taxes: and *maquiladoras*, 104, 115–25;
    Mexican income, 24; and oil prices,
    197
tax reform, Mexican, 32
technical contracts, 138, 141–43
technicians [*maquiladoras*], 104, 107,
    108, 109, 112, 118–19
technological industry, 111
technological investments: 37, 38–39,
    41, 42, 43. *See also* technology;
    technology transfer
technology: and the debt-capitalization
    program, 23; and exports, 39, 41;
    implementation of, 130–35; incen-
    tives for, 176; and the industrial
    sector, 46, 48; and Mexican-
    American trade relations, 6; Mex-
    ican dependency/preference on
    foreign, 41, 45; output of, 139–40;
    and the private sector, 45; and the
    United States, 3, 6–7, 116, 128,
    170–71. *See also* technological in-
    vestments; technology transfer
technology transfer: and the automo-
    tive industry, 128, 149–64; and
    capital return, 133–34; and con-
    tracts, 138, 141–43; controversy
    about, 128; cost of, 121, 128; and
    imports, 139, 140; internal, 129,
    130, 138–39, 143; and labor, 121,
    134, 139–40, 143; and machinery/-
    equipment, 134, 136–37, 139–40,
    141–43; and the manufacturing sec-
    tor, 128, 129–43; and the *ma-
    quiladoras*, 109, 111–12, 113, 121;
    and multinational corporations,

129–43; overview of, 6–7; and
    ownership of firms, 130–43; and
    performance, 130–35, 143; and
    research and development, 138–39,
    141–43; and sources of technology,
    3, 6–7, 129–30, 135–38, 141–43; and
    wages, 121. *See also* technological
    investments; technology
terms of trade, 45
Texaco Oil Corporation, 192
Texas: 66–67, 71–72. *See also name of
    specific city*
textiles industry, 130–43
Third World debt program [Baker
    plan], 26, 32, 38
Tijuana, Mexico, 11, 66
Toluca, Mexico, 155
tourism in Mexico, 5, 24, 106
trade: and the Baker plan, 26; and the
    building industry, 176; and myths,
    167; unstability of world, 45; wars,
    45. *See also* trade, Mexican
trade, Mexican: and domestic demand,
    37; and drug trafficking, 63,
    91–101; and economic growth, 22,
    24, 43; and industrial moderniza-
    tion, 41, 48; and investments,
    38–39, 41; levels, 39; liberalization
    of, 24, 26, 32, 37, 183; need for
    research concerning, 50; patterns,
    46–48; and the private/public sec-
    tor, 46; problems concerning, 37;
    and productivity/quality, 44–45;
    surpluses, 19–20, 39, 41–42, 46,
    47–50; and terms of trade, 45; and
    tourism, 5; and wages, 37; and U.S.
    exports/imports, 3, 4–6, 24, 37. *See
    also name of specific topic*, e.g. ex-
    ports, Mexican; GATT
training and development [*ma-
    quiladoras* work force], 109–11,
    118–19
Trist, Eric, 166

unemployment/employment: and the
    automotive industry, 154; in the
    border region, 75; and illegal aliens,
    67–68, 70, 104, 105–13; and the
    manufacturing sector, 133; in

About the Editor and Contributors

Khosrow Fatemi is Professor of Business at Laredo State University and the editor of *The International Trade Journal*. His research interests are in the areas of international trade and economic development, energy, and regional economic issues, particularly those pertaining to North America and the Middle East. He is the editor of *International Trade and Finance: A North American Perspective* (1988) and has published in *The Wall Street Journal, The Middle East Journal, Issues in International Business,* and others.

Richard Ajayi is Assistant Professor of Finance at Temple University. His research interests and publications span the areas of international finance and management, management of financial institutions, and insurance and risk.

Ronald M. Ayers is Associate Professor of Economics at University of Texas at San Antonio. His publications include work in the areas of labor economics, the construction of a statewide economic profile, and managerial problems in the southwest borderlands. He has also consulted with government and industry regarding economic and financial matters.

José G. Barrera-Flores is Professor of Economics at Iberoamerican University in Mexico City.

Dale S. Bremmer is Assistant Professor of Economics at Arkansas State University. He received his Ph.D. in economics from Texas A&M University in 1985.

Robert Carbaugh is Professor of Economics at Central Washington University. He is the author of several articles in professional journals and the coauthor of *The International Monetary System.* He is also the author of *International Economics,* a widely used textbook.

J. Jay Choi is Associate Professor of Finance and International Business at Temple University. Before joining Temple, he taught at Columbia, New York University and the University of Pennsylvania. He has published widely on finance, international finance, and the financial management of developing countries.

Barbara R. Chrispin is Professor of Business at California State University, Dominguez Hills, Carson, California.

Loretta Fairchild is Associate Professor of Economics at Nebraska Wesleyan University, Lincoln, Nebraska. She has published several articles in both Spanish and English comparing local and foreign manufacturers in Mexico and Colombia. Her current research is a microlevel, longitudinal study of technology transfer to Mexico.

Edward Y. George is Professor of Management at the University of Texas at El Paso and a former director of the University's Bureau of Business and Economic Research. He has been actively involved in the study of the maquiladoras and economic development issues since 1978. He was a Fulbright scholar in 1974-1976 and 1982-1983, researching economic development in Africa.

Walter E. Greene is Associate Professor of Business and Director of Small Business Institute at Pan American University in Edinburg, Texas. He is a retired U.S. Air Force officer and has taught at several major universities. He has published extensively in refereed journals and conference proceedings, and has several cases in management, marketing, and business policy textbooks.

David L. Hawk is Professor and Director of the Building Engineering and Architectural Research Center at New Jersey Institute of Technology at Newark, New Jersey. Trained as an architect, planner, and systems scientist, he holds a Ph.D. from the Wharton School of Finance. He has taught and carried out research in various countries including England and Sweden.

Randall G. Kesselring is an Associate Professor of Economics at Arkansas State University. He received his Ph.D. in economics from the University of Oklahoma in 1980.

Robert E. Looney is Professor of National Security Affairs at Naval Postgraduate School at Monterey, California. He is the author of 15 books on various aspects of economic development and has been an advisor to the governments of Iran, Saudi Arabia, Mexico, Panama, and Jamaica.

Edgar Ortiz is Professor of Finance at Universidad Nacional Autonoma de Mexico and Centro de Investigacion y Docencia Economicas. He has published several books and articles in refereed publications. He is a former president of North American Economic and Finance Association.

Emmanuel I. Osagie is Assistant Professor of Economics at Southern University, Baton Rouge, Louisiana. He holds a Ph.D. in Agricultural Economics with research interests in economic and agricultural development, and Third World debt issues.

Ana Maria Perez Gabriel is Professor of International Law and Federal Tax Law at Universidad Autonoma de Tamaulipas at Nuevo Laredo, Mexico. She received her Law Degree from the National Autonomous University of Mexico, and has a Masters of Comparative Jurisprudence from the University of Texas at Austin, Texas. She has also been a practicing attorney since 1962.

Jerry Prock is Professor of Finance and Chairman of Department of Finance and General Business at Pan American University in Edinburg, Texas. He is a frequent contributor to the research on border finance, institutions, real estate, and economics.

Marc Scheinman is Associate Professor of Marketing at Pace University, Pleasantville, New York.

Farhad Simyar is Professor of Accounting and Chairman of Department of Accountancy at Concordia. He has published extensively on international business and energy issues. He taught at Iran Center for Management Studies, Stockholm School of Economics, and University of Ottawa before joining Concordia.

Kim Sosin is Associate Professor and Chairman of the Department of Economics at the University of Nebraska at Omaha. Her areas of research are technological change, monetary practices, and macroeconomics. She is currently working on a microlevel, longitudinal study of technology transfer to Mexico, and also structural change in money demand.